*The Work of Art*

# *The Work of Art*

## Immanence and Transcendence

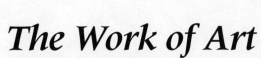

*Gérard Genette*

*Translated from the French*
*by G. M. Goshgarian*

Cornell University Press
*Ithaca and London*

*L'Oeuvre de l'art: Immanence et Transcendence* was published in French,
© September 1994, Éditions du Seuil

Translation copyright © 1997 by Cornell University

First published 1997 by Cornell University Press.
First printing, Cornell Paperbacks, 1997.

Printed in the United States of America

TCF This book is printed on Lyons Falls Turin Book, a paper that is
totally chlorine-free and acid-free.

Cloth printing      10 9 8 7 6 5 4 3 2 1
Paperback printing 10 9 8 7 6 5 4 3 2 1

**Library of Congress Cataloging-in-Publication Data**

Genette, Gérard, 1930–
  [Ceuvre de l'art. English]
  The work of art / Gérard Genette ; translated from the French by
G. M. Goshgarian.
    v.   cm.
  Includes bibliographical references and index.
  Contents: [1] Immanence and transcendence.
  ISBN 0-8014-3159-X (alk. paper).—ISBN 0-8014-8272-0
(pbk. : alk. paper)
    1. Aesthetics, Modern—20th century.   2. Art—Philosophy.
I. Goshgarian, G. M.   II. Title.
BH202.G4613   1997
111´.85—dc21                                      96-46963

# Contents

v

# *Translator's note*

MY EDITORIAL PRACTICE HAS BEEN AS FOLLOWS: (1) WORDS ENCLOSED in brackets in the text are my interpolation when they represent a French equivalent. Words placed in brackets in the footnotes are my interpolation when they represent a French equivalent, explain a reference, or provide supplementary bibliographical information. All other bracketed material in the text or notes is Genette's. (2) Words or phrases followed by an asterisk are in English in the original text. (3) All ellipsis points are Genette's. (4) When Genette quotes from a work that has appeared in English, the English text has, when available, been quoted directly. (5) Titles of works of art are given in English, ordinary usage permitting. (6) Translations of French works quoted by Genette are mine unless othewise indicated.

G. M. G.

*The Work of Art*

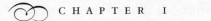 

# CHAPTER I

# *Introduction*

THIS VOLUME IS THE FIRST IN A PROJECTED TWO–VOLUME STUDY OF the status and function of works of art. The present volume deals with the mode, or rather *modes* of existence of artworks; the second will deal with aesthetic relations in general and our relation to works of art in particular. A bit further on, I explain my reasons for adopting this order, which is neither arbitrary nor absolutely inevitable. I also discuss the assumption that the artistic is a province of the aesthetic, an assumption that is not universally accepted, no more than is the distinction, often ignored, between these two domains.

The reader will perhaps be surprised to find a mere specialist in literary studies setting out to explore, without having provided (much) advance notice, one or two disciplines usually reserved for philosophers, or, at least, specialists in practices one spontaneously tends to consider artistic, such as painting, or . . . painting, since that art is frequently, if implicitly, equated with Art as such: everybody knows what the label "History of Art" refers to. My justification for engaging in this semi-illicit activity is my already stated and fortunately banal conviction that literature too is an art (too), so that poetics is a province of the theory of art, and therefore, surely, of aesthetics. The present intrusion is thus no more than an extension or ascension to the (logically) next highest

level, one motivated by a desire to arrive at a clearer view or better understanding of matters by widening the field of vision: if literature is an
art, one is likely to learn something more about it by finding out what
*kind* of art it is, what kind the others are, and, indeed, what an art in
general is—in a word, by attending a little more closely to the *genus
proximum*. I am well aware that enlarging the scope of an inquiry in this
way is a move that can in principle be repeated endlessly, for if art is,
in its turn, a human practice (a statement one can hazard without undue
risk), it becomes incumbent upon us to say what *kind* of human practice it is, what kind the others are, and so on. Even if the Peter Principle destines us all to rise recklessly to our level of incompetence, lack
of time, if nothing else, may be counted upon to prevent us from ven-
turing too far up that dangerous slope.

I should doubtless also explain my general title here. It is a deliberately ambiguous one, since it aims to cover simultaneously (or, rather,
successively) the simple existence of works, and also what they do—in
a sense, the work they themselves perform. *The work of art,*[1] then, refers
to the artwork for the nonce; later it will also come to designate, more
ambitiously, the work done by this work, which is of course the work
performed by art itself. By *art,* in the singular, for a reason I can indicate
but not yet go into: the plural ("the arts") seems to me inevitably to
imply a more or less canonical list of practices bearing the stamp of an
essentialistic definition (even if the list is said to be "open-ended," and
even if one rejects, a fortiori, the traditional notion of a "system of the
fine arts"). Thus it is assumed that there are a certain number (finite or
not) of arts, which are characterized by specific and generic features that
set each of them, and the set of all of them (present or to come), apart
from other human activities, enabling us to decide that a certain activity is artistic, while another is not. However far removed I consider myself from a skepticism that chooses to see in the arts, as Wittgenstein saw
in games, nothing more than a vague nebula definable only in terms of
"family resemblances" between one art and the next,[2] I believe, with oth-

1. [*L'œuvre de l'art,* the French title of this book, suggests something like "the work art does";
a "work of art" in the ordinary sense is *une œuvre d'art.*]
2. This negative position, whose proponents invoke the Wittgenstein of the *Philosophical
Investigations* (trans. G. E. M. Anscombe, 3d ed. [Oxford: Basil Blackwell, 1968], pp. 31ff.), is
adopted by, among others, Paul Ziff, "The Task of Defining a Work of Art," *Philosophical*

ers, that the common definition applicable to the arts, as, indeed, to games themselves,[3] is of a typically functional kind, and that all sorts of practices or productions can take on, or cease to perform, the function in question. Paradoxically or not, it seems to me that *the artistic,* by virtue of its overall operation, can be defined with greater assurance than any of the "arts" taken individually—as can be seen today in the many cases when one feels reasonably certain that an object or act is (or is meant to be) "art," though one is not able or even particularly concerned to say *which* art it belongs to. In their own domain, poeticians have long been aware that certain "literary genres" are often harder to identify than is literature in general: I am hard pressed to say whether a certain text is a novel, but I have no doubt that it is literature. (This situation, where uncertainty about the species does not entail any uncertainty about the genre, is, in fact, among the most banal. To know whether a particular animal is a dog, I do not have to know its breed; indeed, its breed can be, objectively speaking, highly indeterminate.) Insisting on the plurality of arts and genres can thus lead to classificatory quandries and conceptual dilemmas,

---

*Review* 62 (1953): 58–78; Morris Weitz, "The Role of Theory in Aesthetics," *Journal of Aesthetics and Art Criticism* 15 (1956): 27–35; and William Kennick, "Does Traditional Aesthetics Rest on a Mistake?" *Mind* 17 (1958): 317–334. Weitz's contribution is the most forceful and best argued. It is explicitly rejected by Maurice Mandelbaum, "Family Resemblances and Generalization Concerning the Arts," *American Philosophical Quarterly* 2 (1965): 219–228; George Dickie, "Defining Art," *American Philosophical Quarterly* 6 (1969): 253–256; *Aesthetics: An Introduction* (Indianapolis: Bobbs-Merrill, 1971), and "Defining Art II," in Matthew Lippman, *Contemporary Aesthetics* (Boston: Allyn and Bacon, 1973): 118–131; Richard Sclafani, "'Art,' Wittgenstein, and Open-Textured Concepts," *Journal of Aesthetics and Art Criticism* 29 (1971): 333–341; and Joseph Margolis, *Art and Philosophy* (New York: Harvester, 1978). It is implicitly rejected by all those whose approach rests on a positive definition of the concept of (the work of) art, such as Dickie, Arthur C. Danto, *The Transfiguration of the Commonplace: A Philosophy of Art* (Cambridge: Harvard University Press, 1981) ("institutional" or sociohistorical definitions, whatever the—considerable—nuances differentiating the two positions), or Nelson Goodman, *Languages of Art: An Approach to a Theory of Symbols* (Indianapolis: Bobbs-Merrill, 1968) and "When Is Art?", in David Perkins and Barbara Leondar, eds., *The Arts and Cognition* (Baltimore: Johns Hopkins University Press, 1977), pp. 11–19 [also in Goodman, *Ways of Worldmaking* (Indianapolis: Hackett, 1978), pp. 57–70] (a functional definition based on modes of symbolization, called "symptoms of the aesthetic"). The main features of this debate are accessible enough for me not to have to review them here. Like the second group of writers (and many others), I obviously place myself de facto in the camp of those who, undaunted by the "Wittgenstinian" critique, claim that they can prove, by walking, that motion is indeed possible.

3. See, for example, Roger Caillois, *Les jeux et les hommes* (Paris: Gallimard, 1958), which seems to me the best refutation-in-the-act of Wittgenstein's aporias in this domain.

both equally artificial. On the whole, the Crocean theme[4] of the oneness of art is liberating in this regard, because in order to define, not the arts, but the artistic character of this or that activity or object, it mobilizes a criterion which is not, to be sure, "visible," like the one Wittgenstein bizarrely calls for[5], but rather relational (of course, the criterion we plump for need not necessarily be Croce's.) This is doubtless part of what is meant by Jakobson's famous formula to the effect that the subject of poetics is "not literature but literariness."[6] It seems to me that Nelson Goodman's no less famous formula jibes with Jakobson's: not "what is art?", but "when is art?"[7] Less the *arts,* then, than art (without a capital A, in the rather modest sense in which one says that "there is art" in this or that); and less art, when all is said and done, than *artistry.*

## Provisional Definition

The inevitable drawback (I will come back to it) to this state of affairs is that it makes the definition of the subject-matter of the present volume depend on matters to be examined in the next. The definition that follows must therefore be regarded as hypothetical or provisional: *a work of art is an intentional* [intentionnel] *aesthetic object,* or, what comes to the same thing, *a work of art is an artifact (or human product) with an aesthetic function.*[8] These two formulations are equivalent, because an intentional object

---

4. Among others, Schumann was already given to saying, in a formulation which is, to be sure, too abrupt, that "the aesthetics of an art are those of all the arts; only the materials of each differ." Cited in Edouard Hanslick, *Du beau dans la musique,* trans. Charles Bannelier (1854; Paris: Christian Bourgois, 1986), p. 168 [tr. *On the Musically Beautiful,* trans. Geoffrey Payzant (Indianapolis: Hackett, 1986). I have translated Bannelier's French translation of the sentence Genette quotes.]

5. "Don't think, but look!" Wittgenstein, *Philosophical Investigations,* p. 31.

6. Roman Jakobson, "La nouvelle poésie russe" (1919), in *Questions de poétique* (Paris: Seuil, 1973), p. 15 [partial translation as "Modern Russian Poetry: Velimir Khlebnikov," trans. J. Rosengrant, in Edward J. Brown, ed., *Major Soviet Writers: Essays in Criticism* (New York: Oxford University Press, 1973), p. 62].

7. Goodman, "When Is Art?" I have already drawn a parallel, at least implicitly, between these two propositions in my *Fiction et diction* (Paris: Seuil, 1991), pp. 12–15 [tr. *Fiction and diction,* trans. Catherine Porter (Ithaca: Cornell University Press, 1993), pp. 2–6]. There is no getting around this question, which I will return to later.

8. This is the definition given by J. O. Urmson, among others: "I believe that a work of art

can be only a human artifact, unless one puts forward a theological hypothesis (which I refrain from doing) about the divine intentions embodied in natural things, or else an anthropomorphical hypothesis about the aesthetic intentions embodied in things produced by animals, like quails' eggs or spiders' webs. The two formulations are equivalent, again, because *aesthetic object* means "an object in a position to produce an aesthetic effect," while "function" means "intentional effect." The inclusion of both *artifact* and *function* in our definition might be deemed redundant, inasmuch as there are no artifacts without functions (human beings do not produce anything without functional intent), but the function of an artifact is not always aesthetic and is not often exclusively aesthetic; indeed, an artifact's functions do not always include an aesthetic one. On the other hand, an artifact without an (intentionally) aesthetic function (an anvil, for example) can produce an unintended aesthetic effect, which is to say that it can be perceived [*reçu*] as a (simple) aesthetic object, much as a natural object—a flower, for instance—can. Thus there are, in a progressively inclusive relation, three levels of aesthetic objects: aesthetic objects in general, artifacts that happen to produce an aesthetic effect, and artifacts which have an intentionally aesthetic effect, that is, an aesthetic function. These last would be works of art properly so called.

The second formulation, *artifacts with an aesthetic function,* best accommodates our purposes here, since it clearly puts two distinct objects before us: the notion of artifact and that of aesthetic function. These two objects (of study) can be introduced by way of two questions: first, "what does this artifact consist in?," and, second, "what does this aesthetic function consist in?" Nothing logically prescribes the order of the two questions, even if the initial formulation seems to make *artifact* the subject and *aesthetic function* the predicate. In fact, works of art are not more properly particular kinds of artifacts than they are particular kinds of aesthetic objects: the two categories stand in a relation of intersection which does not entail the logical priority of one over the other.

---

can most usefully be considered as an artifact primarily intended for aesthetic consideration." J. O. Urmson, "What Makes a Situation Aesthetic?" *Proceedings of the Aristotelian Society,* supplementary vol. 31 (1957) [also in Joseph Margolis, ed., *Philosophy Looks at the Arts* (New York: Scribners, 1962), p. 22].

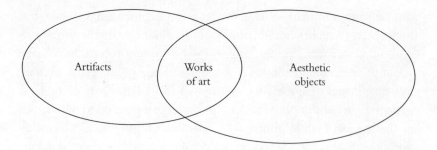

Moreover, if one regards each of these two questions as forming the object of a specific study—the *ontology* (an entirely provisional term) of artworks in the first case, and, of course, *aesthetics* in the second, nothing prevents us, in principle, from starting with the latter, or even, like Kant and others, from confining our attention to it.

However, I can see a reason to begin with the first question, even if it is of a rhetorical or pragmatic kind: namely, the fact that the aesthetic function is the (main) purpose of a work of art—that the work, like any means, serves an end, and that this subordination implies the existence of a scale of importance, suggesting that any inquiry into the subject follow a certain order.[9] The present volume might accordingly be considered a mere preliminary. But—it may perhaps be said without abusing the *captatio benevolentiae*—we will see that matters are, fortunately, a bit more complicated than that.

Our first question, then, to put it in Scholastic terms, is that of the so-called ontological[10] status of works of art—more simply, that of their mode, or, doubtless better, their "*modes* of existence."[11] At least one aspect of this question has been fully treated by contemporary philosophy, and I will be taking that into account, but I need to begin by signalling two

9. Goodman himself puts off his discussion of the "symptoms" of the aesthetic to the last chapter of *Languages of Art,* though he has subsequently, in "When Is Art?" forcefully posed the question of the priority of function over status as regards both importance and pertinence.
10. As one instance, among others, of the (surprising) use of this adjective in contemporary analytic aesthetics, we might cite the third section of Joseph Margolis's anthology *Philosophy Looks at the Arts* (3d ed., Philadelphia: Temple University Press, 1987). Later I will explain my reservations about this cumbersome term, which I propose, at a minimum, to recast.
11. This is, as we will see, the expression employed in Étienne Souriau, *La correspondance des arts: Éléments d'esthétique comparée* (Paris: Flammarion, 1947).

choices of method and principle that set my position apart from those illustrated, with many a fine distinction, by this recent tradition.

## Restricted "Ontology"

To begin with, one does not seem to me well advised to treat the artistic or nonartistic character of an object as an "ontological" feature, thus placing the whole of the theory of art under the banners of ontology. This, as I see it, is the position taken by Arthur Danto, who thus describes[12] the difference between two physically indistinguishable objects, of which one is an artwork (for example, Duchamp's *Bottlerack*), while the other is not (an identical bottlerack in the basement of the BHV[13]). I will defer my discussion of the assumptions underlying this dichotomy—essentially the notion that the ready-made as such[14] can be characterized as a "work of art"—and the theoretical consequences that follow from it. I want simply, at least for now, to indicate my concern to define "mode of existence" as narrowly as possible; or—but this comes to the same thing—I want to situate as far outside the realm of the "ontological" ("what is X?") as possible everything I consider functional ("what is X used for?" or "how does X work?").

One circumstance would seem to militate against this distinction: as artifacts are all intentional objects, it is impossible to define them, even provisionally, without mentioning their function in the definition. Thus it is impossible to say *what* a hammer is without saying what it is used for: a hammer *is for* driving in nails. One possible way of responding to this objection is to say that it is not absolutely impossible to define (or at least to *describe*) a hammer in a nonfunctional manner, as (for instance) a mass of metal at the end of a wooden handle; after all, an archaeologist who discovered one a few millennia from today would describe it in precisely those terms until he determined its function.

12. For example, in *The Transfiguration of the Commonplace,* pp. 3, 41–42, 138–139.
13. [The Bazar de l'Hôtel de Ville, a department store located near Paris City Hall (l'Hôtel de Ville) with a hardware department in the basement. Duchamp bought the bottlerack that became *Bottlerack* there.]
14. See Chapter 9 below. But let me state here and now that my aim is to take issue, not with this way of describing ready-mades, but rather with the practice of applying the description *to the objects exhibited* in and of themselves and as such.

Another response might be that the intentionally constitutive function of an artifact is not constant: nothing prevents us from sometimes, or even always, utilizing a hammer as a paper-weight, and vice versa, without in any way modifying the appearance or perceptible physical nature of either. Thus even the function of an object that is "essentially" functional (a tool) is always potentially variable, while its physical nature remains virtually inalterable (I will discuss this "virtually" at greater length later). This remark doubtless applies a fortiori to works of art, whose practical or aesthetic function can change with circumstances (the Parthenon is no longer a temple; *Olympia* is no longer a provocation), without any change in their mode of existence. The pairs (or series) of indiscernible objects mentioned by Danto, whether real or imaginary, are in one sense (or from this point of view) superfluous ad hoc experiments: the same industrial object does not have the same function before and after it has been promoted to the rank of a ready-made: a simple bottlerack has become . . . something that I would not call a work of art as readily as Danto does, but that is at least, quite obviously and whatever one may think of it, a "museum piece." Yet its physical nature is not, as far as I know, particularly affected by the fact, any more than the physical nature of the famous Jastrow drawing is modified when one stops "seeing" it as a rabbit and begins "seeing" it as a duck.[15]

The "mode of existence" of artworks will here be reduced to this extrafunctional invariant. But let us rather simply say their existence, whose *modes* constitute the works' "ontological status"—though I will write (*onto*)*logical* instead, whenever I cannot avoid the adjective, for it seems to me that these differences in mode are of a logical rather than ontological kind in the full or heavy sense of the word, which the parentheses are meant to lighten. I have also just replaced *physical* with *extrafunctional,* because the former adjective, which might be appropriate for a hammer, bottlerack, or even a drawing, cannot be used to describe other kinds of objects, like a poem or symphony, whose "nature" or "being" is precisely *not* physical. This difference, which will of course crop up again, is, precisely, at the heart of the question of the "mode of existence" of works.

15. See p. 238 below.

The second choice bears on a work's mode of existence thus narrowly defined; it seems to me that we would now do well to divide it into two aspects. The existence of a work—like that, doubtless, of any object—may be approached in two distinct ways. The first constitutes an approximate (and provisional) response to the crude question: "What does this work consist in?" *The Venus of Milo,* for example, consists in a block of white marble of such and such a form, which may currently be viewed, on a sunny day, in the Louvre (one might say a bit more or less about it, without, for the moment, entering into the question of this statue's representative function). Under optimal conditions, a direct, full, and authentic perception of this work can occur only in the presence of this object, which happens to be physical. I say, "under optimal conditions," because any number of different factors can interfere with our perception of it. The noblest, and the one most legitimately bound up with the artistic nature of this work, may be dubbed, with reference to a famous passage in Proust,[16] the "Berma effect"; we might define it as "traumatic anesthesia brought on by the overwhelming sensation that one is in the presence of what is presumably a masterpiece." Compared with any other (indirect) manifestation of the work known as the *Venus of Milo,* this block of marble is evidently *the thing itself,* and it is in this sense that the work "consists" in it.

But *to consist in* must not here be interpreted to mean, exhaustively and without further distinction, "to be in every respect identical and reciprocally reducible to." As has often been shown, certain predicates apply to the physical object, not the work, and (above all) vice versa: Carpeaux's *Dance* can be described as "light," but the block of stone it consists in cannot. Thus some prefer to say that works are "physically embodied"*[17] in objects, the way an individual is incarnated in a body;

16. Marcel Proust, *À l'ombre de jeunes filles en fleurs,* in *À la recherche du temps perdu* (Paris: Pléiade, Gallimard, 1987), vol. 1, pp. 437ff. [tr. *Within a Budding Grove,* in *Remembrance of Things Past,* vol. 1, trans. C. K. Scott Moncrieff and Terence Kilmartin (New York: Random House, 1981), pp. 480ff.].

17. See Joseph Margolis, "The Ontological Peculiarity of Works of Art," in *Art and Philosophy* (Atlantic Highlands, N.J.: Humanities Press, 1980), pp. 17–24. To the best of my knowledge, this formulation first occurs in the title of an article by Margolis, "Works of Art as Physically Embodied and Culturally Emergent Entities," *British Journal of Aesthetics* 14 (1974): 187–196.

but this formulation brings with it a number of awkward metaphysical hypotheses, and, most important, it cannot possibly be applied to works of music or literature, which consist in *nonphysical* objects, and therefore can "be embodied," if one insists on using that word, only in physical *manifestations* of those ideal objects: *The Charterhouse of Parma* "consists" (approximately) in a text, and "is embodied," if one likes, in copies of that text.

This logical objection at least clears a path for a dissociation, and thus for an evocation of *another* mode of existence. When Marcel, after coming home disappointed from Berma's "real" performance, reconstructs it in his mind, and gradually, retrospectively, and more or less sincerely discovers its artistic value, which the emotion of the "live performance" had blinded him to, it may be said that he is in the presence of another mode of manifestation of this work, compounded of memory, retrospective analysis, and conformist wishful thinking*. Today, a film or video recording might provide him the occasion or stimulus for such an experience of the work. Similarly, an overly sensitive art lover can contemplate, "in peace and quiet," a good cast replica of the *Venus of Milo* or a good reproduction of the *View of Delft,* things which, if they can never "replace" the originals, may nevertheless allow him to make observations he would never have made in their presence.

Hence one cannot say, in the full sense, that a work *consists* exclusively and exhaustively in an object. Not only because works can operate, at a distance and indirectly, in a thousand good or bad ways, as I have just pointed out, but also because it sometimes happens that a work consists not in a *single,* but in *several* objects deemed identical and interchangeable, like the various casts[18] of Rodin's *Thinker,* or even in objects acknowledged to differ appreciably from one another, like the different versions of Chardin's *Saying Grace,* Flaubert's *Temptation of Saint Anthony,* or *Petrushka*—and for certain other reasons as well, which we will consider in due time. For now, this hint should suffice to suggest that the mode of existence and manifestation of works is not restricted to "consisting" in an object. They have at least one other mode of existence, which is to *transcend* this "consistence," either because they

---

18. [*Épreuve.* Genette frequently uses this word, which can be translated as "proof" (in the sense, for example, of page proof) to refer to casts of a sculpture, proofs or prints of an engraving, prints of a photo, etc. No English word works equally well in all these contexts.]

are "embodied" in several objects, or because their reception can extend far beyond the presence of this/these object(s), and, in a certain way, survive its (or their) disappearance: our aesthetic relationship with the Tuileries of Philibert Delorme, or even with Phidias's *Athena Parthenos,* both of which have been destroyed, is not simply nil.

I therefore propose to defer my discussion of this second mode of existence, which I will call *transcendence,*[19] and to call the first, symmetrically, *immanence.* I by no means wish to suggest thereby that works do not consist in anything at all, but rather to recall that their existence consists in an immanence *and* a transcendence. A considerable number of obscurities, disagreements, and, occasionally, theoretical impasses seem to me to stem from a rather widespread failure to distinguish between these two modes of existence. I will therefore adopt the opposite stance and procedure here, drawing as sharp a distinction as possible between the study of immanence, the object of Part I of this book, and that of transcendence, the object of Part II. The disadvantage of this choice—for no choice is without its disadvantages—is that the schema I will begin by proposing may seem narrow or even reductive. It will certainly be partial and provisional, pending the complement or corrective to be provided by what comes later. For the moment, then, I can only beg the reader's indulgence.

## The Two Regimes

The modes (a provisional term) of immanence of works of art have heretofore been treated as modes of existence *simpliciter.* I do not here intend to survey the history of this approach, of which I probably do not have exhaustive knowledge. Leaving aside fine distinctions (especially terminological and methodological ones), I want rather to give an overall account of what seem to me to be its achievements, which reflect a kind of convergence over essentials. That an eminently quarrelsome tribe

19. I do not mean to give this term here, any more than elsewhere, a "spiritual" or even a philosophical (for example, Kantian) connotation. I use it in its etymological (Latin) sense, which is eminently secular: to transcend is to go beyond a limit, to overflow a closed space; as we will see later, the work in transcendence is a bit like a river which has overflowed its banks and which is, for better or for worse, only the more powerful as a result.

should have arrived at such an (unacknowledged) consensus is not really miraculous; the general agreement is rather, I think, dictated by the obviousness of the facts, which leave no room for theoretical innovation.

This common position likes to come forward[20] in opposition to two somewhat spectral doctrines that are, quite properly, dismissed as equally wrongheaded. Partisans of the first position, which is never imputed to anyone in particular, are said to maintain that all works of art consist exhaustively in physical or material objects. The main weakness of this doctrine, the argument runs, is that it cannot be applied without distortion or contortion to types of art such as music or literature, whose productions are immaterial (we will see later in what sense and on what grounds). Adherents of the other doctrine, which is not unreasonably, if with some simplification, attributed to "idealist" aestheticians like Croce or Collingwood, are said to affirm that all works of art, including works of plastic or visual art, exist in the full sense only in the mind of their creator—*cosa mentale,* as Leonardo had already said; the material objects that manifest works, from temples to books, are merely crude embodiments and rough traces. The pitfall of the latter theory is, at a minimum, that it weds the destiny of works to the ephemeral existence of an artist, denying them any real capacity for intersubjective communication. Moreover, the two theories make the same obvious error: they ascribe the same mode of immanence to types of works as (onto)logically distinct as works of plastic art, which come from the hand of the artist and are irreplaceable in their physical uniqueness, and literary or musical texts, of which every correct inscription or performance constitutes an occurrence that is, artistically speaking, as fully representative as the original manuscript.

Most art theorists situate themselves midway between these two antithetical monist extremes, adopting a dualistic position that partitions the field of artworks into two types: works whose *object of immanence,* as I will call it, is a physical object (as in painting or sculpture), and works with ideal objects of immanence: works of literature and music, among others. This division is already to be found in Étienne Souriau, who posits, in the name of an "existential analysis of the work of art," the principle of a "plurality of modes of existence," subdivided

20. Especially in Richard Wollheim, *Art and Its Objects* (Cambridge: Cambridge University Press, 1968 [2d ed. 1980]).

into the "physical," "phenomenal," "reic" (*réique*), and "transcendental." Of these, "physical" existence answers most nearly to our question about (onto)logical status. It gives rise to a fundamental distinction: "Certain arts give their works a unique, definitive body: statues, paintings, buildings. Others are both multiple and provisional: this is the case with musical or literary works. [Works of this type] have spare bodies."[21]

Richard Wollheim's equally dualistic position is not clearly spelled out, but can be inferred from his rejection of both monist theories, and also from his way of applying the Peircian distinction between type and occurrence (or token*) to music and literature. (We will encounter this distinction again.) Thus a text is a type whose every written/printed copy or oral recitation is a token. The unique works of painting offer no equivalent for this (onto)logical dissociation.[22] Nicholas Wolterstorff[23] extends this two-leveled status to cover the artworks* of printmaking and cast sculpture, divided up into types (which he prefers to call *kinds**) and their occurrences, which may be either (material) objects* in the case of object-works* like Rodin's *Thinker*, or occurrences in the case of occurrence-works* like works of music; literature has the status of an occurrence-work* because it can be performed orally, but also that of object-work*, because it exists in graphic forms. The field of artworks* is thus that of the arts with multiple products; these are the arts which monopolize Wolterstorff's attention—although he is not immune to a certain monist temptation to extend his analysis to the singular works of the plastic and visual arts, described as kinds* with a single example* whose uniqueness is simply due to technical limitations that are, perhaps, temporary: once reproductive techniques make

21. Souriau, *La correspondance des arts,* p. 48. The work's "phenomenal" existence is related to the seven "sensory qualities" that characterize the arts of color, light, line, bulk, movement, articulated sound, and musical sound; "reic" existence distinguishes "representational" arts, such as literature and painting, from those which are simply "presentational," such as music or architecture; I do not quite grasp what "transcendental" existence is. A "system of the fine arts" laid out on p. 97 displays in a circular figure the fourteen kinds of artistic practice defined by the intersection of the phenomenal and reic parameters. Thus this figure does not take into account the "physical" distinction that interests us here, although it would not be difficult to classify these fourteen arts using the physical criterion, at the price of splitting up those of them which possess, as we will see, both types of "bodies," much as Souriau himself has to split an art like painting up into representational and (abstract art) "presentational" practices.

22. Wollheim, *Art and Its Objects,* esp. §1–39.

23. Nicholas Wolterstorff, *Works and Worlds of Art* (Oxford: Clarendon, 1980).

it possible to produce perfect copies, the *Mona Lisa* or *Venus of Milo* will become artworks* no less multiple than *The Thinker* or *The Charterhouse of Parma.* We will again encounter this much debated issue—as well as the question as to whether the (real) multiplicity of *The Thinker* or a print like Dürer's *Melancholia* is of the same order as that of a literary or musical work.

Joseph Margolis's complex, extensive contribution to this debate[24] seems to me to be marked by the opposite inclination, a tendency to shift all artworks toward the status of plastic productions with a unique object. This tendency makes itself felt, for example, when Margolis defines the literary work as the "prime instance"* produced by the author, and says that everything which comes after is merely a series of copies; or, again, when he objects to Goodman's dichotomy (which we will soon be examining more closely) on the grounds that "all works of art are to some extent autographic";[25] or, finally, when he contests the distinction between *making* and *creating* proposed by Jack Glickman—"particulars are made, types are created," says Glickman, arguing that art consists, not in making, but in creating.[26] A simple housewife (the example is not Glickman's) *makes* a salmon filet with sourwood seasoning, but the artist/chef Pierre Troisgros has (I think) *created* the type which we call his recipe for this dish. Insensibly amalgamating two concepts that all those with an idealist bent have difficulty keeping apart, Glickman plainly exhibits a tendency to assimilate creation to invention, a debatable move.[27] But Margolis's objection is of another sort: on his view, the distinction between *making* and *creating* is not valid, because one cannot create a recipe without actually *realizing* [*exécuter*] the dish the recipe is a recipe for. Doubtless, that is how most culinary creations come about, but to me it seems obvious that this relationship between conception and realization is not the only one: a creative cook *could* think up a recipe and leave it to his kitchen-boys to make it, or else put off making it himself to a more propitious moment, without

---

24. Margolis, "Works of Art as Physically Embodied," *Art and Philosophy;* "The Ontological Peculiarity of Works of Art."
25. Margolis, *Art and Philosophy,* p. 69. [Translated from Genette's French translation.]
26. Jack Glickman, "Creativity in the Arts," in Margolis, ed., *Philosophy Looks at the Arts,* pp. 168–185. The sentence quoted is on page 178.
27. See below for a discussion of this assimilation in Luis Prieto, "On the Identity of the Work of Art," trans. Brenda Bollag, *Versus* 46 (1987): 31–41.

in any way invalidating his creative act. I will not carry the difficult parallel between culinary creation and the production of literary or musical works any further for the moment (one cannot compose a poem or melody "in one's head" without mentally arranging the words or notes, which, accordingly, do not stand in the same kind of relation to the work as does a recipe to a culinary work), but, at a minimum, it seems to me certain (and obvious) that an architect does not need to realize his plans himself in order to have created the building he prescribes in them, and that a playwright does not have to realize his stage directions himself in order to have created stage business. On two or three occasions, then, Margolis tends to edge the status of certain ideal works toward that of works of physical immanence. It should be added that, in his case, this inclination is compensated for by the accent he puts on the "emergence"* of the work as opposed to the objects in which it is "embodied"; but it would be simpler, perhaps, if there were nothing to compensate for in the first place.

The most balanced or judiciously disposed version of this *doxa,* and the one that is the most fully worked out and skilfully argued, is, in my opinion, Nelson Goodman's.[28] But this nominalist philosopher makes it a point of honor not to utilize notions as "Platonic" as the opposition between types and tokens, or, a fortiori, between physical and ideal objects. Hence his classificatory criterion is purely empirical: it so happens that in certain arts such as painting, the production of fakes or forgeries*—that is, passing off a faithful copy (or a photographic reproduction) of a work as the original[29]—is a really existing practice, one which is as a general rule profitable, and, sometimes, punishable and actually punished by law, because this activity is meaningful. It is likewise the case that in other arts, such as literature or music, forgery is not practiced, because a correct[30] copy of a text or score is simply a new

---

28. See Goodman, *Languages of Art,* chapters 3–5.

29. Although Goodman devotes a few instructive pages to the Van Meegeren case, one should not confuse forgery so defined (a fraudulent copy of a singular work) with forgery by imitation, or pastiche; the latter consists in producing (fraudulently or not) an "original" or at least new work *in the manner* of another artist—as Van Meegeren produced new works "in the Vermeer manner." Pastiche is practiced in all the arts, and can in no case serve to discriminate between two regimes of immanence.

30. I say a *correct* copy here, and not, as with painting, a *faithful* copy. The difference between these adjectives involves fundamentals. I will come back to it.

copy of that text or score, neither more nor less valid, from a literary or musical point of view, than the original. What might very well be practiced, however, and has in fact been practiced in certain periods,[31] is the production of "pirated" copies of a work, that is, editions which, because they violate the copyright held by the author and his legal publisher, are fraudulent from a *commercial* point of view. But if these copies are correct—that is, if they exactly match (sameness of spelling)* the original—they are just as valid textually. In other words, in certain arts, the notion of *authenticity* is meaningful, and is defined by a work's *history of production,* while it is meaningless in others, in which all correct copies of a work constitute so many valid *instances* of it. Goodman christens arts of the first sort autographic, not altogether arbitrarily, and those of the second sort allographic;[32] he can thus avoid falling back on descriptions that are, in his eyes, too metaphysical. We will, however, see that this distinction in fact coincides with one which counterposes material to ideal works, or, more exactly (in my view), works of physical immanence (material objects or perceptible events) to works of ideal immanence—that is, works consisting in a type common to several correct occurrences.

Without yet entering into a detailed account of these two regimes,[33] I must point out that, for Goodman, this basic distinction does not affect two other, less important distinctions. One of these contrasts the arts in which each work is a unique object, such as painting or carved sculpture, to those in which each work is or can be a multiple object, that is, a series of objects held to be identical, like the copies of a text, or else equivalent, like the casts of a sculpture (these two kinds

31. Witness, for example, Balzac's legitimate complaints about the "Belgian forgeries" of his books.

32. The original motivation for introducing these now widely used terms, which have ontological sobriety to recommend them, was evidently the difference in status between unique "autographic" manuscripts and works with multiple copies, dubbed, a contrario, "allographic." The common root *graph-* matters less here than does the contrast *auto-/allo-*, which is relevant to all the arts.

33. I will henceforth use this term, rather than *mode,* to distinguish autographic from allographic, inasmuch as these two kinds of functioning are mutually exclusive for a given work, which cannot be autographic and allographic at the same time, just as a country cannot simultaneously be a republic and a monarchy—even if there exist, in the one case as in the other, mixed or intermediate practices, some of which will soon claim our attention. By *modes,* in contrast, I mean types of functioning that are compatible and complementary, such as immanence and transcendence, or the various sorts of transcendence, which can coexist.

of multiplicity are quite distinct, as Goodman is very much aware, but the distinction between them is not pertinent at this point in his discussion[34]). The other of these lesser distinctions contrasts one-stage arts, like painting or literature (the object produced by the painter or writer is *ultimate,* and defines the work), with two-stage arts (or, as the case may be, arts involving more than two stages), such as printmaking or music: the printmaker's plate or the composer's score merely represents a stage awaiting execution, whether by the original artist or someone else. I am not sure that the last two cases have exactly the same status, and I will return to them in connection with the allographic regime; but for Goodman, at any rate, the three distinctions are independent of one another, and cut across one another nonhierarchically.

A final reminder: if music and literature (among other arts) are allographic, the act of writing, printing, or performing a text or score is for its part an autographic art,[35] whose usually multiple products are physical objects that can be forged or counterfeited. It is not possible to "counterfeit" *Rameau's Nephew* or the *Pastoral* Symphony without producing a new, correct copy of these works, but one can produce a fake of an edition or performance of them, or of their manuscripts. One can, that is, give out (or mistake) a faithful imitation of an edition, performance or manuscript for the edition, performance or manuscript itself, just as, in painting or sculpture, one can make forgeries or errors of attribution— and, as Goodman says, for the same "reason," namely, the autographic nature of these ways of realizing works which are themselves allographic.

But to say that a given "art," as defined in the prevailing terminologies of the "system of fine arts," *is,* without further distinction, autographic or allographic, would be a considerable oversimplification of both Goodman's theory and the reality it sets out to describe. We have already seen that "sculpture," a fully autographic art (for the time being, at any rate), can be subdivided into two rather distinct types: carved sculpture, involving objects that are in theory unique, and cast sculpture, with potentially multiple objects. Architecture, as Goodman himself says,[36] can belong to the autographic regime, when it produces, in artisanal fashion, unique, irreproducible objects (Goodman's example is

34. Goodman, *Languages of Art,* pp. 112–115.
35. Ibid., pp. 117–119.
36. Ibid., pp. 218–221.

the Taj Mahal); but it can also belong to the allographic regime, when it produces the sort of prescriptive diagrams we call plans, whose realization can be as multiple (and multiple in the same way) as that of scores or literary texts. "Multiple" is to be taken here not in the sense which applies to the various casts of *The Thinker,* assumed to be identical and interchangeable, but rather in the sense that the admitted diversity of these copies or performances is held to have no adverse affect on essentials, namely, that which *is prescribed by* the text, score, or plans. Music itself can be taken to illustrate both regimes (though not in the same work): it is allographic in the case of a scored composition, autographic in the case of a complicated improvisation, in which elements that cannot (easily) be scored in a notational system, such as the timbre of a voice, mingle with elements that can—including, as a rule, melodic line or harmonic structure. Many aspects of oral literature also belong at least partially, and for analogous reasons, to the autographic regime. Thus the borderline between the two regimes sometime runs right through "an art," partitioning it into two (onto)logically distinct practices, whose unifying principle (when there *is* unity) is of a different order. On this very empirical point, subject to considerable fluctuation in actual practice, Goodman puts forward a historical hypothesis,[37] according to which all arts were originally autographic, but, gradually and to different degrees, "emancipated" themselves by adopting notational systems wherever possible. The most recalcitrant of the arts, from this point of view, would appear to be painting. We will have occasion to deal with this question later on: though it may seem peripheral, crucial theoretical questions in fact hinge on it.

We have insensibly drifted from an empirical defining criterion (pertinence or nonpertinence of the notion of authenticity) to another, which, though equally empirical, is presented by Goodman as the "reason" or explanation for the first:[38] allographic practices are characterized by the utilization of a more or less strict system of notation, such as language, musical notation, or architectural drawings. Whatever the (appreciable) differences between the ways these various systems work, the availability of a notation is simultaneously the index and instrument of a distinction between those characteristics of a realization which are

37. Ibid., pp. 120–123.
38. Ibid., p. 115.

(considered) obligatory and those which are (considered) optional; a notation defines the work solely in terms of its necessary features, even if its contingent features are legion—we should, doubtless, say "literally innumerable," as the case of music makes plain. But the freedom one has in realizing literature is no less extreme. Thus the text of a novel as noted in the original manuscript does not define the speed at which it is to be read, whether aloud or silently, nor does it specify any typographic choices. As to the other variations in realizations of the work that we can either observe or, elaborating on those just mentioned, imagine, they are quite as innumerable, and yet in no way affect the text as such, i.e., its sameness of spelling*. Poetic texts, as is well known, are usually characterized by a denser web of prescriptions (bearing, for example, on layout), but they never seek to, and never can, specify *everything*.

Now the distinction between the prescribed and the nonprescribed,[39] and thus between that which is pertinent (to the definition of a work) and that which is contingent or impertinent, indicates that an allographic work is defined and identified, exhaustively and exclusively, by the set of features contained in its notation. This set of features (here I abandon Goodman's terminology for more ordinary usage, which Goodman would doubtless object to) constitutes what is traditionally known as the specific or qualitative identity of a thing (in Scholastic terms, its *quiddity*)—*specific*, not individual, because it shares each of these features with ... all the other objects that also exhibit it (the *Jupiter Symphony* shares the feature "symphony" with all other symphonies, the feature "C major" with all other compositions in C major, etc.), and the finite set of these features with ... every other object that happen to display the same set of features. Of course, there is every chance that only the *Jupiter Symphony* will exhibit *all* the features which define its complete specific identity; another score that also happened to exhibit the same features would be, quite simply, *the same score*. I do not say *the same work*—even if one takes these features to include "having been composed

---

39. I do not say the difference between what is prescribable and what is not, for there are virtually no a priori limits to prescribability: certain playwrights like Beckett are much more directive than others when it comes to stage productions or stage business. Nothing, in principle, prevents composers from specifying details like the make or even the serial number of an instrument. Writers too can spell out choices about typography or paper quality; and so on. But the fact—for this is a simple question of fact—is that no one ever tries to prescribe everything.

by Mozart"—for if Mozart had, at two distinct moments in his life, twice produced, unintentionally (and not from memory or by copying his own work), the same score, these two occurrences of the same score could in certain respects be deemed two distinct works, like Cervantes' *Quixote* and Pierre Ménard's, if only on account of the operal[40] (but not notational) feature "involuntary reminiscence," a feature that would be exhibited by the second score, but not the first. We will come back to these questions, which are apparently meaningless for Goodman, but mean a great deal to me and others.

I do not, then, say "the same work"; but I do say "the same score," or "another copy of the same score"[41]—that which it is regardless of the circumstances of its production and the physical particularities of its actual form, provided only that it display all the features of specific identity defined by the ideal score of which it is (by this very fact) a copy. However, two copies of the same score (or, naturally, of the same text) or even of the same edition will necessarily differ from the standpoint of their numerical or individual identity (*haecceitas,* or thisness), which assures that: 1) the score lying on the left half of this table is the score to the left, that on the right half the score to the right; 2) I would know which was which if somebody switched them around in my presence; 3) if I do not know which is which because I was not paying attention, the question would at least make sense; and 4) the two copies can in no case be at the same place at the same time.[42] Being endowed with a numerical identity distinct from specific identity is thus peculiar to physical objects, one of whose specific features consists in having a location in space (*res extensa*). Lack of numerical identity—which we have whenever two entities sharing all the same pertinent features of specific identity are ipso facto absolutely identical—is, in contrast, the peculiar characteristic of ideal objects: a text or score is an ideal object, in that

40. [*Opéral,* a neologism derived from opus and operate. Genette glosses this word in Chap. 13, n. 42.]

41. The word *score* is clearly problematic, because it sometimes designates the *notation* of a work in its ideality, and at other times denotes a physical, and by definition particular, copy of this ideal score. Here I am using it in the first sense.

42. On the (classic) distinction between the two types of identity, see, among others, P. F. Strawson, *Individuals: An Essay in Descriptive Metaphysics* (London: Methuen, 1959), pp. 35–37; on the relevance of this distinction to the identification of works of art, see Prieto, "On the Identity of the Work of Art."

two texts or scores endowed with the same specific identity are quite simply the same text or score, and cannot be differentiated on the basis of (among other things) location in space, the reason being that, unlike copies of them, which are physical objects, texts or scores—ideal objects—are *not located* in space.

One consequence of this state of affairs—unless it is merely another way of describing the same state of affairs—is that a physical object (a painting, a cathedral, a copy of a text or score) can undergo a partial change of specific identity without undergoing any change in numerical identity. A book or painting can burn up and a cathedral can collapse, but the resulting pile of ashes or stones would be what has *become of*, or what is *left of*, *this* book and not another, *this* building and not another, etc. Conversely, the specific identity of an ideal object (a text, a score) cannot change in the slightest without the object's becoming a different ideal object—*another text, another score*. Let us say, then, without taking our description of this dichotomy any further, that autographic objects of immanence are capable of *being transformed,* while allographic objects of immanence cannot be transformed without being *altered,* in the full sense of the word—without, that is, *becoming other(s).*[43] The mural called *The Last Supper* continues to be the mural called *The Last Supper* as it gradually fades, and will still be *The Last Supper* even after no one can make it out. The text of "Meditation" in the 1862 edition (*Le Boulevard* and *Almanach parisien*), which reads, "Be good, my sorrow, quiet your despair . . . ,"[44] is a *different* text (of the same work) than the manuscript text (1861) and the text to be found in the other editions, which reads, "Be good, my Sorrow, quiet your despair . . . ." Thus material objects of immanence, however singular they may be, and even if they are unique,[45] are always at least diachronically plural, inasmuch as

43. [The Latin for other, *alter,* like the French for other, *autre,* is discernible in *altérer,* to alter.]
44. [Charles Baudelaire, "Receuillement," *Œuvres,* vol. I (Paris: Pléiade, Gallimard, 1975), pp. 140–141 (tr. "Meditation," in *The Flowers of Evil,* trans. and ed. James McGowan [Oxford University Press, 1993], p. 347).]
45. French [like English] is not very helpful when it comes to making this crucial distinction: if unique [*unique*] is unambiguous, particular or singular [*singulier*] is not, since this adjective, frequently used to describe a unique object ("The *Mona Lisa* is a particular work") can also be applied to any object considered in its numerical identity, even when what is in question is an object in a series, indistinguishable from thousands of others ("this particular [but not unique] copy of *The Charterhouse of Parma* belonged to Balzac"); a cast of *The Thinker* is a particular but not a unique cast. Henceforth, I will try to reserve "unique"

their specific identity never stops changing as they age, while their numerical identity remains unchanged. In contrast, an ideal object of immanence is absolutely unique, since its specific identity cannot change without bringing about a change in its numerical identity. Such an object is, however, *multiple* in the very special sense that it can have untold realizations or *manifestations.*[46]

It seems to me, then, that allographic (ideal) objects are exhaustively defined by their specific identity (since they do not possess a numerical identity distinct from it), and that autographic (material) objects are essentially defined by their numerical identity, or, as Goodman says, by their "history of production,"[47] since their specific identity changes constantly without canceling our sense of their "identity" tout court. It is in advancing the second proposition that I part company with Prieto, who seems consistently to make possession of a specific identity in compliance with the original the necessary condition for authenticity. This is perhaps owing to the nature of the examples he chooses to build his argument on—for instance, a particular 1930 portable Erika typewriter utilized by a certain group of Resistance fighters, which one cannot reasonably look for anywhere else than among the series of 1930 Erika portable typewriters, just as the Geneva Library's lost copy of *Das Kapital* can hardly be identified among (in the full sense of the word[48]) a collection of copies of *Mein Kampf.* But we have seen that a material object can undergo a considerable number of transformations without undergoing any change in its numerical identity, and if the particular Erika typewriter being sought had been repaired, in a clinch, with a Remington keyboard and Underwood carriage, a search based on specific identity would have every chance of leading the searchers astray by orienting them in a more selective way than was called for.[49]

for objects which have no doubles, while using "particular" or "singular" exclusively in the distributive sense.

46. I use manifestation as a term with a broader extension and more restricted connotation than performance: a musical text can be manifested by either a performance or a written notation; a literary text, by an oral performance or an inscription.

47. Prieto clearly demonstrates the link between the two notions by insisting on the part played, in establishing the numerical identity of an object, by continuity of perception, or, failing that, by certificates or pedigrees* attesting to numerical identity.

48. [*Parmi,* "among," literally means something like "belonging to," "of the number of."]

49. I prudently refrain from changing *all* the Erika's parts, since that would make it into a new version of Jeannot's famous knife, which, given its purely relational definition, is, rather, an ideal object, like the Paris-Geneva express train so dear to Saussure. [Jeannot is a stock

The same holds for autographic works of art. Suppose that, after learning from an unimpeachable source that the *Mona Lisa* in the Louvre is merely a superb copy which Arsène Lupin substituted for the original in 1903, one sets out to track down the real *Mona Lisa*. After a long search, one discovers in the Aiguille Creuse at Étretat,[50] the hideout and personal museum of the gentleman thief, a sooty painting, covered with stains, half gnawed away by the mice, and adorned, as if by anticipation,[51] with a mustache—in short, an object displaying virtually none of the features of the *Mona Lisa*'s specific identity, though a precise historical detail, say, one of Leonardo's fingerprints, proves beyond the shadow of a doubt that its numerical identity is the *Mona Lisa*'s. Here again, it is evident that basing the search on specific identity would have been a poor way of going about things—all the more so if the *Mona Lisa* had been reduced to a heap of ashes, preserved, perhaps, in a crystal urn. More generally, it seems to me that Prieto, in his partially justified quarrel with "collectionism," or the fetishism of the authentic, shifts the status of material works much too close to that of ideal works by assuming that both are exhaustively defined by their specific identity of "creation," and by treating physical authenticity as a purely commercial or sentimental value lacking all aesthetic relevance.

Obviously, the independence of the two criteria of identity is illustrated, inversely, by the fact that an ideal object of immanence remains unaffected by the "history of production" of its physical manifestations. I would certainly not say, with Goodman, that an exceptionally speedy or lucky monkey who happened to type out a text strictly identical to that of *The Charterhouse of Parma* had produced the same *work* as Stendhal, for a literary work is a (language) *act* whose definition encompasses many things besides its text; this point brings us back round to the distinction between immanence and transcendence. But I would

---

comic character who repeatedly changes, first the blade, then the handle of his knife, which thus evokes anything transformed so often that it has none of its original parts.] If all the parts of the Erika had been subsequently replaced, its numerical identity would, as a result, doubtless be *scattered* over all the parts that had been gradually replaced and thrown out. 50. [The Aiguille Creuse or "Hollow Needle" is a 75-yard-high needle-rock that juts spectacularly up out of the sea opposite the cliffs of France's Alabaster Coast near the village of Étretat. In the popular Sherlock Holmesian novel of the same name (Maurice Leblanc, *L'Aiguille Creuse* [Paris: P. Lafitte, 1909] [tr. *The Hollow Needle,* trans. Alexander Teixeira de Mattos (London: Bodley Head, 1960)]), the master thief Lupin stashes his loot there—old masters he has had replaced with perfect copies.]
51. [Of Marcel Duchamp's *L.H.O.O.Q.*]

unhesitatingly say that the monkey had produced the same *text,* that is, the same object of immanence, which is exhaustively defined, since it is an ideal object, by its specific identity—here textual.

I hope I have established the denotative equivalence (differences in connotation aside) between the Goodmanian dichotomy autographic/allographic and the classical opposition material objects/individual[52] ideal objects, or types with occurrences (or copies). I also hope that I have at least made plausible, pending a more satisfactory argument, the distinction between the two modes of existence I have called immanence and transcendence. I will continue to put off my examination of transcendence, even if we will, nolens volens, encounter the reason for drawing the distinction in the interim. I will, then, first consider under the specific term *immanence* what is ordinarily treated, indiscriminately, as "mode of existence" or "ontological status." Since the opposition material/ideal bears on immanence alone, and sometimes divides artistic practices that are in all other respects homogeneous, I will generally avoid speaking of autographic or allographic *arts* or works (transparent metonymies aside), reserving these adjectives for the *objects of immanence* of such works; "autographic art," for example, will henceforth mean nothing more for us than "an art whose works have autographic, or material, objects of immanence." Moreover, the category of greatest relevance for us will be one that often cuts across a considerable number of traditional artistic distinctions: that of the *regime of immanence,* autographic or allographic.

But before proceeding to examine each of these two regimes in turn, I want to point out or recall that the distinction between them is not as clear-cut in practice as in theory. Thus we will also be dealing with *mixed* cases such as concrete poems, which wed the ideality of a text to the materiality of a particular sort of writing; *intermediate* cases, such as autographic arts with multiple objects; and *ambiguous* cases, like the arts of performance which are autographic as far as the numerical identity of each particular performance is concerned, but allographic with regard to the specific identity common to all instances of the same series—without excluding developments, whatever their causes may

52. I will return in due course to the crucial distinction this adjective implies.

be, which shift works, and sometimes arts, from one category to the other. A demolished building or burned painting of which we have nothing but descriptions becomes, in its own way, an ideal work in transcendence [*en transcendance*], because transcendence, as we can now see, is itself a form of ideality. Suppose that one hundred painters, starting out from Pausanias's description,[53] undertake to reconstitute Polygnotus's painting *The Battle of Marathon,* which once adorned the Poikile in Athens along with a few others. Description being what it is, namely, necessarily approximate (and in this particular case quite cursory), all one hundred paintings would be faithful reconstitutions, and yet each would differ from all the others; moreover, all would probably differ from the original. But they would all be *The Battle of Marathon* as described by Pausanias, which has become, thanks to him and historical misfortune, an allographic work.[54]

As the reader will have noticed, I have just transposed a page of Diderot which is so thoroughly germane to our discussion that I feel compelled to reproduce it at length. There will thus be at least one page of real French in this book:

> A Spaniard or Italian desirous of owning a portrait of his mistress, whom he could not expose to the gaze of any painter, settled for the only choice left him, and undertook to make a very long, very precise written description of her. He began by determining the exact size and shape of her head; then he took the measure of her forehead, eyes, nose, mouth, chin, and neck; finally, he reexamined each part of her, sparing no pains to ensure that his description

53. *Description of Greece,* Book I, Chap. 25, "Of the Poikile and Its Paintings" [tr. of Books I and II by W. H. S. Jones (Cambridge: Loeb Library, Harvard University Press, 1918), pp. 127–133. Genette is, à la Arsène Lupin, having a bit of fun at the expense of the unsuspecting. The chapter of Pausanias he cites does not include a description of *The Battle of the Marathon* in the Poikile. Moreover, in Book V, Chap. 11, this painting, frequently attributed to Micon, is attributed to Panainos. Pausanias's best-known account of a painting by Polygnotus, in Book X, Chap. 25, concerns a pair of frescoes at Delphi which depicted the sack of Troy and Odysseus's adventures in Hades. See Pausanias, *Description of Greece,* vol. 4, trans. W. H. S. Jones (Cambridge: Harvard University Press, 1935), pp. 513–555.].
54. At least this imaginary example has to do with a work that was once real; conversely, of imaginary works like Achilles' shield in the *Iliad,* we possess several competing and, naturally, divergent "reconstructions." There is nothing paradoxical about this: lost works inspire so much respect that no one wants to take the risk of reconstituting them—unless some glaring exception I have forgotten about is there to poke a hole in this fine princi-

would engrave in the painter's mind the real image he himself had before his eyes. He omitted neither colors, nor forms, nor anything bearing on her character: the longer he compared his description with his mistress's face, the more accurate he found it; he believed, above all, that the more details he charged it with, the less he would leave to the painter's invention; he ignored nothing he thought the brush should capture. When he felt that his description was complete, he made one hundred copies of it and dispatched them to one hundred painters, enjoining each to transfer to the canvas exactly what he himself had committed to paper. The painters set to work, and in time our lover received one hundred portraits, all of which exactly resembled his description, and none of which resembled any of the others—or his mistress.[55]

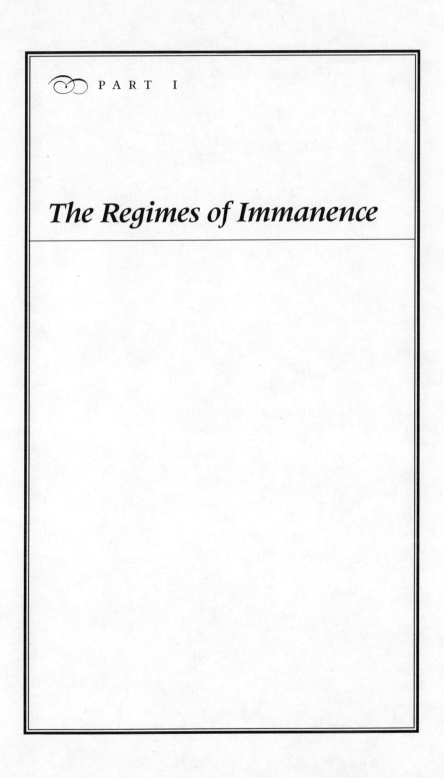

PART I

# *The Regimes of Immanence*

# CHAPTER 2

# The Autographic Regime

AUTOGRAPHIC OBJECTS OF IMMANENCE, WHICH CONSIST IN physical things or events, fall, naturally, within the province of the senses, lending themselves to direct perception through sight, hearing, touch, taste, smell, or a combination of two or more of the senses. Yet classifying the arts these objects belong to on the basis of the organs they affect, as has often been done in the history of aesthetics, appears to me a rather pointless exercise,[1] while hierarchies of value like the one Hegel proposes strike me as decidedly gratuitous.[2] As to a classification based on the materials used by the arts, though I do not know if one has ever been essayed, it seems to me that the distinctions and, above all, the connections it would make would not be lacking in comic effect: such a classification would, for example, assign Vermeer and Bocuse[3]—strange bedfellows* indeed—to the same cubicle, inasmuch as both use oil (though, to be honest, I doubt it is the same oil in both cases). I will leave this possibility aside, without glossing over the fact

1. See, for example, Étienne Souriau, *La correspondance des arts: Éléments d'esthétique comparée* (Paris: Flammarion, 1947).
2. G. W. F. Hegel, *Aesthetics: Lectures on Fine Art* (1832), trans. T. M. Knox, 2 vols. (Oxford: Clarendon, 1975), 2: 621–628. The "division" and hierarchy proposed by Kant, *The Critique of Judgement,* §§51–53, is even shakier.
3. [Paul Bocuse is a celebrated chef.]

that it is not simply laughable: painting sometimes calls for incredible kitchenwork, and the recipes involved play a part in determining what kinds of products are turned out, how they are preserved, and even, on occasion, the way they are consumed. We will encounter at least one instance of this.

It would be possible to think up another thousand more or less "Borgesian" taxonomies, but, for a reason I would be hard put to account for, it seems to me that the most suitable is one that distinguishes two sorts of "material objects":[4] those consisting (I am going to use dangerously simple words) in *things,* and those consisting in *facts,* or events—more precisely, in *acts.* Paintings, sculptures, and cathedrals are things; improvisations or executions of music, dance steps, and pantomimes are acts, and thus facts. A display of fireworks is a deliberate, organized event, which, as such, might perhaps be regarded as an act.

This frequently encountered distinction is very fragile, and obviously comes up against doubtful cases: is a stream of water like the one Proust attributes to Hubert Robert's fountain in *Cities of the Plain* a thing or an event? If we answer "a thing," the reason is doubtless that it persists in time; but events too persist (more or less), while a stream of water does not persist forever. Nor, as a matter of fact, does a painting: "statues die too." And if one prolonged, for hours, weeks, or years, a fireworks display that was as repetitive as a stream of water (this would surely be possible, if costly), would it become a thing? But is a stream of water necessarily repetitive? And what does "repetitive" mean? All this confronts us with very thorny problems indeed. In due course, I will at least try to put forward a more precise definition of the kind of duration, or, rather, durations at issue here.

But the fact that the distinction is not watertight and that there exist undecidable cases may be nothing more than the empirical manifestation of a deeper reality, which certain philosophers convey in the following simple, and, to my mind, very obvious proposition: there are no things, there are only facts. This is basically what Wittgenstein says at the beginning of the *Tractatus,* while Quine constantly suggests that we read verbs (whether verbs of action or stative verbs) under (the)

4. The very fact that we can speak without redundancy of "material objects" indicates that "object" is here taken in the broad (and, moreover, classic) sense of object of attention, a sense englobing ideal objects as well.

names (of things), on the grounds that names or nouns are always the result of a more or less legitimate "reification." This "deeper reality" is, as I see it, of a more physical than metaphysical kind: "things" are the stable (that is, relatively fixed and durable) appearances taken on by certain shifting configurations of atoms, which nonetheless continue to lead their unwearying dance beneath the surface. In short, things are a special kind of event.

Having recalled this established truth, we will continue (or resume) using "thing" to designate those relatively stable concatenations of events traditionally called *bodies* or *res extensae*—including, among other things, animate bodies like yours or mine. Lalande's *Vocabulaire* cautiously sanctions this usage: *"Thing* expresses the idea of a reality which is considered in a static state, and as detached or detachable, a reality constituted by a system of qualities and properties assumed to be fixed. Things are thus counterposed to facts and phenomena. The moon is a thing, eclipses are facts.'"[5]

I will, then, distinguish two kinds of material objects (of immanence): things[6] and events (most events being acts in the domain[7] we are considering); if need be, I will use, in the following restricted senses, *real* (of or relating to things[8]) and *factual* (of or relating to *facts*), *evential* (of or relating to *events*)—and also *performantial,* since most factual works belong to the *performing arts\**. But I will draw a further distinction, among real objects of immanence, between those which consist in a unique object, like the *Mona Lisa,* and those consisting in several objects assumed to be identical, like *The Thinker* or *Melancholia.*

---

5. André Lalande, *Vocabulaire technique et critique de la philosophie,* 10th ed. (Paris: PUF, 1988), S.V. "Thing."

6. Here "object" would be both the more usual and the more elegant term, and I will occasionally use it in this sense. But we need to maintain the official acceptance of the word at the highest level, which subsumes every kind of immanence, ideal immanence included.

7. The domain, that is, of works, or artistic objects. In the broader domain of aesthetic objects, we again find acts or gestures ("the sower's noble gesture" [a frequently cited phrase from Victor Hugo's "Saison des semailles"], which lays no claim to having aesthetic value, and others, less sublime but possibly more graceful), and even events that are not human activities, like, precisely, Lalande's eclipse.

8. Hence in a very restrictive and more or less etymological sense. In the broad sense, of course, ideal objects are plainly quite as real as material ones.

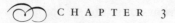 CHAPTER 3

# *Unique Objects*

$A$UTOGRAPHIC WORKS WITH A UNIQUE OBJECT OF IMMANENCE ARE essentially products of a transformational manual practice,[1] obviously directed by the mind and carried out with the help tools or more or less sophisticated machines, but not, in principle, prescribed by already existing models (material or ideal) that these works would merely serve to realize. The existence of such a model would authorize the production of several more or less identical objects, a form of production proper to other kinds of practices (multiple autographic, or even allographic), to be examined below. This reservation by no means implies that one must exclude, a priori, the endless variety of artisanal products from the domain of art, for every sort of human product that has an aesthetic function comes under our definition, irrespective of any judgment as to its aesthetic value. The reservation does, however, exclude nearly all such products from the domain that interests us at the moment, which is in no way privileged because its products are one-

---

1. Transformational, because human products are never created ex nihilo, but rather from some preexisting material, and therefore some object. On this point see Luis Prieto, "On the Identity of the Work of Art," trans. Brenda Bollag, *Versus* 46 (1987): 36–37. Conversely, the "destruction" of an autographic work, like that of any material object, is never anything but another transformation—for example, of the *Mona Lisa* into a heap of ashes.

of-a-kind, except perhaps on the commercial or symbolic plane, where rarity carries a premium. Cabinetmakers, goldsmiths, jewelers, ceramists, basketweavers, saddlers, and fashion designers all produce objects with aesthetic (and other) functions that it is perfectly legitimate to consider works of art; but they almost always work from a model which they have either in front of them or in their mind's eye, and which can be repeatedly utilized, with the full approval of their clientele and society at large. The exceptions represented by the "unique specimens [*modèles*]" (a somewhat contradictory term) of certain jewels, items of furniture, or creations of high fashion do, however, fit into the category under consideration here, either because they cannot, for material reasons, be reproduced, or else (the more common case) because restrictions have, for obvious reasons, been deliberately imposed.

These two motivations, rather hard to sort out, are also responsible for the uniqueness of the works characteristic of the canonical "plastic" arts in their autographic regime, such as drawing, painting, carved sculpture, architecture, and also photography. In the case of the first three arts, matters are perhaps too self-evident to require lengthy discussion. As is well known, drawing (more precisely, a certain imaginary sketch by Hokusai) serves Nelson Goodman as an emblem of pictorial representation reduced to the bare essentials, as contrasted with diagrammatic notation (more precisely, an electrocardiogram that Goodman assumes, for the sake of argument, to be physically indistinguishable from the Hokusai sketch). Drawings can also be used to illustrate, in contradistinction, again, to diagrams, the autographic regime of immanence:[2] if, in diagrams, all that counts is a set of points defined with respect to an ordinate and an abscissa, the characteristic property of a drawing (figurative or not) is that it is impossible to distinguish pertinent from contingent features, because here the slightest details count—thickness of line, color of the ink, nature and state of the support. This repleteness of pertinence plainly implies that no replica (I use the word in the broad sense here) of a drawing can be considered strictly identical with it,

---

2. It can further be used to illustrate, here too in contradistinction to a diagram, one of the "symptoms" of the aesthetic function: predominance of exemplification over denotation, or relative syntactical repleteness, for example. The fact that these criteria are interchangeable is a delicate point we will encounter again some day. See Nelson Goodman, *Languages of Art: An Approach to a Theory of Symbols* (Indianapolis: Bobbs-Merrill, 1968), pp. 192–193.

which further implies that the work must be regarded as necessarily unique.

One could raise two objections to this analysis. The first would be that it is hard to see how a drawing can simultaneously be said to be exactly identical with a diagram and yet impossible to reproduce exactly. The response, it seems to me, is that the first case is purely hypothetical, while the second falls within the realm of real possibility; furthermore, to conclude that a sketch is "indiscernible" from a diagram, we must, precisely, disregard its diagrammatically irrelevant features, which make for its material uniqueness. The second objection is that if this holds for every material object considered from an aesthetic point of view, it is hard to see how there can exist multiple and yet strictly identical material objects of immanence, like the objects of immanence of Rodin's *The Thinker*. The obvious answer is that there are no such objects, but that a cultural convention pretends, for a number of good reasons, that there are. But let us not get ahead of ourselves.

## *Painting*

Painting, especially in its most painterly*[3] forms, certainly provides the most obvious examples of material works which cannot be multiplied, and it is no accident that Nelson Goodman regards it as the art which most stubbornly resists evolving in the direction of the allographic regime—even, I would add, in the direction of the multiple autographic regime. One reason for this obviousness is the greater visual and material complexity, generally speaking, of the products of this art, which inclines one to the spontaneous conclusion that "no one (not even the artist) can" turn out a perfect copy of a Vermeer or a Pollock. If a painting is not always more complex than a drawing, it is nevertheless "deeper," or, to use the common expression, denser. A rather striking example goes to show how what I earlier called painterly "kitchenwork"

---

3. There is unfortunately no workable French equivalent for this English adjective, which designates the substantial properties of painting qua material, as contrasted with its *pictorial*, that is, its formal and (sometimes) representative properties. The distinction is roughly the same as that between *peindre et dépeindre* ["paint" and "depict"].

contributes to making the products of painting unique.[4] The work I have in mind, entitled *Zuflucht* [Refuge],[5] is by Paul Klee. It is officially described as "oil on cardboard," but that is a considerable oversimplification. On the back of the cardboard, one finds the following note:

Technique:

1. cardboard
2. white oil-based lacquer
3. while (2) still sticky: gauze and a coating of plaster
4. tinted with red-brown watercolor
5. zinc-white tempera mixed with glue
6. fine-line drawing and watercolor hatching
7. lightly fixed with an oil-based varnish (diluted with turpentine)
8. highlighted in places with zinc-white oil
9. coated with gray-blue oil; wash of madder lake in oil

In a case of this kind, making a "perfect copy" would require that one exactly reproduce not merely all the perceptible detail, but also the process of production it resulted from; one would thus have to repeat a list of operations converted, by dint of being repeated, into a "recipe"— a procedure that tends to come under the allographic regime, as we will see. To which it must be added that such lists are rather rare, as are, consequently, the occasions when a copyist can exactly imitate the procedures followed by his model. Little matter, the objection might run, as long as the reproduction of the visible result is beyond reproach— that is, ultimately indiscernible from the original. In fact, chemical reactions being what they are (though I do not know what that is), the two works, products of two different methods of "preparation," would probably evolve ("age") differently, and thus sooner or later cease to be indiscernible.

4. A factor contributing to uniqueness or to the material impossibility of making a perfect copy is not necessarily a guarantee of authenticity in the strict sense that (in principle) governs attributions. That a painting in the Rembrandt manner is unique and cannot be copied does not guarantee that it is a painting by Rembrandt. The authenticity of the workshop is often more collective than individual, involving the prestige of a distinguished master more than the physical act of painting. The old masters often painted their paintings the way Caesar built his bridges. Even the words "from the hand of," found on attestations of authenticity, are imprecise: from which hand?

5. 1930, 50 x 35.6 centimeters, Pasadena, Norton Simon Museum; the technical specifications are cited in Pierre Boulez, *Le pays fertile* (Paris: Gallimard, 1989), p. 163.

## Architecture

The idea of a building constructed without any sort of plans has long been incompatible with our conception of architecture, even if we have all had occasion to throw together a slapdash toolshed or shack in the backyard. Conversely, the idea of two or more (conventionally) "identical" buildings built from the same plans, which is the empirical test for a fully allographic architecture, is associated with a state of the art we tend to regard with disdain. Goodman, taking due note of our uncertain notion of what architecture is, describes it (in its current regime) as a "mixed and transitional" art.[6] *Transitional* may be taken in a diachronic sense (inasmuch as architecture is evolving from its original autographic regime toward a completely allographic one, like, perhaps, all the other arts, and today finds itself at some point along the way), while *mixed* may be interpreted synchronically: architecture today exhibits purely autographic forms (toolsheds), fully allographic forms (series of HLMs[7]), and all manner of intermediate forms typical of modern "high" architecture—for example, buildings with a unique instance which, though built from plans, include details that cannot possibly have been thought out in advance. Whatever historical prognosis one can or cares to make, the diagnosis that architecture belongs to a mixed regime is obviously correct and not especially noteworthy. I will come back to the question of the empirical limits of the allographic regime; they are essentially bound up with the fact that, first, many modern works we could perfectly well multiply by repeatedly realizing their plans are in fact not multiplied, and, second, that such a practice would violate our sense of the status great works of architecture are supposed to have, even if they are contemporary—say, Mies van der Rohe's Seagram Building, to cite one of the best modern works straightaway.

The distinction between autographic and allographic architecture is, then, relative, a distinction of degree. Thus Goodman is not wrong to illustrate autographic architecture modestly, and, as it were, nega-

6. Goodman, *Languages of Art,* p. 221.
7. [*HLM or habitation à loyer modéré,* originally a designation for low-rent housing built and administered by the state, is now used to refer to all moderately priced multi-unit housing.]

tively, contenting himself with the remark that "we may bridle at considering another building from the same plans and even on the same site [as the Taj Mahal] to be an instance of the same work rather than a copy."[8] In other words, we *tend to* regard this building as an autographic work, rather than an allographic work with a unique instance. But what would we say of a replica of the Seagram, "built from the same plans," that was (re)erected in, for example, Hong Kong? Legitimate second instance or unimaginative copy?

I have no idea whether there exist "plans" for the Taj Mahal in the prevailing sense—both prescriptive and antedating the building—but nothing is proven if there are none: we might, after all, very well lose the plans for the Seagram. The real question is, rather, whether a descriptive, retrospective account of a building, like the notation of an improvised melody after it has been played, would be sufficiently precise and complete to prescribe an authentic "instance" in its turn. The real answer is, certainly, *more* a matter of convention than technique: the difference between instance and copy is, here, a question of consensus and tradition, and the relevant data are purely empirical. *The fact is* that Postman Cheval[9] left no plans for his castle, no more than Gaudi did for the Church of the Sagrada Familia; this makes it hard, not to finish the work now that the artist is dead, nor even to finish it "in the original style" (since the style of a part can always be plausibly generalized or projected onto the whole), but rather to finish it in conformity with the creator's intentions, since it would seem that nothing provides a sufficiently precise account of them, even supposing that the artist himself had a perfectly clear idea of what he meant to do, which is doubtful, given that his methods were largely improvised. In contrast, buildings are "always" (as we say) being built or rebuilt from the plans of an allographic architect after his death: take a look, without leaving Barcelona,[10] at Mies van der Rohe's German Pavilion.

8. Goodman, *Languages of Art,* p. 221.

9. [Ferdinand Cheval, a postman who devoted himself to building, between 1876 and 1912, a fantastic castle in the southern French village of Hauterives.]

10. [Barcelona is also where the Sagrada Familia is located.] The German Pavilion, built for the 1929 World Fair and then torn down, was reconstructed in 1986 to mark the centenary of the artist's birth.

## *Sculpture*

Unlike architecture, like painting, carved sculpture might seem to offer a fairly reliable model of an autographic art whose products are necessarily unique; "necessarily" here means "by virtue of material and technical necessity"—there being no two identical blocks of stone or blows of the chisel. But one needs to point out, in the first place, that carving is not quite the only technique whose productions cannot be prescribed. The same holds for many other kinds of sculpture, such as Gonzalez's or Calder's, whether forged, made of noncast metals, assembled with bolts or rivets, etc.—not to mention objects constructed with mixed materials, or César's compressions, which provide the perfect illustrations of a partially random art. Secondly, to approach the matter from the opposite angle, "direct carving" (of stone, marble, wood) is not always as "direct" as the name suggests. "Direct carving," says a craftsman, "does not necessarily mean setting out, chisel in hand, in quest of adventure, following wherever successive blows of the hammer and new encounters may lead. This very 'modish' notion is comparatively recent. Among sculptors, the term 'direct carving' means, above all, that the sculptor does his carving himself, without the help of a stonemason or pointing machine, using a maquette that represents a rough model or preliminary sketch of the planned work." [11]

Doubtless the "direct" nature of the act of carving is no more called into question by the fact that sculptors use maquettes than is the direct nature of painting by the fact that painters make sketches [*esquisses*] [12] or preliminary drawings; this does not even suffice to make carved sculpture a "two-stage" art (otherwise, every art would be—at a minimum— a two-stage art, except for automatic writing in the strict sense of the term, should it exist, which I strongly doubt). But what is to be said about cases where a craftsman, working from, say, a plaster maquette made by the artist, realizes a work the artist does not deign to correct with the chisel, as Rodin, toward the end of his life, often did not, because stone "bored" him? In that case, we have a two-stage art, like cast sculpture; nothing, except perhaps custom, requires it to remain on the

11. Jean Rudel, citing Luthringer, in *Technique de la sculpture* (Paris: PUF, 1980), p. 34.
12. Rather than *ébauche,* which seems to me inappropriate here. I will come back to this point later. [*Ébauche* means preliminary draft and strongly connotes something unfinished.]

level (I do not say the slippery slope) of an autographic art with multiple products. If one grants that a craftsman, working from a plaster
model, can realize a statue in marble, then why not two, three, or a
thousand, the more so as this type of work is not hampered by the material limits (wear and tear on the model) cast sculpture does? Here as
before, the answer is *convention*.

But not all carving, of course, is direct. This is the where the technique known as "pointing" enters the picture; practiced from time im-
memorial, it has, over the centuries, seen steady improvement due to
the utilization of increasingly mechanized methods. "Pointing" says
Rudel, "means transferring an often small plaster, clay, or stone model
to a block of stone or marble, using reference marks and special instruments. Over the centuries, the initial, rather simple procedure has become increasingly precise. Beginning in the Renaissance, large-scale
direct carving was as a rule abandoned in favor of pointing, a task usually entrusted to specially trained craftsmen; this continued to be the
case until the beginning of the twentieth century, which saw a return
to carving."[13]

It will have been understood that pointing has, as a result of these
improvements, moved rapidly toward acquiring the status of the *imprint*
[*empreinte*], which, as we will see, governs all the reproductive techniques
of cast sculpture. It is, at the very least, a semi-imprint, and there is doubtless nothing to prevent machines like the ones locksmiths use to copy
keys from some day producing replicas—scaled up, life size, or scaled
down—quite as "faithful" as actual casts, and in unlimited quantities, barring deterioration of the model. The real limitations are, then, self-
imposed or dictated by custom. I do not suppose that Rodin authorized
the reproduction of "his" sculptures in marble, and it is well known that
a few (rare) sculptors, like Michelangelo and Brancusi,[14] refused to contemplate using any technique other than direct carving. Thus when one
says, following Goodman, that carved sculpture is an autographic art with
unique products, "carved" must be understood to mean "actually produced by direct carving wherever technical constraints require, and conventionally considered to have been so produced in all other instances."

13. Rudel, citing Luthringer, *Technique de la sculpture*, p. 46.
14. Moore, however, who began by doing carved sculpture, later switched to modeling.

I do not much know to what technique we should attribute the sculptures Renoir, as an old man, verbally "dictated," by dint of prescriptive descriptions, to his student Guino, who later acquired the status of a "coauthor" in court.[15] This case brings us back to Diderot's fable: if Renoir had simultaneously directed several students in this fashion, we would today possess several versions of all these works, each different from the others and all, in this very special sense, "authentic."

## Photography

Because it typically involves the two stages of developing and printing, the art of photography in its standard state—but perhaps one should say "in its classical state," with a touch of nostalgia—may serve as a paradigm for the multiple autographic regime as defined by Goodman, who says that "the autographic arts are those that are singular [only] in the earliest stage":[16] a photographic negative is singular, the prints taken on paper are, if one desires, multiple. This is the status of printmaking as well—and for good reason—a point I will come back to in due time. But considerable technological diversity, both diachronic and synchronic, lies concealed behind the generic term *photography,* inasmuch as "outmoded" techniques can persist or be revived for various reasons (aesthetic reasons among them); the recent revival of the daguerreotype offers an example. Some of these techniques give rise to objects that are in principle unique. The negative prints made on paper by Niepce (around 1820) were singular, and, moreover, short-lived, until Daguerre discovered a method for fixing and developing them. Even the daguerreotype (1838) consisted in a unique impression (a negative, but legible as a positive in a raking light) on a metal plate; proofs of it could not be "pulled," so that it could not be multiplied. Bayard's positives, made directly on paper (1839), were still unique; they could not be printed more than once. Apparently, it was the calotype, invented by Fox Talbot (1839, paper negatives made transparent with wax) which inaugurated the two-stage technique with multiple prints characteristic of the classic state. Many

15. "This led to so great a drop in popularity that prices fell by 75%." Maurice Rheims, *Apollon à Wall Street* (Paris: Seuil, 1992), p. 226.
16. Goodman, *Languages of Art*, p. 115.

different kinds of light-sensitive surfaces were utilized (until Eastman introduced celluloid in 1888), and the final prints were made on paper. But we know that Polaroid's one-step "instant" photos (1947) were, once again, unique prints. In each of these cases, of course, the object could be multiplied via a "reproduction"—a photo of a photo—but Goodman would say that this was a copy, rather than an authentic instance like the prints made on paper in the classical state. Nevertheless, since any proof pulled on paper is an imprint, and since a photo, and therefore a reproduction, is also a (phototonic) imprint, we must again admit that these distinctions, which can take on decisive importance at the legal or commercial level (where an original print must not be confused with a reproduction on a postcard or in an album), are of an institutional rather than a genuinely technical nature.

This very superficial examination has left aside countless intermediate forms, such as those between drawing and painting (pastels, pen and ink drawings, sanguines), painting and sculpture (cutouts, crushed relief, polychrome sculptures, paintings on shaped supports), sculpture and architecture (to which "art" do the Pyramids, Dubuffet's towers, the Statue of Liberty, or the Sydney Opera House belong?), or painting and photography (retouched photos). We have also neglected the equally great diversity of techniques peculiar to each art: consider, in painting, the differences between wash drawings, watercolors, frescos, tempera painting, gouaches, oil paintings, enamels, acrylics, and the variety of pigments, supports, ingredients, and the instruments used to apply them—square and sable brushes, palette knives, thumbs, spray guns, the sticks and watering cans used to make drip paintings, the human body in the case of Yves Klein, and so on. Consider, again, the number of objects and materials that, for a few decades now, have been produced, found, "installed," picked apart, piled up, or spread out; they provide the bread and butter of the exhibitions and museums, under a label which is usually, and very appropriately, vague. As I said earlier, we still know, or think we do, that all this is "art," but we no longer know which art it is, and are beginning to see that specifying this is by no means an essential condition of aesthetic pleasure—or displeasure—or even of the artistic relation. I do not here list these symptoms (for the most part already rather old hat) of an explosion in the so-called plastic arts, among others, in order to give vent to my dismay or astonishment over a revolution that has not been the first and will doubtless not be the last in the history of art. I mention them, rather, to bring out the polymorphous, hetero-clite, and constantly shifting nature of practices the theory of art strives to account for, and the no less precarious—and in any case relative—nature of the new categories it claims to have contributed to the history of art, of which "ontological status" is, despite the intimidating name, not the least evanescent. A pile of coal exhibited by Yannis Kounellis at the Entrepôt in Bordeaux[17] can pass for the "unique," untransportable object par excellence, one no description will enable us to reconstitute exactly as it was: nothing is more singular than chance. But this physically irre-ducible singularity can be revoked with a single word: the sovereign artist, duly consulted, need only respond, disdainfully, "Any old pile will do the trick." Town dumps are overflowing with irreplaceable objects. The major "symptom" of the aesthetic, "every detail counts," has its devil-may-care counterpart in another, which counterbalances but does not invalidate it: "anything goes"*. But that is another story, which will call for our attention a bit later.

To be sure, the definition of the status "unique product" as we are using the term here neglects all the inevitable transformations of iden-tity that occur in the course of time, whether as a result of gradual aging or sudden alteration; at a minimum, such transformations endow even the most singular works with a certain diachronic plurality. I have elected to consider this point in the chapter on transcendence, for rea-sons that will appear when we come to it.

17. 1991.

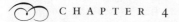 CHAPTER 4

# Multiple Objects

*I* WILL BEGIN THIS CHAPTER BY CITING A PASSAGE FROM NELSON Goodman that has already been mentioned; it seems to me to state the essentials on the theoretical level:

> The example of printmaking refutes the unwary assumption that in every autographic art a particular work exists only as a unique object. The line between an autographic and an allographic art does not coincide with that between a singular and a multiple art. About the only positive conclusion we can draw here is that the autographic arts are those that are singular in the earliest stage; etching is singular in its first stage—the plate is unique—and painting in its only stage. But this hardly helps; for the problem of explaining why some arts are singular is much like the problem of explaining why they are autographic.[1]

We will ignore the last sentence, which, with its discouraged tone, is unusual for Goodman; it does not bear on our new subject, but rather on autographic works in general, as well as their unique (when they *are* unique) products. Furthermore, I am not certain that their unique,

---

1. Nelson Goodman, *Languages of Art: An Approach to a Theory of Symbols* (Indianapolis: Bobbs-Merrill, 1968), p. 115.

autographic nature needs to be *explained:* there is nothing surprising about the fact that a human activity should produce a singular material object by transforming already existing materials. What is surprising, and does call for explanation, is rather the fact that an artistic practice should produce the *ideal* objects that allographic works immanate in[2] (but we have not gotten that far yet), and also, perhaps even more surprisingly, the "identical" material objects that multiple autographic works immanate in. More surprisingly, if one bears in mind that two material objects cannot be strictly identical at the physical level, even if industrialism has, for more than a century now, been accustoming us to treat as identical countless mass-produced objects which are such only from a certain (practical) point of view, and in an entirely conventional sense at that.

But Goodman pays virtually no attention to this question of (specific) identity, and rightly so. The multiple prints of an engraving can differ appreciably; it is thus not their "uniqueness of identity" which defines them as "authentic" prints,[3] but their provenance. The essential point is that certain autographic works consist in several objects, undoubtedly more or less interchangeable from an artistic point of view, and that the existence of such works depends on the fact that their "history of production" includes two stages: one produces a singular object—if it did not, the work would not be autographic, which means, let us recall, capable of being counterfeited—while the other produces multiple objects, taking the singular one as its point of departure.

The singular object obtained in the first stage is thus the means of producing the multiple objects of the second; it remains to be seen how this means functions (Goodman does not say), if not at the level of technical details, which doubtless differ considerably, then at least as far as its operating principle is concerned. Exploring a few typical examples may be helpful here; but we need, first of all, to clarify the way we are using the notion of stage.

Considered in an absolute sense, every creative process involves not two, but many stages. The various materials Klee applied in preparing *Refuge,* mentioned earlier, give us some sense of this, as do the untold

2. [*Immaner,* a neologistic back-formation from *immanent,* "immanent."]

3. As Goodman insists elsewhere, in another connection (different inscriptions of the same text), "there is in general no degree of similarity that is necessary or sufficient for replicahood." *Languages of Art,* p. 131, n. 3.

preliminary drawings and sketches for countless pictorial works, or, again (in the allographic regime), the outlines, rough drafts, and other "pre-texts" leading up to a page of Flaubert or Proust. But the word *stage* will here be used more specifically to refer to one particular genetic operation: that which determines the production of an object that is preliminary (instrumental), and thus not ultimate, yet definitive and capable of producing, in its turn, the ultimate object of immanence, as if it produced it itself by means of an (as it were) automatic technique. The product of the first stage is thus not simply a sketch or draft, but a *model* elaborate enough to guide, or even inflexibly control, the next stage, which, because it involves only realization, *may* be delegated (though this is not necessarily the case) to a simple craftsman who has no creative function. We noted, in discussing pointing techniques in carved sculpture, that a somewhat similar situation was created when a Rodin or a Moore contented himself with modeling a plaster model that someone (who might be the artist himself) then realized in marble. Such a model is something else entirely than the preliminary maquette a true "carver" like Michelangelo or Brancusi might make for himself, for the latter sort of rough version is merely a tentative draft the sculptor is free to interpret or reject as he sees fit, whereas a model, in the full sense (there can, of course, be any number of intermediate cases), has an imperative, binding character that leaves no margin for initiative or variation. This is obviously even truer of cast sculpture, printmaking, or photography, whose second stages are purely mechanical, and take place independently—in principle, as in the previous instance—of the human mind.

## Cast Sculpture

The techniques and materials utilized in cast sculpture are diverse and constantly evolving, but the general principle this art rests on is always the same. The artist produces a model by manipulating a malleable substance like clay, wax, or plaster;[4] a negative mold is then produced by

4. Two examples taken almost at random: the *Balzac* by Rodin which created the famous scandal after being shown at the 1898 Salon was the original plaster, still on exhibit at the Rodin museum. It was not until 1926 that (at least) two bronzes were taken from it. One

packing bonded sand around this positive model, after which molten metal (generally bronze) is poured into the mold. When it has cooled, the mold is broken open and the molded metal removed.[5] For the next casting, a new mold has to be made from the model, and so on. Tradition, backed up, in France, by a law in force since 1981, limits the number of casts that can thus be made to twelve (of which four are "artist's casts"); these twelve are, consequently, considered to be "authentic," that is, to make up the multiple work. The reasons for this limitation are, once again, partly technical (the model deteriorates, and the casts decline in quality) and partly commercial: taking too many casts would diminish the value of the whole set, reducing it to the level of a series of mass-produced objects. The casts are conventionally regarded as identical (at least initially, for they can subsequently develop in very different ways); the order in which they are produced apparently counts for little. Their identity is very roughly guaranteed by the homogeneity of the material they are made of: two metals of the same grade obviously stand a better chance of resembling one another than do two blocks of stone or wood. As soon as the number of casts exceeds the legally determined limit, one has crossed over into the realm of forgery,[6] of which there are essentially two kinds, involving additional casts or duplicate molding. Duplicate molding consists in utilizing one of the authentic casts as a model for a new mold. It is illegal for the same reasons unauthorized casts are; in both cases, the forgery consists in presenting these objects, produced in different ways, as authentic. The law does authorize duplicate molding, however, if the results are treated as

---

was for the museum in Antwerp; the other would be placed at the Vavin Crossroads in 1939. A third cast was made in 1954 for the Museum of Modern Art. As for Houdon's bust of Voltaire, the original plaster is in the Salon d'honneur of the French National Library; the marble statue made from it is today in the Théâtre-Français [Comédie française]. This double example shows clearly that the distinction between unique and multiple works does not always coincide with that between cast and carved sculpture.

5. Thus the "two stages" are, in fact, three, and generally even more, since the most frequently used method appears to involve making a clay model and a mold, then a plaster model and a second mold, after which the bronze is poured. A recent technique makes use of a polystyrene model sculpted with a knife; the metal fills all the space in the mold originally occupied by this model, which is burned away. In this technique, the model is obviously utilized only once; further casts are obtained by duplicate molding.

6. On the various kinds of forgery in this domain, and the definition, a contrario, of authenticity, see François Fabius and Albert Banamou, interviewed by Isabelle de Wavrin, "Rodin, Claudel, Barye et autres bronzes. Attention danger," *Beaux-Arts* 71 (1989).

"cast replicas" and identified as such. The principle that informs dupli-cate molding, all legal considerations aside, typifies the principle under-lying reproduction; we will encounter this category again in a broader context, in connection with the transcendence of autographic works in general. For reproductions of unique works are, of course, also pos-sible; thus the technique of duplicate molding has made it possible to turn out reproductions of carved sculpture in synthetic stone, either for teaching institutions like the Museum of French Monuments, or in order to protect endangered works by replacing them with reproduc-tions *in situ*.[7]

## Printmaking

Printmaking techniques are at least as diverse as those of cast sculpture: relief engraving in wood, linoleum, or plastic, in which the design is produced by cutting away everything that is not to be left in raised relief; intaglio engraving on a copper plate with a drypoint burin, or etching with aqua fortis or aquatint (leaving aside the mixed techniques exemplified by, at least, Picasso); lithography, in which lines traced in grease-based crayon are selectively inked; and serigraphy, in which ink is applied directly to paper through unmasked areas on a silk screen. But, whatever the technique, the first stage consists in the production of a unique "plate" (or screen), and the second in inking this plate and then using it to take an impression on a certain number of sheets of paper, which then constitute so many authentic prints, whether they are pulled by the artist himself or a craftsman. Here again, the limits on the procedure are at once technical (wear and tear on the plate)[8] and institutional (limited editions to avoid depreciation); here again, fraud is a matter either of pulling extra prints, or passing off as originals third-degree reproductions made from one of these prints, a photograph, or—why not—a new plate made by tracing the original.

7. Or hand-made copies, as with Carpeaux's *Dance,* which has been removed from the Gar-nier Opera House and replaced with a copy by Paul Belmondo; the original has found refuge in the Orsay Museum. I will come back to the theoretical difference, which is in any case obvious, between copies and reproductions.
8. For various material reasons, wear and tear is generally a more important factor in print-making than in cast sculpture; especially in drypoint, burrs soon wear down.

Photography in its classical form, with multiple prints, proceeds on the same principle: a light-sensitive surface receives a photonic imprint (negative) comparable to the engraving cut or etched into a plate, while the process by which this imprint is transferred to paper, through contact or projection, is comparable to the pulling of a print. In photography as in printmaking, the final imprint is reversed; hence the use of the (entirely relative) notion of negative to refer to the printing surface. This reversal is most conspicuous in photography, but it also leaps to the eye in certain prints, when words or a signature, traced in normal fashion on the plate, show up backwards on the print. The technical reason for limiting the number of prints is doubtless less compelling in photography, since there is negligible wear and tear on the negative, but, here as elsewhere, commercial considerations play a part in drawing the line between good printings and bad, or reproductions and authentic prints.

It should pointed out that, in all these cases, the object is autographic, so that one can forge not only its second phase (forged copies), but also its initial state: one can use the authentic originals to produce a fake original plaster "by Rodin" or a forged plate "by Callot," and one can even turn out a fake negative "by Cartier-Bresson" (and sell it as a real one). In this last case, it would "suffice" to find the subject of the photograph again, or else to reconstruct it, and then to photograph it from the same angle, at the same distance, in the same light, with the same lens, etc. I do not say this would be easy, I do not know whether it would be profitable, and I do know that it would be illegal, but those are all secondary questions.

## Tapestry-Making

A final type that I think we should consider for the sake of its minor deviations from the others is tapestry-making,[9] which, again, unfolds in two stages; the product of the first is a singular model, that of the second a realization that is, at least potentially, multiple. In the first stage, a painter produces a painting that will serve as a model, called a "car-

---

9. I mean, of course, tapestry-making from a model. There also exist, or at least could exist, tapestries improvised in a single stage without a model, which (would) thus have a unique object of immanence.

toon," even if those by Bayeu or Goya are generally oils on canvas.[10] In the second stage, the weaver makes the tapestry after the cartoon, transposing it as faithfully as he can into the colors of his wool. What he has done once, he can, in theory, repeat indefinitely, although it seems to me that custom looks far less favorably upon the multiplication of the end product here—even if we know of at least one instance in which four copies of a tapestry were made straightaway.[11] At any rate, this offers us an opportunity to recall that, in all arts of this kind, the multiplicity of the object is only a possibility that is not necessarily always exploited. It is entirely possible to take a single bronze,[12] a single print, or a single photographic print from the original model, and then destroy the model for greater security. There certainly have been such cases, even if they came about by accident (it is also possible to decide not to go beyond the model stage, which would bring us back to the single-stage autogaphic regime with a unique object). It is not even certain that the sole reason for introducing two-stage procedures was, in every instance, a desire to produce multiple works. They may simply have been adopted for the artist's convenience, if, like Rodin, he had a preference for modeling clay, or else because of the difficulty connected with obtaining direct positives in photography (but these can be obtained today with reversal-type film, and one does not generally feel the need to multiply slides). I do not see how engraving can be regarded as having any purpose other than multiplication—though there is the notable exception of the Degas monotypes in the Picasso collection: the special technique utilized to make them (the plates themselves were retouched with ink or paint) ensured that, in principle, only one proof could be pulled.

The essential difference between tapestry-making and the other arts with multiple products seems to me to reside in its principle of realization. To specify the nature of this difference, I will borrow Prieto's crucial distinction between realization (or reproduction) from a *matrix* and on a *signal*. A printmaker, sculptor, or photographer produces an

10. [Cartoon in French is *carton*, which also means cardboard.]

11. The tapestry in question is *Women at Their Toilet,* made after a collage by Picasso at the Gobelins' Tapestry Factory from 1967 to 1976; two of the tapestries were in color and two "in gray."

12. This was the case with Picasso's *Harvester* (1943), a bronze "monotype."

object that serves as a matrix in a mechanical process of realization, whether multiple or not; a musician or architect (and, I would add, a writer) produces an object which acts as a signal for an intellectual process of realization that presupposes an interpretive reading based on a code (a musical notation, diagrammatic or linguistic conventions). It will already have been understood that Prieto appeals to these two principles of realization to distinguish two groups of artistic practices: they correspond to our autographic multiple arts in the one case, and our allographic arts in the other—and it is quite certain that realization on a signal is eminently characteristic of the latter category, as we will have ample occasion to confirm. One can, however, just as easily reproduce a text, building plan, or score by utilizing one of its instances of manifestation as a matrix in a mechanical procedure such as photocopying. Conversely, it is possible to reproduce a painting, sculpture, or building (or even, as I just suggested, photographs, and, of course, films—whence the practice of the *remake,* which we will meet again) by utilizing it as a signal for a replica, or *copy,* that is as faithful as possible. Reproductions from a matrix or on a signal can be made in all sorts of arts—with the single proviso that *realizations* in music (the passage from a score to an interpretation), literature (the passage from writing to speech), architecture (the passage from the plans to a building), and cooking (the passage from the recipe to the prepared dish) can only occur on a signal. But (unique or multiple) works of plastic art are reproduced in both ways; one procedure is just as good or as bad as the other, and neither enjoys theoretical superiority (though one may be more commendable): a good photo of the *View of Delft* can be more "faithful" than a bad copy, and vice versa.

## Imprint and Transcription

I will use *imprint* to designate a realization or reproduction obtained by employing the original as a matrix, and will provisionally use *copy* to refer to a realization or reproduction that utilizes the original as a signal.[13] If

13. Prieto calls them, respectively, *reproduction* and *copy.* As we will see, this makes it hard (though not for Prieto) to draw the necessary distinction between realizations and reproductions.

we leave aside, for the moment, the cases in which these two procedures (which have more to do with the transcendence of works) are utilized for purposes of fraud, or to produce documentation for study purposes, it is clear that unique autographic works are works that cannot, by common consent, legitimately immanate in such realizations, while multiple autographic works are works that can. Cast sculpture, printmaking, and photography obviously proceed by way of imprint, regarded as legitimate within certain technical and/or conventional limits, provided that the matrix is the product of the first stage (model, plate, or negative) and not the second (sculpture, print, or proof pulled on paper). Taking imprints from second-stage products can only give rise to *reproductions.*

The peculiarity of tapestry-making, as we can now see, is that the cartoon plainly functions, not as a matrix to be applied, but as a signal to be interpreted, with the result that what the weaver does comes closer to producing a copy than an imprint. But if his activity is compared to that of a painter seeking to make a *faithful* copy of a painting,[14] it becomes easy to spot a difference that brings out the heterogeneous nature of this notion of copy. Like the painter-copyist in Arsène Lupin's employ,[15] the weaver bases his work on attentive observation of his model (the cartoon); the features of its specific identity prescribe what he does, and, via various copying or tracing operations, guide the way he does it (like a pattern in sewing). But, unlike the ordinary copyist, the weaver plainly makes no attempt to produce an object as similar as possible to his model: no one can mistake a tapestry for the cartoon it is based on, for the features characteristic of the cartoon are obviously *transposed* in the tapestry, if only because of the difference between the materials each is made of. Certain features of the model are, then, retained because they are regarded as pertinent to this transposition, while others are ignored because they are regarded as peculiar to the model; transposing the second set of features is regarded as either impossible and/or pointless. In this respect, the weaver's activity tends to resemble the copyist's—not, this time, in the sense that applies to painting,

14. Let me make it clear that *faithful* is not a pleonasm here, since many copies, especially those made by great artists, are a great deal freer than those made, for example, by forgers, whose unlawful craft obliges them to make copies that are as hard to distinguish from the originals as possible. I will come back to the matter of degrees of faithfulness when I discuss transcendence.

15. See Chap. 1, n. 45.

but rather in that in which one "recopies" the text of a manuscript in a different hand or typographic system, that is, by scrupulously respecting the text's literality while neglecting the graphic peculiarities of the copy. Certain more conventional forms, like Lurçat's numbered cartoons, where each color is prescribed by a number that refers back to a code, bring the status of tapestry-making still closer to that of the allographic arts. But it seems to me that even in this case, and, a fortiori, in the prevailing forms of this art, the requirements for an allographic regime are not quite fulfilled, since one still has reason to distinguish between an authentic cartoon and a fake, or between an original tapestry made after this cartoon and a copy made after the tapestry. Thus it seems to me more exact to treat tapestry-making as a multiple autographic art situated very close to the border between the autographic and allographic arts—and hence to regard it as one of the "transitional" arts[16] that, perhaps, await nothing more than a change in conventions to switch regimes.

Doubtless, it is now clear why I said, a moment ago, that my distinction between *imprints* (from a matrix) and *copies* (on a signal) was provisional: the second notion is too vague, or not sufficiently analytic. *There are copies and copies.* In both cases, a conscious (not a mechanical) activity takes an object as a signal with a view to reproducing it; but in one case, the copyist makes an effort to *copy everything* in the model, down to the least little detail, including the material it is made of, its weight, the nature of its support, etc.; in the other, he sorts pertinent from contingent elements, concerning himself with the latter alone. The first attitude is characteristic of the autographic arts, while the second characterizes the allographic arts, even if the example of tapestry-making goes to show that there are ambiguous cases. Thus it would behoove us to devise more precise terminology, by, for example, using the word *copy* exclusively for the first sense, and adopting a more active

16. The production of stained-glass windows is another; it too involves making an object (by applying paint or enamel to glass, or else by assembling pieces cut out of larger sheets of tinted glass) after a painter's "cartoon"; the cartoon is placed under the glass and so remains visible. In sewing, the pattern is placed *on* the material to be cut out, but the method of copying is comparable, and the fact that transposition is involved is just as obvious. In all these cases, the object realized is clearly discernible from its model. But, in the case of sewing from a pattern, we have doubtless crossed, from an institutional point of view, into the allographic regime. One sees, then, just how permeable the frontier is.

term for the second, such as *reading* or *transcription*. An everyday example may serve to illustrate this difference. Imagine a handwritten page—a letter, say, from Napoleon to Josephine. Since the photocopier (which would have produced an imprint of it) is out of order, a historian asks his assistant to copy it out by hand. The assistant attentively *reads* the fiery document, and then transcribes it without making any effort to imitate the handwriting; he is obviously treating it as a *text,* an allographic object, whose sameness of spelling or ideal textual identity is all that matters. A forger in Arsène Lupin's pay bent on counterfeiting the letter would take a completely different tack: he would not only imitate the great man's handwriting, but would also provide himself with identical paper of the same period, a quill of the same type, ink of the same color, etc., so as to produce a true copy (*facsimile*) of the letter, treated, this time, as an autograph: that is, an autographic object (the similarity between the two words is far from adventitious). The forger's copy is *faithful,* whereas the assistant's transcription is merely *correct*. But this "merely," intended to be purely quantitative (the assistant preserves *fewer* features than the forger) might actually, or from another standpoint, be quite misleading, inasmuch as the forger could do his work *without knowing how to read,* turning nothing other than his manual dexterity to account, as he would in forging a drawing by Dürer or Picasso. In that case, deciding whether the assistant or the forger preserves more features becomes a risky business. The truth of the matter is that they do not preserve the same features, and that they are quite simply not dealing with the same object.

But we have strayed a bit from the subject of multiple autographic works: Napoleon's letter is, qua *text,* an allographic object, and, qua *autograph,* a unique autographic object. Like a "faithful copy" of the *Mona Lisa,* a "faithful copy" of the letter could not be anything other than a facsimile made for documentary purposes, or a counterfeit. Prieto's view, let us recall, is that these distinctions have only economic relevance, given the values governing "collectionism," and are not at all pertinent aesthetically, in the proper sense of that word. The distinction is perhaps not as self-evident as Prieto seems to think; but the moment to debate the issue is not yet at hand. For now, we are merely observing empirical realities that owe more to custom than logic; at this level, it is clear that aesthetic and economic notions are closely intertwined. Here the status of multiple autographic works, entirely distinct from that of allographic works, rests on a convention as rigid as it is artificial—the one which makes prints, proofs, or casts [*épreuve* in all three cases] of objects of immanence all equally authentic, whatever their perceptible differences, since their authenticity is in principle guaranteed by the techniques utilized to make the imprint (in tapestry-making, exceptionally, by those utilized to transpose the design), by the practice of printing limited editions, and by the exclusion from the domain of the authentic of every possible sort of "reproduction," that is, production which does not issue directly from the first-stage model. As we will soon see, the conventions governing the allographic arts are of an entirely different order; the fact that copies of allographic works can be turned out in virtually unlimited numbers is by itself striking evidence of this.[17]

One is sometimes tempted to make short shrift of all these subtle distinctions by deciding to treat the work's object of immanence, in all the cases in point, as the (unique) first-stage model (original plaster, plate, negative, cartoon) produced by the artist; this makes all objects produced thereafter authorized reproductions of no greater artistic value than replicas produced by duplicate molding, unauthorized proofs, and other such facsimiles. Such a decision would considerably lessen our theoretical burden, like the symmetrically opposed decision made by Prieto, who regards every work as a conceptual "invention" whose realization(s) are of secondary importance. Thus there would no longer be multiple works, but, in literature, music, and architecture, as everywhere else, only unique autographic works whose objects of immanence would be the autographic manuscript, score, or plan: in sum, Margolis's "prime instance," mentioned earlier. Like all reductive solutions, this one too comes at a price: namely, an inability to account for the multiplicity of existing practices and conventions—here, the fact that the "world of art" (and, with it, the world tout court) treats certain works as if they were unique and others as if they were multiple, regarding the first-stage model for mul-

17. The "limited editions" of deluxe works do not come under the allographic regime, because they have to do, not with the ideality of the text, but with the materiality of its instances; they belong to the multiple autographic regime, just as manuscripts belong to the unique autographic regime.

tiple works as an ephemeral, utilitarian object in the service of the ultimate work, the work properly so called. In some cases, such as that of
Goya's "cartoons," the world of art changes its mind (adopting the cartoon as a work), and the convention shifts accordingly. It is time for theory to take this state of affairs into account, and even to *account for* it. But
it is not for theory to take the lead here and to decree what should be.
Art is a social practice, or, rather, a complex set of social practices; the
"status" of works is dictated by them, and by the notions and views that
accompany them. It would be neither very reasonable nor very profitable
to define the one without paying due attention to the others.

# CHAPTER 5

# Performances

---

THE DOMAIN OF ARTISTIC PRACTICES WITH FACTUAL OR EVENTIAL objects of immanence roughly coincides with that of the arts of spectacle or performance: theater, cinema (as far as the *profilmic,* or what takes place on the set, is concerned), musical or poetic improvisation or performance, dance, mime, public speaking, variety shows or cabaret, the circus, everything in sport that lends itself to spectacle, and, more generally, any human activity the perception of which can by itself produce and structure an immediate aesthetic effect (among other effects)—immediate in the sense that it is not deferred until such time as the activity produces something. (I will come back to this point.)

A first feature distinguishing works of performance from the practices we have so far considered is that the former are more frequently produced collectively; this often mobilizes a group of a certain size, such as a theatrical company, orchestra, dance ensemble, or sports team, requiring those in the group to work together so closely that it sometimes becomes impossible to sort out each individual's contribution to the whole. The collective nature of this activity often creates the need for a specific individual role, that of coordinator or "director": conductor of an orchestra, captain of a team, director of a play or movie, etc.; his or her function differs, in some cases, from that of the others involved in realizing the work. The fact that the work is produced collectively also affects its reception, which is generally assured by a more or less organized group of individuals, called, of course, a public, or, doubtless more aptly, an audience.[1] The collective nature of this reception is much more vital and formative here than in the case of the audience for a literary or even pictorial work, which is little more than an aggregation of individuals.

## Realization and Improvisation

Many of these arts are performantial practices whose function is to create a manifestation, perceptible to the eye and/or ear, of already existing works of the allographic regime: verbal texts, musical compositions, choreographies, pantomimes, etc. This function sometimes makes it difficult to tell, in practice, just what is to be attributed to the preexisting work and what to the performance, but the difficulty in no way diminishes the difference in status between these two types of practice, which I will come back to in a moment. It should, moreover, be pointed out that even if these arts are today generally assigned the task of performing existing works, all of them can function in an improvisatory mode as well, in the mode, that is, of performances independent of any previous work. A musician (a vocalist or instrumentalist) can improvise a musical phrase, an actor stage business or a line, a dancer an enchainement, a bard an epic tale, etc. Witty remarks and flights of eloquence are supposed to burst forth spontaneously; their value falls whenever we suspect that they have been premeditated, or, a fortiori, composed by a "third party." As to the moves of tennis or soccer players, the nature of these games and the largely unpredictable developments of each match guarantee (except when a match is fixed) that they will be improvised, even if it goes without saying that the art of improvisation presupposes, here as elsewhere, a mastery born of long training.

It is therefore tempting to regard improvised performances as the purest state of the art of performance—as spontaneous acts which owe nothing to the work of others and therefore constitute, more than any

1. [Genette employs the French word *audience,* noting that its use in the sense of "public" is an anglicism.]

performance of realization, autonomous objects which deserve to be called works. But matters are not so simple. Doubtless an improvised performance can, in the "best" of cases, be autonomous in the sense that the performer does not realize a text previously produced by someone else (Liszt playing a Beethoven sonata), or even by himself (Liszt interpreting his own *Sonata in* B), but rather lets the music "well up under his fingers" without borrowings or premeditation (Liszt improvising a pure "fantasia"). But, to begin with, the autonomy of an improvisation, even when narrowly defined, is never absolute. In practice—barring cases where things are systematically left up to chance—an improvisation, whether musical or of some other kind,[2] is always based to some extent either on a preexisting theme, which it varies or paraphrases, or on a certain number of formulas or clichés; this rules out all possibility of freely inventing each moment, note after note, without any connecting structure. Certain not very convincing attempts at free jazz aside, jazz has for half a century now provided a good illustration of this close cooperation between the improvised and the composed, despite the extremely rapid evolution of its idiom observable until (at least) 1960. It makes itself felt not only in the arrangements (especially of passages for several musicians) that are worked out in advance and learned by heart, or even written out, but also in the way each improvised chorus follows or takes off from a pattern laid down by the chord progression of the theme. This, in some sort, genetic relationship between a borrowed harmony and improvised melody finds a supplement in the resources provided by stock musical phrases, arpeggios, scales, and scraps of tried and true quotations, all of which go a long way toward facilitating matters—but also toward making them more facile—for the musician as well as his audience.[3]

The same situation can be observed, mutatis mutandis, in every improvisatory practice: a speaker never launches into a speech without some idea of the theme he will treat and a supply of commonplaces and stock phrases. As for the improvisations of ancient or modern bards,

---

2. From what we know of them, the methods of the Commedia dell'arte, fallen into disuse, seem to provide a perfect illustration of the relationship between an already established framework and theatrical improvisation.

3. [*Ba(na)liser le parcours,* a visual pun: *baliser* means to mark out a path with beacons, etc.; *banaliser* means to make banal.]

the work of Milman Parry and Albert Lord has taught us just how much they owe to the ressources of a formulaic style, "descriptive epithets," and such devices as the variable hemistich.[4] Even a tennis player's or chess player's moves are determined, however "unprecedented" each stage of a match may be, by the tactics the situation imposes, and, simultaneously, the repertory of decisions (*serving, going to net, lobbing, bringing out one's knight, castling, sacrificing a pawn,* etc.) that knowledge of the rules and experience of the game authorize or suggest. The famous line ascribed to Picasso applies to all these practices of on-the-spot performance: "Three minutes to do it, a lifetime to prepare."

These circumstances, and a good many others of the same order, do not merely go to show that improvisation never takes place without at least some premeditation and support. They also throw into relief the fact (which is in any case obvious) that the improviser, however great his powers of invention and however original he might be, is always simultaneously both a creator and an interpreter of his own creation, so that his activity invariably has two facets, one of which pertains exclusively to the "arts of performance," and the other to some other, usually allographic art, such as music, poetry, choreography, etc. An improvised work, doubtless—yet one a listener or spectator (to say nothing, as yet, of the techniques of recording) can, with a modicum of competence and skill, write out straightaway in the notation proper to the art in question: written text, score, choreographic plan, and so on. That this should be so shows that the improviser has expressed him*self in the idiom* of an already existing allographic art; as a result, the text (in the broad sense) which did not exist prior to his performance never fails to *result from* it, to be able to outlive it, and, at all events, to distinguish itself from it. When an actor interprets the stanzas of *The Cid,* in his own style, voice, and accent, and with his own particular facial expressions, gestures, and so forth, it is easy for a practiced observer to distinguish between the two works—Corneille's and, say, Gérard Philipe's—for the simple reason that the first can always be considered independently of the second, and, thus, the second independently of the first ("how did he interpret the role?"). When Mirabeau delivered his famous reply to

4. Milman Parry, *The Making of Homeric Verse,* ed. Adam Parry (Oxford: Clarendon, 1971); Albert Lord, *The Singer of Tales* (Cambridge: Harvard University Press, 1960).

the Marquis of Dreux-Brézé on 22 June 1789, with (I suppose) the accent of a delegate from Aix-en-Provence ("we are here by the will of the people," etc.),[5] the sentence which he cannot be said to have "interpreted," inasmuch as it gushed out (I imagine) all at once, and was inseparable from an overall style, physical appearance, movement, and an act—this sentence could nevertheless be extracted from the rest by an analysis made after the fact, perhaps even immediately after. If the Marquis, taken aback by the orator's ardor and pronunciation, had turned to the person sitting next to him and asked, "What did he say?", his neighbor would have repeated Mirabeau's outpouring in standard French (with a Parisian accent); he would, that is, have transmitted the *text,* stripped of the extralinguistic or "suprasegmental" features peculiar to the performance. In both cases, the work of performance properly so called (Gérard Philipe's interpretation, Mirabeau's *actio*) is the performantial event minus the text, in the sense in which Roland Barthes said, "What is theatricality? It is theater-minus-text."[6] The sole difference, it seems to me, resides in the fact that in one case the text (Corneille's) exists prior to the performance, while in the other (Mirabeau) it is produced by the interpreter himself in (more or less) the heat of the moment. This difference, which is plainly of capital importance when it comes to distinguishing the improviser's art from that of a "mere performer," is to all intents and purposes irrelevant to the way we describe the mode of existence of the work of performance considered in and of itself, that is, *without regard to what it performs, preexistent or not.*

It must also be pointed out that it is as a rule impossible for anyone but the artist to say whether a performance is—but we must rather say *to what extent* a performance is—improvised (indeed, it may even be doubted that the artist himself . . . ): when a jazz musician produces a solo, no one in the audience can guarantee that it has not been *entirely* written out, note for note, and memorized the day before (something which, it will be granted, would have no effect on the artistic value of

---

5. [Louis XVI had charged Dreux-Brézé with the mission of ordering the deputies of the Third Estate, Mirabeau among them, to leave the session of the newly formed National Assembly. Mirabeau's famous reply runs, "Go tell your master that we are here by the will of the people and will only leave at the point of the bayonette."]

6. Roland Barthes, "Le théâtre de Baudelaire," in *Essais critiques* (Paris: Seuil, 1964), p. 41 [tr. "Baudelaire's Theater," in *Critical Essays*, trans. Richard Howard (Evanston, Ill.: Northwestern University Press, 1972), p. 26].

the performance, except from a very special point of view, which, generally and a bit naively, attributes extra merit to improvisation). What can be said with certainty, however, is that no*t everything* in the solo was invented on the spot, since music is, after all, the art of combining sounds (as literature is that of combining words) which, by definition, existed prior to the performance.

Improvisation is not, then, a *purer,* but, on the contrary, a more *complex,* state of the arts of performance. Two theoretically distinct, and yet, in practice, often inseparable works mingle in it: a text (poetic, musical, or of some other kind) that can, after the fact, be written out in a notational system and indefinitely multiplied—this constitutes the allographic or ideal aspect of improvisation—and an (autographic) physical act whose material features cannot all be noted, despite the fact that they can be imitated, or even forged. Of an improvisation by Charlie Parker, one can note (and, therefore, publish and/or play again) the melodic line, with its tempo and rhythmic structure, but not the quality of the sound, which (aside from the type and make of the instrument, both easily ascertainable) has its origins in the particular features of breathing and embouchure that no notation can describe or transmit.[7] Yet nothing prevents a sufficiently talented instrumentalist from learning to reproduce this sound, and doing so well enough to pass off one of his own recordings as a lost and recovered recording of Parker's. The same sometimes happens in the case of performances that realize a score. (I will come back to this point.)

In practice, the audience perceives [*reçoit*] these two aspects of what it takes to be (not without reason) a single creation as if they were indissociable; it is hardly necessary to add that this syncretism makes part of the specificity (and charm) of an art like jazz, and, indeed, of poetic and rhetorical improvisation as well. On Nelson Goodman's hypothesis, there are reasons for thinking that all the arts which today are essentially allographic started out in this complex state which a few practices

---

7. I do not mention harmonic structure here (the "chord changes"), which can of course be described in a notation (and often is, in the form of a "chart"), but which in principle forms part, not of an improvised variation, but rather of the preexisting theme, even if this theme has been created by the improviser himself—as it often . . . half is, since a musician frequently produces (and copyrights) a new melodic theme laid over a borrowed (and legally unprotected) harmonic structure.

like those just mentioned still attest to; more radically ideal modes of creation, such as literature and musical composition, then gradually separated themselves out from the others. But, symmetrically, this "emancipation" opens up the possibility of purely performantial practices, like the arts of the actor, dancer, or performing musician. When an opera lover who knows the score of *Cosi fan tutte* by heart goes to the opera to appraise the new prima donna in the role of Fiordiligi, his musical experience and education permit him to distinguish effortlessly between what is Mozart's due and what Miss X's, that is, between what pertains to the art of musical composition and what to the art of singing; these artistic states have been, as it were, preanalyzed by the traditions and conventions of the world of art. We now turn to a consideration of some of their specific features.

## Identities

In terms of their relation to time, a "thing" or material "object" in the ordinary sense, and therefore also a work which immanates in such an object, whether unique or multiple, are characterized by what might be called *duration of persistence:* from the moment of its production to the moment of its utter destruction (I need say nothing more about the entirely relative nature of these two notions), such an object of immanence maintains an invariable numerical identity, which survives all the inevitable modifications of its specific identity. Under ordinary conditions of reception, the object's specific identity is itself taken to be approximately stable, at least throughout the period required for one occurrence of the act of contemplation. I make the trip to the Hague to admire the *View of Delft;* I look at it for an hour; it never occurs to me to wonder if the picture has "changed" in the course of the hour, and even less to try to detect signs of such a change—although it is, after all, not merely probable, but entirely certain that it has. I take it for granted—or at least assume it to be pertinent to my aesthetic experience, without going too deeply into what I mean by this—that the *View of Delft* has persisted in its being for an hour . . . and that I have persisted in mine.

Considered in the absolute, the nature of works of performance is not fundamentally different from this, inasmuch as a thing is a swarm of ordinarily imperceptible events. Yet such works offer themselves up to reception in time in a very different manner: an event does not "persist" before our eyes the way an unmoving object, steadily identical to itself, does; rather, it unfolds, with or without visible movement (a simple change in color or lighting appears as an event without motion), over a certain period of time, in the sense that its constitutive moments succeed one another from a beginning to an end. To watch or listen to it unfold consists in following it from this beginning to this end. I may choose to contemplate the *View of Delft* for an hour or a minute, but I cannot choose the period of time in which I will watch the entire performance of *Parsifal* or a Japanese No play; if I leave the theater after an hour, I will not really have "listened to *Parsifal* for an hour" the way one looks at the *View of Delft* for an hour, but will rather have listened to (and watched) only an hour of *Parsifal*. The duration of a performance (and of any event whatsoever) is not, like that of material objects, a duration of *persistence,* but a duration of *process,* which cannot be subdivided without negative repercussions on this process, that is, the event itself. It is, of course, in this sense that works of performance are "temporal" objects, whose duration of process makes up part of their specific identity; they are objects that can be experienced only in this duration of process, that cannot be experienced in their totality unless one experiences the totality of their process, and that can be experienced only once, because a process is by definition irreversible and, in the strict sense, unrepeatable. Such objects are certainly not "more temporal" than things; they are, rather, objects endowed with a different temporality, which is—how should one put it?—more intimately bound up with their manifestation. I know very well that one can go to the "same" performance of *Parsifal* several times, but I also know very well that that is not quite true. We will encounter this crucial point again further on.

I grant—indeed, I just said—that one also does not see quite the same *View of Delft* twice. In practice, however, it would occur to no one to wonder if today's *View of Delft* is lighter or darker than yesterday's, whereas an enthusiastic (but attentive) Wagnerian could say, without its striking anyone as odd, that yesterday's *Parsifal* was not sung as well as last week's, or that it was conducted more briskly, etc., even though the cast and conductor had not changed. The doubtful or borderline cases are to be sought elsewhere: for example, in the well-known *mobiles* with an internal (Tinguely) or external (Calder) source of motion, since repetitive or chance process enters into the definition of their status; or, again, in the "ephemeral" objects whose installation and exhibition are designed to last for only a limited period of a few days or weeks. Consider, among other such works, the fabric fences that Christo put up in California (*Running Fence*, Sonoma and Marin Counties, 1976), or his "packaging" of the Pont-Neuf in 1985. Here one is hard put to draw a clear-cut distinction between the status of thing and that of event, even if, in all these cases, the hurried public contents itself with a brief visit, thereby plumping de facto for the former, out of laziness.

I have dwelt on this temporal dimension because it is relatively specific. This is not to say that the setting of works of performance matters less than does that of other autographic works, even if it is, by definition, temporary. On a symbolic level, the first concert Rostropovitch gave in Moscow after several years of exile had a different emotional, and thus, to a certain extent, aesthetic charge than the same concert would have had if it had been given in New York or London. From a technical standpoint (and therefore here again, to a certain extent, from an aesthetic standpoint as well), the setting of every performance has its particular perceptual properties: visual, acoustic, spatial, and so on; the same troupe will not perform the same way in an Italian-style theater and a Greek or Roman amphitheater; the same cast will not sound the same at La Scala, at Covent Garden, or in front of the "mysterious abyss"[8] in Bayreuth.

These features, and a host of others, help make up the specific identity of a singular performance, that is, a performance which is unique or else considered in its singularity. (I will come back below to the specific identity of a series of performances considered to be "identical"). Given that a performance unfolds through a succession of moments, one might be tempted to suppose that none of its component elements, lacking duration of persistence, could *evolve* by changing their specific identity over the course of a performance. But, as a matter of fact, certain aspects of a performance can very well undergo such changes, deliberate or accidental, welcome or not: in a symphonic movement which has, in theory, the same tempo throughout, it can happen that the conductor *speeds up* or *slows down;* in the course of a recital or an opera, the timbre of a singer's voice can become *lighter* or (the more fre-

---

8. [A deep pit for the orchestra.]

quent case) *darker;* an actor, pianist, or tennis-player can make *more and more,* or *fewer and fewer,* mistakes, a jazz combo can *warm up,* and so on.

The *numerical* identity of a performance is as determinate as that of any other material fact or object, but this is hardly ever a question under normal circumstances, since it is not easy to attend a performance without knowing *which performance* one is attending. The question could, however, come up in the context of a repetitive series—for example, if a spectator dozed off in the middle of a short, "regular" (repetitive) number, then woke up and asked the person sitting next to him if they were still watching the "same" number, or the next occurrence of it. The question arises much more naturally in the case of sound recordings or recorded broadcasts, which we are more likely to see and/or hear without knowing which performance they are traces of. Thus I can hear, on the radio, a recorded broadcast of *Tristan und Isolde* as performed at Bayreuth this year, and ask which *performance* (of the series) it is; the question can take on a certain importance if it is known, for example, that a certain singer was ill on a given day. Or, again, a musician can record several "takes" of the same interpretation in the studio, then listen to them all in order to pick out the best (specific identity), without knowing beforehand which was which. After making his choice, he might ask *which* one he had chosen, only to be told, as often happens, that it was "the first"—numerical identity, or I understand nothing at all of the subject.

The question of numerical identity is obviously of greatest relevance in cases of forgery or uncertain attribution. It is in this context, of course, that Goodman initially works out his criterion for the autographic regime.[9] But, here again, forgeries in the proper sense of the word (forgeries of a singular object) must be distinguished from mere specific imitations. The fact that a pianist or actress can play a role or a concerto "in the style" of Horowitz or Madeleine Renaud—one Horowitz or Renaud may very well never have played—illustrates the second category, and is in no wise proof that an autographic work is involved, since it is just as easy to write or compose "in the style" of Stendhal or Debussy. The mark of the autographic—that is, of the physically singular

---

9. On the possibility of forging performances, see Nelson Goodman, *Languages of Art: An Approach to a Theory of Symbols* (Indianapolis: Bobbs-Merrill, 1968), p. 113, n. 9, and pp. 117–118.

nature of a performance—is that it is possible to mistake or pass off (on a recording) a faithful imitation, deliberate or not, of a given *specific* (singular) performance by a certain artist *as* that performance.[10]

These questions of identity thus bring us to a consideration of the two means by which a work of performance can, to a certain extent, escape from the temporal condition of an event, that is, from its ephemeral, one-time-only character. Though these two means partially converge to produce the same effect, they differ markedly in kind. I have in mind reproduction by means of *recording*, and *repetition*, or, more precisely, what is conventionally regarded as repetition. Although it is, for obvious technological reasons, the more recent of the two kinds of reproduction, I will begin by discussing recording, whose theoretical implications are (to my mind) of lesser import.

## Recording

By recording, I mean any sort of visual and/or aural reproduction of a performance in any branch of the arts, whatever the technical procedure involved. I do not employ the word *reproduction* (which is, moreover, widely used in this domain) fortuitously: a record, tape, cassette, or film, whether the procedure used to make it is acoustic, photonic, electrical, magnetic, analog, or digital, is never anything other than a more or less faithful documentary record (produced by imprint) of a performance, and not a state of that performance, just as a photograph of the *View of Delft* is merely a documentary record, not a state, of that work. In this sense, as we will see, recordings have more to do with transcendence than with immanence, so that the remarks we have already

10. "It was learned only a short while ago that the recording of Chopin's Concerto No. 1 for Piano and Orchestra, long admired and thought to be a Swiss Radio tape recording of a 1948 concert by Dinu Lipati, is in fact a recording of a 1955 performance given in Prague by the pianist Halina Czerni Stefanska. When the tape was first discovered, it was identified by Madeleine Lipati, who had 'recognized' her husband's manner of playing beyond the shadow of a doubt. After a long inquiry (involving a comparison of sound spectographs?), the Polish pianist was able to reclaim her property" (Françoise Escal, *Le compositeur et ses modèles* [Paris: PUF, 1984], p. 68). It is impossible to miss the parallels between this case of excessively confident (or self-seeking) identification by a spouse, and the one in *The Return of Martin Guerre,* which Prieto aptly evokes to illustrate the difference between the two types of identity.

made about reproductions of material works apply to them as well. As with a work of plastic or visual art, a faithful reproduction of a musical or theatrical performance can provide the occasion or means for a more accurate perception and fuller or more intense aesthetic relation than the "thing itself" apprehended in the unsatisfactory conditions direct contact often involves: poor visibility, bad acoustics, annoying or disturbing surroundings, lack of attention, the "Berma effect," and so forth. Moreover, the frontier between "direct"[11] and recorded is not totally impermeable, no more, doubtless, than is that between direct and indirect perceptions of works of plastic or visual art. Nelson Goodman is not wrong to call the notion of "merely looking" into question:[12] if we accept glasses, why not magnifying glasses or microscopes? If electric lighting, why not raking lights, X-rays, or scanners? If hearing aids, why not electric amplifiers, microphones, loudspeakers, transmitters? If opera glasses, why not the lens of a movie camera, or transmission by radio, cable, or satellite? If live broadcasting, why not short-term delayed broadcasting, long-term delayed broadcasting, tape recorders or video recorders which further delay the delayed broadcast,[13] and so forth? These notions must, in other words, be relativized; we need to envisage, between the "I was there" of the happy few* who were at Salzburg or Glyndebourne, and the "I have it on CD" of the average music lover, all the present and future nuances of the "I was almost there"—the most common mode, alas, of the aesthetic relation.

In theory, be it noted, a recording bears on a singular performance, much as a reproduction can only be of a singular work of plastic or visual art (a duplicate mold of *The Thinker* has, genetically speaking, to be a duplicate mold of one or another cast of *The Thinker,* not of *The Thinker* in general, even if the differences are so slight that, without additional information, we cannot tell, afterwards, *which* cast the duplicate mold was made from). But technological advances have long since made all sorts of cutting, sound editing, and other types of mixing possible, so that today many live recordings are amalgams of takes of sev-

11. *Direct,* which also means "live," as in "live broadcast."

12. Goodman, *Languages of Art,* p. 101–102.

13. [The French term for delayed broadcasting, *diffusion différée,* paves the way for a graphic pun and a glancing allusion to Jacques Derrida: "further delays the delayed broadcast" is, in the original, *sur-diffère la 'différance.'*]

eral different performances in the same series, of which the recording provides a kind of synthetic account or anthology: the first day's overture, the next day's high C, the voice of one performer with the face of another. Recordings can also be doctored note by note in the studio (think of Glenn Gould), and informed music lovers are convinced that not all the notes in a certain aria of Isolde's owe their existence to the same prima donna. (I will come back to this.) Yet the fact remains that no matter how complex the mixing may have been, every note in a diachronic or synchronic amalgam produced in this way is drawn from a singular performance.

However, technical progress is not responsible for another circumstance that is of greater artistic relevance: the emergence of a new convention, in the name of which a group of artists that considers itself well represented by a live* or studio recording,[14] to which it has the same (potentially lucrative) legal rights[15] as it would have to a particular performance, can adopt and authenticate the recording as a work in the full sense of the word. From then on, the status of this reproduction is, as with a print, photograph, or cast sculpture, that of a multiple autographic work—multiple, and, as a rule, unhampered by the technical or else deliberately imposed limitations that restrict the right to take imprints of works of plastic art. Yet it remains autographic, because the work's "prime instance" is always singular, and can be forged in each stage of its development: I can record an interpretation of the *Winterreise* in which I imitate Dietrich Fischer-Dieskau's timbre and style (first-stage forgery), or I can make a pirate recording of one of the same singer's concerts and sell it as if it were an "authentic" recording, that is, one acknowledged and approved by the artist (second-stage forgery).

There is, however, a world of technical and artistic difference between the simple acoustic recordings made with a single microphone in the early years of the twentieth century, and the subtleties of today's digital recordings. Similarly, between a "filmed stage performance" of the 1930s and a film-opera like Rosi's *Carmen* or Losey's *Don Giovanni*,

---

14. The difference between these two modes, which is diminishing on the technical level, is in any case not of fundamental importance from the point of view that interests us here: whether in public or in the studio, and whether or not the performer is free to stop and start again, a performance is always an event that unfolds in time.

15. [Untranslatable wordplay: "sur lequel il a (et, si possible perçoit) . . . des droits."]

there is all the difference between a simple documentary record of a performance, and a complex performance in which the contributions of the artists, on the one hand, and the director and his entire crew, on the other, are so tightly interwoven that they are, in the literal sense, inextricable. In such cases, we are witness not merely to a change in the status of an artistic practice, but to the birth of a new art, to which several other arts of widely varying status contribute: for example, the art of a librettist, composer, several singers, an orchestra, conductor, director, set designer, wardrobe designer, sound engineer, cameraman, and many others, whose names deservedly appear in the credits. In the face of such multi-media monsters, the theory of art would do well to take note of the sometimes derisory simplicity of its analyses.

## *Iteration*

In theory, an improvisatory performance does not lend itself to iteration of any kind. When a jazz musician, from one evening to the next, or from one studio take to the next, "replays" the same piece, this simply means that he takes up the same theme to ring new changes on it. Of course, the capacity (or desire) for renewal varies sharply with the artist, period, school, and also theme, some themes providing a better basis or more room for improvisation than others. The "group improvisations" of New Orleans–style bands were often nothing more than modest paraphrases. In contrast, studio documents testify to the remarkable diversity of approach of a Charlie Parker. Certain chord progressions (like that of *Cherokee,* an obsessively repeated theme of the 1940s) lend themselves to innovation more readily than others which are too simple (a contemporary musician cannot do much with a chord chart of the 1920s) or too rich: Thelonius Monk's often intimidate other artists, while John Coltrane's *Giant Steps* has discombobulated at least one. At all events, improvisation is not the only kind of creativity there is in jazz; a great many major jazz works—for example, certain suites by Duke Ellington or Gil Evans—are wholly composed. For the most part, however, improvisation, in jazz or elsewhere, and whether musical or of some other kind, is, as such, of the order of the singular, in the full sense: in other words, it is unique.

The same cannot be said of performances of realization. An allographic work is susceptible of an indefinite number of good or bad *correct* performances (in compliance, that is, with the indications in the text or score), leaving aside the incorrect ones; furthermore, *a* performance, defined by its conformity to the text as well as its specific identity as performance, is always considered, by the conventions of the world of art, to be repeatable within the limits of that conformity and that identity. To take a deliberately simple example, let us say that a touring pianist or actor who plays the *Hammerklavier* Sonata or the role of Harpagon before a different public every night *can* be said to offer "the same" interpretation of the work in question night after night, with negligible variations. An aficionado who follows him from performance to performance will have no trouble detecting significant differences from one to the next. Yet this by no means prevents the artworld from making pertinent use of a synthetic (all iterative entities are synthetic) notion like "Pollini's *Hammerklavier*" or "Michel Bouquet's Harpagon", considered solely with respect to their specific features, that is, those features common to all occurrences of them, and distinct, when taken en bloc, from other synthetic notions such as Schnabel's *Hammerklavier* or Dullin's Harpagon. This common character, identified in purely specific terms (it is hard to see what might constitute the *numerical* identity of such an entity) make the iterative series something purely ideal, a class of which each particular performance is a member; their common features could doubtless be recorded, if not in a notation in the strict sense, then at least in a sort of script that would go beyond the indications in the text—the stage directions in *The Misanthrope,* for example, or the specifications of tempo in the *Hammerklavier.*[16] Thus one is entitled to consider an iterative series of performances (Pollini's *Hammerklavier*) as a subclass of what Goodman calls the "compliance-class" constitutive of an allographic work (Beethoven's *Hammerklavier*). The term generally used to designate the stable identity of such a series (reiterable in what is called a "reprise" in French and a "revival" in English) is *production;* Monroe Beardsley judiciously suggests that we extend

---

16. For the theater, there exists a series of scenographic scripts, like the one Jean-Louis Barrault wrote for *Phèdre* or Jean Meyer for *The Marriage of Figaro;* they were published in the (unfortunately discontinued) series "Mises en scène" put out by Éditions du Seuil.

it to cover all entities of this sort.[17] Thus it is common usage to say that the Paris Opera is "reviving" a production of the Geneva Opera. In actual fact, the term often refers to nothing more (but this is already a great deal) than the (relative) identity of two stage productions. There can obviously be considerable variation in the way the term is applied, but there is nothing to prevent us from calling a more compact series a "production," with a view to designating the broadest possible identity, accidentals aside. The *Ring* cycle directed by Chéreau and Boulez at Bayreuth in 1979 or by James Levine at the Metropolitan Opera from 1988 to 1990 are examples of such productions.

This usage, duly attested in prevailing cultural practice, entitles us to regard works of performance as capable of sustaining, by dint of reiteration, an intermediate mode of existence, located somewhere between the autographic and allographic regimes. I restrict myself to saying "capable of," because a performance that remains unique (as a result of accident, decision, or discouraging failure) obviously will not attain this status; I say "intermediate," because it seems to me that too many facets of the art of performance (for example, an actress's face, a dancer's physique, the timbre of a singer's voice) elude even verbal notation for a truly allographic "emancipation" ever to become a real possibility—and I say this without the slightest trace of disappointment. A second reason is that the specific identity of a series of performances can *evolve* the way the specific identity of a material object does, in contrast to that of texts or musical compositions, which is invariable, barring revisions. Thus we say that a certain production is "becoming more solid" as time goes on, that a singer in this production "is putting more and more into his role," or that the conductor "keeps slowing down the tempo"—yet we do not lose our sense of the identity of this production, just as a painting continues to be the same even if the colors change. But this variability has its limits, since, unlike that of material things, it is not underwritten by an invariable numerical identity. Making too many changes in the cast, for example, can call the identity of a stage production into question, while the identity of the same performer's interpretation of a work can undergo a sharp break, as is attested by certain recordings made at wide

17. Monroe C. Beardsley, *Aesthetics* (1958), 2d ed. (Indianapolis: Hackett, 1981), p. 56.

intervals: for example, the recordings of the *Goldberg* Variations made by Gould in 1955 and 1981, or Fischer-Dieskau's recordings of the *Winterreise,* which date from 1948 and 1985.[18] In such cases, we prefer to speak of *two* interpretations, which may be as different from one another as if they were the work of two different performers. All these hesitations or liberties of usage testify to (among other things) the uncertain nature of iterative identity.

Such identity doubtless has an intermediate status for more than one reason and in more than one sense. It lies between the autographic and allographic as far as ideality is concerned, but also between immanence and transcendence, inasmuch as iterative performance does not, unlike a multiple autographic work, proceed from a mechanical imprint capable of ensuring sufficient identity between two impressions that are in principle indiscernible, but rather from an endless effort of renewal: instinctive or deliberate faithfulness to an interpretive style constantly clashes, on the common basis of a text to be performed, with a legitimate desire to revitalize and improve. Iterative performances thus tend to recall the practices of more or less free self-imitation that give rise to works with replicas. Like Chardin's *Saying Grace,* "Gérard Philipe's Rodrigo" or "Boulez's *Parsifal*" are works of plural immanence that do not nessarily set out (as *The Thinker* does) to attain the empirical indiscernibility of objects of immanence.[19] As such, they exceed their immanence, and manifest their transcendence.

To sum up, in broad outline: a performance is a physical event, and, as such, a unique autographic object; but, by way of recordings, it gives rise to a multiple autographic art, and, by way of iteration, to a plural autographic art. These two facts are also facts of transcendence, the first by way of indirect manifestation, the second by way of plural immanence. We will of course encounter these notions again a bit further on, in a context that is more specifically theirs.

18. To be honest, this last case is complicated by the fact that the pianist was not the same in both cases (it was Klaus Billing in one instance, Alfred Brendel in the other). Fischer-Dieskau has apparently made five separate recordings of this song cycle (and others), two of them with Gerald More; comparativists tend to lose their way here.

19. I am here speaking of these interpretations as iterative performances, not singular recorded performances; the multiple instances of the latter are, for technical reasons, just as (doubtless even more) difficult to distinguish from one another as are the twelve casts of *The Thinker.*

# CHAPTER 6

# The Allographic Regime

T HE GOODMANIAN THEORY OF THE ALLOGRAPHIC REGIME[1] IS
introduced, let us recall, by way of an empirical and apparently
almost fortuitous detail, and works its way back to the causes which
account for it. This starting point is the fact that certain kinds of works,
and therefore certain arts, do not lend themselves, as others do, to
forgery in the strict sense, that is, the act of fraudulently passing a copy
or reproduction off as the authentic original—not because that would
be impossible, but rather because it would, in a sense, be too simple, and
so meaningless, there being nothing easier than to recopy or reproduce
the text of, say, Baudelaire's "The Death of Lovers"; and, above all, because the product (a new copy of this poem) would finally be neither
more nor less valid than its model, and so would in no wise constitute a forgery of this text, the nature of which is to be indefinitely reproducible. Again, if the copy is handwritten, the fraud might consist
in passing it off as the original autograph, or, if it is a printed text, as a
copy belonging to a particular edition; but the forgery in such cases
would bear, not on the allographic object known as the text, but rather

---

1. The term "allographic regime," defined on pp. 16–17 above, is of course not to be found
in Goodman, who simply describes certain arts as autographic and others as allographic.

on the unique autographic object known as an autograph manuscript, or else on the multiple autographic object known as an edition. Passing off a copy or facsimile as an authentic manuscript or copy of an edition is a meaningful act, for this facsimile *is not* what one claims it is. However, it makes no sense to speak of "passing off" the *text* of this facsimile for the text thus reproduced, because the two texts are strictly identical, or, more precisely, because there is only *one* text, which "is reproduced" or, rather, *"manifested,"* in material forms that may or may not be identical, by the original manuscript, the authentic printed copy of the original edition (and any other authorized edition), and such fraudulent facsimiles as may have been made—and also by any transcription produced in different handwriting or lettering, as long as it is "orthographically" (literally) correct, complies, that is, with its model. Thus if one assumes (as is perfectly obvious at this level) that a literary work consists in its text (and not in the variable manifestations thereof), it follows that such a work cannot be forged, or that a faithful forgery or exact transcription of one of its correct manifestations is, quite simply, another correct manifestation of the work.

This state of affairs, which, mutatis mutandis, is also characteristic of music and certain other artistic practices, tautologically defines these practices as allographic, but cannot be said to *explain* the existence of this regime of immanence. Rather, it provides an *index* of it, insofar as it is one of its consequences or effects, even while it serves (as we will see) as an instrument of it. The explanation we are after is not to be sought in the fact that the products of arts of this kind are multiple. As we have already seen, certain arts which have multiple products (or *proofs*)[2], like printmaking or cast sculpture, are no less autographic for that, since each proof must be certified as authentic and is accordingly defined by its "history of production," whereas an inscription of "The Death of Lovers" or the score of the *Jupiter Symphony* would, even if composed at random, constitute instances of these works quite as valid as those obtained from the original manuscript by transcription or photocopying. Goodman also discusses and rejects another possible explanation,[3] which turns on the idea that autographic arts have only one

2. [See Chap. 1, n. 18.]
3. Nelson Goodman, *The Languages of Art: An Approach to a Theory of Symbols* (Indianapolis: Bobbs-Merrill, 1968), pp. 113–114.

stage* of production (the work the painter produces is *ultimate,* for no one has subsequently to "realize" it), while allographic arts have two (the composer produces a score which a performer, who may be the composer himself, must then play). This criterion discriminates no better than does one based on the fact that an art has multiple products, for certain autographic arts (precisely those with multiple products) also have two stages, whereas an allographic art like literature has only one: the manuscript or typescript (etc.) produced by the writer is also, from our present vantagepoint, ultimate; later it will (or will not) be *multiplied* by impression, but this quantitative operation does not affect its text's mode of existence any more than an oral performance does. The borderline between the two regimes does not, then, lie here.

Moreover, it seems to me that the distinction between one-stage and two-stage arts does not take quite the form Goodman says it does. The contrast between the regimes of music and literature is by no means as clear-cut as he seems to think. Indeed, it is far more fluid. There have been and continue to be situations in which literature tends to functions in two stages (in the theater, for example), and there are others in which music, by necessity or choice, functions in one stage, which yields a score musicians read but do not play. Furthermore, there exist purely oral forms of "literature,"[4] as well as unwritten musical forms, whose single stage is not that of a notation awaiting (a possible) performance, but rather that of a first execution (possibly) amenable to a notation. In short, the relationships between these two modes of manifestation are not, perhaps, most accurately described in (diachronic) terms, as "stages," but rather in synchronic or achronic terms; we will encounter this point again. One can pertinently apply the notion of stage, it seems to me, only to autographic arts with multiple products, where the model, plate, or negative produced by the artist necessarily *precedes* the proofs later taken from it by imprint. On the other hand, in literature, music,

---

4. Paul Zumthor, *La lettre et la voix* (Paris: Seuil, 1987), objects, not unreasonably, to the use of the term literature to describe this sort of practice, since the etymology of the word so clearly marks it as referring to the written mode alone. I will use it nonetheless, for lack of a better and like nearly everybody else, as a convenient way of designating what these two modes of manifesting texts have in common at the level of the necessarily crude distinction between "arts." (The more accurate term would doubtless be "verbal art.") The word *text* will, of course, also be used here in a sense that applies to both oral and written literature.

and indeed, as we will see, all the allographic arts, the order in which performance and notation occur is in no sense prescribed by a relation of cause and effect. The multiple autographic arts are thus the only ones that may properly be said to have "two stages," and, as Goodman clearly suggests, it is only in the second that their products can be multiplied.[5] The allographic arts are not intrinsically two-stage arts, but rather arts amenable to two different modes of manifestation, the order of which is relatively unimportant. This remark, which I will expand upon later, by no means implies that an explanation of the allographic regime "by stages" should not be rejected—quite the contrary.

The true explanation ("the reason," as Goodman puts it) hinges on a distinction, characteristic of the allographic regime, between differences which "do not matter" and the pertinent differences that permit us to differentiate between two inscriptions, or two performances, of (for example) a literary or musical work; or else it hinges—but this ultimately comes down to the same thing—on a distinction between the "the properties constitutive of the work" and "contingent properties"[6]— the latter being properties of, not the work, but one of its manifestations. The properties constitutive of a literary work—I am inclined to say "of its *text*," but the distinction is not yet pertinent at this point in our discussion—are those which define its "orthographic identity"; but the English expression "sameness of spelling" has the advantage of not putting undue emphasis on the written mode. What is at stake here can be summed up as the work's linguistic identity before any bifurcation between the written and the oral, an identity any inscription or presentation has to respect if it is to count as correct. The "contingent" properties of an inscription or presentation are those which characterize the mode of manifestation alone: typographic options, timbre, rate of delivery, etc. Similarly, in a musical score, it is the features of the typographic realization that count as contingent; in a performance, the (variable) features peculiar to the interpretation, such as the tempo adopted (if it is not prescribed), the timbre of a voice, or the make of an instrument. We can see that the descriptive adjectives "constitutive" and "con-

---

5. He says so *a contrario* in a sentence we have already quoted: "autographic arts are those that are singular in the earliest stage; etching is singular in its first stage—the plate is unique— and painting in its only stage." *Languages of Art,* p. 115.

6. *Languages of Art,* pp. 115–116.

tingent" must be understood with respect to the work (or, rather, its object of immanence), that is, as meaning "proper to the object of immanence" and "proper to a given manifestation," the latter considered either with respect to its generic features (for example, the features common to every copy of the same edition of *The Charterhouse of Parma* or to all occurrences of Alfred Brendel's interpretation of the *Waldstein* Sonata), or, a fortiori, its singular features: the torn page in my copy of *The Charterhouse,* a certain false note in a certain occurence of Brendel's interpretation of the *Waldstein.*

This distribution between the properties of the object of immanence and the properties of its manifestations accounts for the empirical fact which we identified, at the beginning of this chapter, as a touchstone for the allographic regime. If a literary or musical work cannot be forged, the reason is that the presence of all its "constitutive" properties in a would-be "fake" suffice to make this new object a correct manifestation of (the object of immanence of) the work, one quite as correct, from the present vantagepoint, as all the most officially authenticated manifestations: an autograph manuscript, an edition "revised by the author," a performance conducted by the composer, etc.—and this regardless of the "contingent" properties peculiar to this manifestation, such as being a photocopy of the kind prohibited by the Law of 11 March 1957,[7] a falsified document, an instance of shameless plagiarism of Brendel's interpretation, etc. A contrario, the indiscernibility between constitutive and contingent properties (between immanence and manifestation), characteristic of the autographic regime, entails that the slightest variation in properties counts as conclusive evidence (and a feature) of a forgery: for example, in the case of a copy of *The View of Delft* otherwise assumed to be "perfect," the fact that it was painted in 1990.

But this distinction between the two sets of properties doubtless calls for explanation in its turn. Nelson Goodman, although he was to devote a whole chapter of *Languages of Art* to a very close examination of the "requirements" a notation has to satisfy, and although he sometimes ascribes too large a role (in my view) to written modes of manifestation, nevertheless takes pains to avoid treating the availability of a notation as the key to this situation, of which it is more an effect

7. [French laws are ordinarily identified by the date they were promulgated.]

than a cause. "While availability of a notation," Goodman said in 1978 in response to a remark of Wollheim's, "is usually what establishes an art as allographic, mere availability of a notation is neither a necessary nor a sufficient condition [for the allographic regime]."[8] It might be asked how the "availability of a notation" can "establish" a state of affairs without being a sufficient condition for it. Here again, the response is undoubtedly that it has more the character of an effect than of a cause: there can be allographism without notation (non-necessary condition), but there cannot be notation without allographism, a necessary condition for notation that is, consequently, a reliable index of it, and thus plainly a sufficient condition, not for the allographic regime, but for the judgment that an art is allographic.

But the 1978 text is in fact more restrictive than this formulation suggests, since it evokes the availability of systems of notation in the autographic arts, such as the numbering of paintings in certain museums (comparable to the use of call numbers for books in libraries),[9] where 76.21 unambiguously designates the twenty-first work acquired in the year 1976. In that sense, of course, the availability of a notation is not a reliable index of an allographic regime, but it seems to me that Goodman stretches the concept of notation too far when he applies it, a bit sophistically, to any unambiguous system for identifying an object, identified in this case by the numerical identity it possesses as a singular object, the way everyone in France is identified by his or her INSEE number.[10] As to the notations characteristic of the allographic arts, they

8. Nelson Goodman, *Of Mind and Other Matters* (Cambridge: Harvard University Press, 1984), p. 139.

9. In question here are particular instances, not "titles," as the professionals say, since, when a library has several copies of the same book, every book bearing the same title has its own call number.

10. [The number which everyone in France (in theory) is assigned by the INSEE, or Institut national de la statistique et des études économiques, also serves as a Social Security number.] As a matter of fact, some of these identificatory schemes include descriptive features, and thus features of specific identity, such as the subject-classification of the Dewey decimal system, which uses a decimal notation (700 = the arts, 800 = literature, etc.). But, for one thing, to make such a classification descriptive of *each and every* book, we would have to complicate it to the point of making it the numerical equivalent of its text; for another, a completely arbitrary numbering system would be, certainly, less transparent, but just as unambiguous. The systems that classify books by format obviously bear no relation to the texts of the works they classify, and it is hard to imagine the feature "twenty-first acquisition" being taken for an intrinsic property of the painting thus identified.

clearly record, not numerical identities (which their objects, being ideal, do not have), but rather specific identities, defined by the set of these objects' "constitutive properties," which they make it possible to "reproduce" in new manifesations that conform to the originals. If we limit the concept to this function, the availability of a notation once again becomes, it seems to me, a reliable index of allographism, and thus, in terms of diagnosis or definition, a sufficient condition. That it is not a *necessary* condition for allographism is something Goodman affirms without arguing the point, but we find confirmation of the fact in the allographic character of an art like literature, which does not possess a notation in the strict sense, and even more readily in that of artistic practices like dramaturgy (stage production), where simple verbal *scripts**  preserve a record of works.

I will come back to the difference between scripts and literary texts; suffice it to say, for the moment, that a text is a verbal object (of immanence), and that a script (for example, a recipe or stage directions) is a verbal denotation for a nonverbal object like a dish or stage business. If one grants that certain allographic works do not have, or, at least, do not yet have, notations any more rigorous than such verbal denotations, then one surely must grant that notation in the strict sense is not a necessary condition for this regime. "What is *necessary*," Goodman insists, "is that identification of the or a [possibly unique] instance of a work be independent of the history of production; a notation as much codifies as creates such an independent criterion."[11] I would be inclined to say that a notation codifies *rather than* creates such a state of affairs, which, to repeat, defines the allographic regime, of which notation is both an effect and an instrument: when such circumstances (for example, the ephemeral nature of performances or the collective character of certain creations[12]) impel an art to move toward the allographic

11. Goodman, *Of Mind and Other Matters,* p. 139. For lack of a better word, I have here used *"exemplaire"* [copy, exemplar] to translate "instance," which Goodman employs in a broader sense than the French word has, inasmuch as he can speak of unique instances, such as a singular painting; but *"exemple"* [example] would be even more misleading. This case aside, I use *exemplaire* only to refer to the multiple manifestations of allographic, but not autographic, works, in the sense in which one says that one is printing three million *exemplaires* of a book or score. ["Exemplaire" in the latter sense is generally rendered by "copy" in the present translation.]

12. Ibid., p. 140. Cf. Goodman, *Languages of Art,* p. 121.

regime, the invention and gradual refinement of a system like classical musical notation cannot but promote and sustain this mode of existence. But allographic regimes can arise and persist in the absence of such a notation, muddling through until something better comes along, as choreography did for centuries before the recent invention of one or more notations deemed unambiguous. Furthermore, it goes without saying that a notational system can be more or less strict, passing, like our musical notation, through stages or modes of varying degrees of refinement; again, it is evident that it can coexist more or less harmoniously with other, less precise descriptive systems, like verbal indications of tempo or expression.

Notation, then, is manifestly not the determining cause of (nor even the sole means of expression for) the distinction between constitutive and contingent properties. It remains to say what that cause is. Goodman traces it back to certain practical necessities like the need to preserve ephemeral productions or enable several people to work together to realize them: in other words, the need "to transcend the limitations of time and the individual."[13] The precondition for such "transcendence" is that there be agreement as to the properties two literary or musical performances must necessarily have in common, or that must be included in an architectural work by the person charged with its (sometimes deferred) execution; there must also be agreement about the means used to record a list of such properties. However informal these may be, they can hardly be improvised as one goes along, or from one work to the next, because they presuppose, at a minimum, the establishment of a classificatory scheme and a nomenclature common to all the productions of a given practice, like the repertory of steps and movements in dancing, or of materials, forms, and procedures in fashion design, cooking, or jewel making. The allographic regime is thus, intrinsically, a *phase* which an art enters en bloc (though perhaps not completely)[14] and, doubtless, after a period of development; it is the end product of an evolutionary process and the object of a "tradition" which "must first be established, later to be codified [I would add, *or not*] by

13. *Languages of Art*, p. 121.
14. "Perhaps not completely," because, even today, there still exist, for example, artisanal architectural practices, more or less like those Gaudi relied on to build the Church of the Sagrada Familia, as well as improvised musical forms lacking notations of any sort.

means of a notation."[15] Its definition is thus inextricably bound up with a diachronic hypothesis, according to which "initially, perhaps, all arts are autographic,"[16] some, if not all, later gaining their "emancipation not by proclamation but by notation"[17]—or some other means. The fact that an art belongs to one or the other of the two regimes is not due to "anything more than a tradition that might have been different and may change."[18] This doubtless implies that circumstances—for example, the variable relations between the necessary and the possible—can reverse the course of things, so that an allographic art can eventually become autographic again, like, to some extent, photography, which, we saw, has partially reverted from the status of a multiple autographic to that of a unique autographic art as a result of various technological developments. We will later have occasion to note indications of a similar tendency in the recent evolution of musical practice.

15. Nelson Goodman, *Problems and Projects* (Indianopolis: Bobbs-Merrill, 1972), p. 136.
16. Goodman, *Languages of Art*, p. 121.
17. Ibid., p. 122.
18. Goodman, *Of Mind*, p. 140.

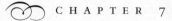 

# *Reduction*

W E HAVE SEEN THAT THE ESTABLISHMENT OF THE ALLOGRAPHIC
regime in an artistic practice comes about as the result of a
process of development, and also of a "tradition" which itself consists
in a set of conventions peculiar to each of the practices involved; we
will encounter these conventions again. As to the actual work-by-work
application of the allographic regime, it comes about as the result of a
mental operation that does not depend, a priori, on any established
notation, and that, indeed, is by no means restricted to artistic practices—unless one regards *every* practice as potentially artistic, a way of
looking at the matter which, though it does not appear to me at all
unreasonable, would be premature at this point. Such a mental operation takes place, for example, every time a physical act (a bodily movement or vocal emission) is "repeated," and every time a material object
is "reproduced" in some way other than by mechanical imprint. To be
sure, no iteration of a physical act or material object can be strictly
identical to the original, so that taking something for an acceptable
reproduction requires neglecting or "disregarding" a certain number of
characteristic features of the first occurrence which disappear with the
second, to be replaced by others peculiar to the second occurrence,
regarded in their turn as equally negligible. I raise my right arm and ask

someone present to "do the same thing"; he too raises his arm, and if he is paying attention, even raises "the same arm" I have, that is, *his* right arm. Materially speaking, these two gestures have nothing in common, and the expression "the same arm" is, in one sense, comically absurd: his arm is not mine. Yet I declare myself satisfied with this (modest) performance, in the name of an identity of movement we will describe, very loosely, as "partial," given that we regard the two acts as identical or homologous, mutatis mutandis: my partner's raising his right arm is to him as my raising of mine is to me. Physically, however, everything has been *mutatum;* in reality, the identity of the two acts comes down, like all identity, to an abstraction—to whatever two acts of raising the right arm have in common. If I myself raised my right arm "twice," it could be said, (very) approximately, that the physical elements involved were the same in both instances; but one never "repeats" exactly the same act, so that the only wholly identical element would be, again, the abstraction called "raising one's arm," or, at a minimum, the more restricted but still abstract abstraction, "Genette is raising his arm." If I utter the sentence "it's nice out," or sing the first eleven notes of *Au clair de la lune* and ask my volunteer assistant to do the same, nothing he produces in his voice will be identical to the sounds I have emitted, apart from the verbal entity "it's nice out," in the spoken mode, or the musical entity "do-do-do-re-mi, etc.," in the sung version, possibly raised an octave, or even, if the assistant has a bad ear, a third, a fourth, or worse. If I draw a simple figure on the board, a square, for example, and my assistant complies with my request to draw the "same" figure in his notebook, the two figures will doubtless have nothing in common beyond the general definition of a square.

In each of these experiments, the (ephemeral) act or (durable) object produced is itself a singular physical object (in the broad sense) which, because it is not exactly reiterable, belongs to the autographic regime; whether or not it can claim the status of art depends on an intention and/or effort of attention that does not interest us for the moment. As I have already said, a mental operation, not a mere physical act, would be required to bring these acts or objects into the allographic regime, since it is not enough for X to raise his right arm after Y, say "it's nice out," sing *Au clair de la lune,* or draw a square for these acts or objects to be accepted as true replicas of their model: they have rather to be considered with respect to what they have in common with this model, and that is an abstraction. The threshold of what is required can of course be lowered, if one is prepared to accept either of the two arms, any sentence, melody, figure, etc.; or it can be raised, if we require that the arm be raised in a special way, that the sentence contain a certain accent, that the melody be sung at a particular tempo, that the square be of a certain size; but all we do in such cases is change the level of abstraction or the extension of the common concept. If, however, the second occurrence is not sanctioned and, as it were, legitimized by this mental operation, it will be perceived, not as a "second occurrence" of the same act or object, but simply as another act or object connected to the first by, at best, a vague relation of resemblance. This is of course what happens if, for some reason, the first (and hence, in this case, the sole) occurrence is regarded as a unique, unrepeatable object, defined not only by its specific identity, which, by definition, can be shared, but also by its numerical identity, which, by definition, cannot—if, in other words, the first occurrence is regarded as definitively autographic: for example, when my raising my arm, uttering the sentence "it's nice out," or singing the melody *Au clair de la lune* is treated as the indivisible performance of a dancer, actor, or singer because it is considered impossible or impertinent to separate the act from its choreographic, verbal, or musical "content." In this instance, the act of iteration would no longer be regarded as a "second occurrence" (indeed, the very notion of occurrence would no longer apply), but rather as a more or less "faithful," and, depending on the case, amusing or fraudulent "imitation." The difference between the first and second sets of cases does not depend on the degree of similarity between occurrences, but, rather, on the status assigned the first occurrence, which either does or does not authorize the mental operation that the status of the second (or any subsequent occurrence) depends on in its turn. Let me go back to the example of the geometrical figure to make up a variation on it that will doubtless illustrate matters more vividly. Say that Picasso draws a square on a wall, and asks his grandson to copy it. If we imagine, fancifully enough, that this happens during a geometry lesson, Pablito will regard the figure with an eye to the specific and thus transferable identity it has qua "square," and will in his turn, and in his own fashion, draw another square. In a different context (a drawing lesson, perhaps), Pablito will regard the figure as a "Picasso"—for he already knows what that means—and quite rightly declare that he is incapable of reproducing its "inimitable" line. The same square functions in the second case as an autographic object, essentially defined by its numerical identity or "history of production"; in the first, it functions as an allographic object with an indefinitely transferable specific identity. In the one case, an "imitation," however meticulous and true to the original, can never be anything other than a fake; in the other, even a slipshod imitation counts as a perfectly valid new occurrence. The two distinct contexts here function as the "traditions" Goodman speaks of, that is, as *usages* which, in all essential respects, determine the difference between the two regimes.

As the preceding examples perhaps suggest, more or less clearly, these determining situations are not merely differentiated by blanket definitions like "geometry lesson" or "drawing lesson." Allographic situations always comprise, if to different degrees, instruments of (specific) identification that autographic situations can very well do without: standing before a certain figure drawn by Picasso, I can lose myself in an act of synthetic contemplation devoid of all analysis; informed after the fact that it is only a simple geometrical figure, and told to reproduce it as such, I have to pick out its constitutive (geometric) properties from among the contingent ones (contingent from the present standpoint) Picasso's style has graced it with, and there can be no doubt that I would find it easier to accomplish the task if I already had at my disposal the concept of, for example, *square.* I would be similarly helped if, upon hearing certain sounds coming out of a human mouth, I disposed of notions like *speech, the French language, sentence, words, music, melody, sounds, intervals,* etc., which would be of great use in analyzing these sounds into either the contingent (timbre, accent) or constitutive (words, tones) properties of the verbal or musical object. These notions would further help me reproduce the constitutive properties, clothed in the, again, contingent properties of my own voice. The set of ideas that help me make this transposition constitutes the repertory of linguistic or musical identifications; every allographic practice is reinforced by competence of a similar sort. To a layman, the movements of a dancer or matador can seem uncoordinated, random, and perfectly resistant to an analysis that would analyze them into contingent properties, on the one hand (characteristic either of the artist's style or of some particular feature of his

performance), and properties constitutive of the passage he is executing, on the other; but a connoisseur will recognize them as an entrechat,
grand jeté, veronica, or final thrust *a recibir,* that is, as so many codified
movements constitutive of the practice in question, and identifiable
amid the chance events or special twists proper to this or that particular performance,[1] just as a competent listener can identify the words
of a sentence or the intervals of a melody in a vocal emission. The same
sort of repertory (vocabulary and syntax) helps one pick out the basic
elements (forms and materials) of a work of architecture, the ingredients and methods used to prepare a dish, the bouquet and taste of a wine,
the material and design of a dress, and so on. This type of competence
does not always enable us to produce new occurrences ourselves; but it
generally suffices to allow us to identify two different instances of the
same "constitutive property."

As we have noted in passing, none of the operations I have just
mentioned depends on the availability or utilization of a notation in the
strict sense, which would presuppose artificial, sophisticated graphic
conventions: knowing how to read music is by no means indispensable to reproducing a musical phrase "by ear," while the repertory of
techniques proper to each practice can simply be described in words
and handed down by oral tradition. What is more, the operation that I
have so far called "mental" can be perfectly silent, implicit, or even unconscious. When I "repeat" a sentence or melody in my own voice, or
when I "reproduce" a gesture or figure in my own style, I do not always
feel that I am or need to be analyzing these objects of perception into
constitutive and contingent properties. Benefiting, doubtless, from my
acquired competence, I usually conduct this analysis "without thinking
about it," without taking note of the fact: here the adjective "mental"

1. Moreover, the role played by the circumstances surrounding a realization varies, sometimes as a function of the more or less physical nature of the performantial practices involved. In the most "intellectual" of the arts (or sports), such as chess, the pertinence of such
circumstances is almost nil. There are a thousand more or less effective, more or less elegant
ways of executing what is called, in tennis, "volleying"; in chess, on the other hand, "moving one's queen to F8" can be an inspired move or an ill-advised one, depending on the
situation, but cannot be well or poorly performed, from the point of view of the game itself:
it is exhaustively defined by its function, whereas its physical realization is entirely negligible. The reason is doubtless that it is actually more the physical manifestation of an intellectual act than a performance—it would be enough to declare "Queen to F8," as is in fact
done in write-ups of a match or games played at a distance.

should not necessarily be taken to imply participation of the conscious mind. It would perhaps be more accurate to say that what I do presupposes certain cerebral events and certain chemical or electric reactions between my neurons, the intellectual or reflexive counterpart of which rises to consciousness only when something goes wrong, or when I am making an exceptional effort to demonstrate something. I am not even sure that the operation of selective iteration requires, in general and a priori, closer attention than does the faithful reproduction of an object with all its properties. If I am asked to repeat "exactly" a word (of a language) I do not know and have just heard pronounced for the first time, I have to strain to reproduce the slightest details of the sound, since, by definition, I cannot tell which are pertinent and which not. If I know the word, the analysis of it goes on, as it were automatically, "somewhere" between my ear and my mouth, and I need pay no attention at all to the details. Identification completely frees me, so to speak, of the need to pay attention. In short, it is less tiring to understand something (for that is what is in question here) than to parrot something mechanically back at someone. But this is of course because one has previously *learned to understand.* The notion of competence, which encompasses that of the mastery (become unconscious) of a code, encapsulates all this in a word.

Thus the passage of a work (object or event) from the autographic to the allographic regime presupposes, indeed *consists in,* a more or less conscious mental operation that analyzes an object into its constitutive and contingent properties, picking out only the first with a view to producing—or, at least, to the *possibility* of producing—a correct iteration that will in its turn display these constitutive properties, accompanied by new contingent properties. X sings *Au clair de la lune* in his own tessitura and timbre, Y produces, in his, a new series of sounds that has nothing in common with the first except the melodic line of *Au clair de la lune,* defined in terms of pitch intervals and units of relative duration. Once again, the number of properties defined as constitutive can vary according to circumstances; one can, for example, treat rhythmic values as contingent, while demanding that the key be maintained, or we can do the opposite, etc. Such variation in the requirements imposed can only be limited by collective cultural norms. But I have described iteration as merely *possible,* because the potential for it created by the allographic regime can easily remain unrealized. In our cultural regime, the text of an original manuscript that has not yet been reproduced and perhaps never will be is not for that reason perceived as being any less iterable as far as its constitutive properties are concerned, in a form that would disregard the contingent properties it has qua manuscript—a typographic transcription, for example. What defines the allographic state is not actual (selective) iteration, but iterability—in brief, the possibility of distinguishing between the two sets of properties.

This possibility, already illustrated by the imaginary example of Picasso's square, is not a "natural" fact definitively distinguishing certain objects from others, but rather a fact determined by culture and usage—a more or less institutionalized, codified consensus that results from an encounter, or balance, between needs and means. Certain objects are relatively easier to analyze in this way than others, but "relatively" means "in a way that depends on the pressures of necessity and, simultaneously, available competence, individual or collective." I may find it easier to analyze a phrase by Mozart than a Chinese dish, but this does not mean that Mozart's music is *in itself* more amenable to the allographic regime than Chinese cooking; it seems quite plausible that a Cantonese gourmet would have difficulty with what I find easy, and vice versa. At any event, and all things considered, necessity knows no law [*nécessité fait loi*], but nobody is required to do the impossible; the general tendency is to consider as constitutive those properties which, in a given time and place, can by common consent be picked out by a process of abstraction and recorded through denotation. Until the metronome was invented, specifications of musical tempo were either absent (so that the tempo was always ad libitum), or stated in words (andante, allegro, etc.), with all the imprecision and ambiguity typical, as Goodman shows, of discursive language; musicians "made do"—that is, did without. Thanks to the metronome, Beethoven was able to include precise—and, apparently, inapplicable—indications of tempo with his last works. There is no stopping progress, but—since (to bring this string of clichés to an end) mankind only sets itself such problems as it can solve—the solution to this problem is miraculously simple: constitutive properties are always identifiable, because, at each stage of development, the properties that are considered constitutive are those that can be identified. The noble adjective "ontological" is decidedly ill suited to realities as fluctuating and typically practical as these—unless they are to be regarded as exemplifying what Quine calls "ontological relativity."

As we have seen, the properties singled out as constitutive (according to varying criteria) have nothing material about them: what is common to my *Au clair de la lune* and my assistant's, or to Pablo's square and Pablito's, is a fairly abstract entity, even if its extension varies with the rigidity of the requirements imposed. Our founding operation could thus be called *abstraction*. But this term seems inappropriate to me for reasons that will become clear later. For the time being, let us simply adumbrate them, by observing that, if "square" in general is most assuredly a concept, the same is not true of a melody or the text of a poem, objects that are quite as singular, after their fashion and in their regime, as Picasso's square after and in *its*. Allographic objects are, like the analogies that spark reminiscences in Proust, "ideal, but not abstract"; I will therefore call them (as I have already done above), not abstractions, but, more broadly, ideal objects, or, to use a somewhat shorter and much more fashionable term, *idealities*. Again, so as to remain on the terrain of a pseudo-Husserlian vocabulary, I propose to christen our founding operation *allographic reduction*,[2] inasmuch as it consists, properly speaking, in reducing an object or event, after analysis and selection, to the features it shares or could share with one or more other objects or events whose function is likewise to manifest the ideal immanence of an allographic work in physically perceptible form. "Constitutive" properties are those of an (ideal) object of immanence; the "contingent" properties (of this object) are, of course, constitutive of its various manifestations. For example, the structure AABA (among others[3]) is constitutive of *Au clair de la lune;* being sung in a tenor voice is constitutive of certain of its manifestations. Beginning with "for a long time . . ." and ending with " . . . in the dimension of Time" characterizes (not exhaustively, but doubtless

2. In contrast to the Husserlian reductions (phenomenological, eidetic, transcendental), which are conscious, technical procedures, this reduction, be it here recalled, is quite common and often not the result of conscious thought. It is, in sum, a reduction in the most ordinary sense of the word, one which does not, perhaps, require the participation of a human brain: presented with two stimuli, Pavlov's dog (and even mine) is perfectly capable of isolating the pertinent feature common to both.

3. Among others, of course, for this "form" is typically generic. A complete statement of the constitutive properties of *Au clair de la lune* alone would call for other predicates, whose conjunction, as we will see, determines it as an ideal *individual*.

exclusively, Oulipian[4] variations aside) the text of *Remembrance of Things Past;* being set in Garamond on an 8-point body characterizes certain of its manifestations. It is therefore appropriate—and, indeed, high time— to substitute the more precise term *properties of immanence* for "constitutive properties," and to replace "contingent properties" with "the generic or individual properties of a given class of manifestations or of one particular manifestation"—or, for greater facility, *properties of manifestation.* For, although an object of immanence is unique, its manifestation branches out, virtually without limit, into genus, species, and varieties of all sorts, until it reaches this or that physically perceptible, material individual which serves as its sole physical manifestation: the last Pléiade edition of *À la recherche du temps perdu* is one of these classes, my personal copy of this edition is one of these individuals. This edition is itself an ideality, as imperceptible at the physical level as the text of the novel. Only copies of it (or of them) are perceptible. We must therefore do more than differentiate between properties of immanence and properties of manifestation; among the latter, we need to draw a further distinction between the properties of the intermediate, optional forms of manifestation, which are no less ideal ("being set in Garamond on an 8-point body"), and the properties of material objects (copies or instances) of manifestation ("being on my table at this moment"). We now turn to an examination of these structural and functional relations between immanence and manifestation.

4. [The Oulipo, or Ouvroir de littérature potentielle (Workroom of potential literature), a literary group founded in 1960, experimented with constraint as a means of stimulating creativity. Probably its most celebrated innovation was the "lipogram," a text in which the writer avoids all words containing a certain letter of the alphabet.]

# CHAPTER 8

# Immanence
# and Manifestations

*I*T IS CHARACTERISTIC OF AUTOGRAPHIC WORKS, IT WILL BE RECALLED, to give us no reason to distinguish between their immanence and manifestations, since their object of immanence is physical, perceptible, and therefore manifest in and of itself. In contrast, allographic works possess the two modes of existence we have called ideal immanence and physical manifestation (and others as well). These two modes are, as it happens, (onto)logically distinct, but their logical relation is quite complicated. If a work's "constitutive" properties are the properties of its object of immanence (for example, a text), and its "contingent" properties those of its object of manifestation (for example, a book), it cannot be said that its object of manifestation does not comprehend its constitutive properties; moreover, we have seen that what permits us to distinguish constitutive from contingent properties is an analysis which takes all of a work's properties into account. To put it somewhat naively, the object of manifestation exhibits both the constitutive and contingent properties, while the object of immanence exhibits only the former—and is, indeed, nothing other than their sum: my copy of *The Charterhouse of Parma* contains, let us say, two hundred thousand words and is four hundred pages long; its *text* also contains two hundred thousand words, but is no number of pages long, for "being x number of pages long" can be predicated only of physical manifestations, not of ideal immanence, whereas "containing x number of words" is common to both modes. Naively, again, it may be said that the manifestation contains (the properties of) the immanence, which does not, for its part, contain (the properties of) the manifestation. This relation of inclusion accounts for the metonymic shifts which allow us to say, in ordinary conversation, that a book has moved us, when what is in question is obviously its text, or else that *The Charterhouse* is in the library, when what is involved is obviously a copy of it.[1] On the concrete level, of course, we always deal with objects of manifestation, restricting our attention now to what is purely immanent "in them" (reading relation), now to the manifestation alone (bibliophilic relation).

The mode of immanence is unique, barring transcendence, if one assumes (among other things), as I will be doing constantly but provisionally in this chapter, that every literary work has only *one* text, or that every musical work has only one (ideal) score, or that there is only *one* recipe for cassoulet. A manifestation, in contrast, can take very different forms, not only because editions of the same text, score, or recipe can differ considerably on the material level, but also because a vocal or instrumental performance can provide just as good a (some would say a better) manifestation of the literary or musical work than the text or score, and a culinary work in a dish, a manifestation equal or superior to one in a cookbook. I posit on principle that an allographic work has (at least potentially) two distinct modes of manifestation, of which one is, for example, that of musical performances, recitations of texts, built buildings, or the meals we find on our plates, while the other is that of scores, books, building plans, or recipes; and, further, that these two modes of manifestation, whose respective relations to the mode of immanence differ appreciably, do not, a priori, stand in any fixed order or cause-and-effect relation. This last point is not universally granted, and I will come back to it. Somewhat further on, I will also come back to the *potential* nature of the two modes of manifestation every work has, and to the possibility that it might have a third. For the moment, suffice it to recall that certain scores have never yet been played, that certain improvised musical works or works of oral literature have never yet been written down ("an old man who dies is a library gone up in flames"), and that

1. See Charles L. Stevenson, "On 'What Is a Poem,'" *Philosophical Review* 66 (1957): 329–362.

Borges, while out walking, sometimes composed an entire poem "in his head"; it would be "dictated," that is, recited by Borges and "committed to paper" by his secretary, only several hours later.

The relationship between the immanence and its two (perceptible) modes may be symbolized by a triangle with immanence at the apex, and each of its two manifestations at the other two corners. Thus we have:

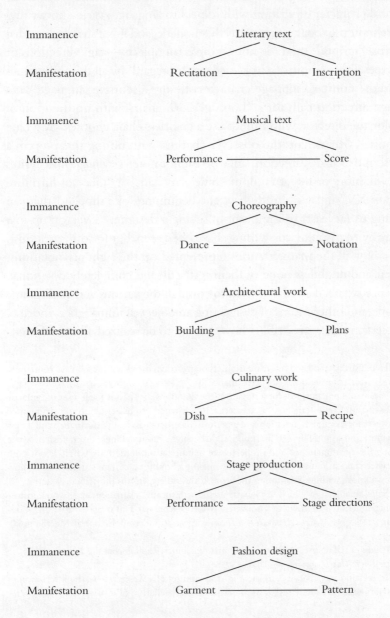

| Immanence | | Literary text | |
| Manifestation | Recitation | —————— | Inscription |

| Immanence | | Musical text | |
| Manifestation | Performance | —————— | Score |

| Immanence | | Choreography | |
| Manifestation | Dance | —————— | Notation |

| Immanence | | Architectural work | |
| Manifestation | Building | —————— | Plans |

| Immanence | | Culinary work | |
| Manifestation | Dish | —————— | Recipe |

| Immanence | | Stage production | |
| Manifestation | Performance | —————— | Stage directions |

| Immanence | | Fashion design | |
| Manifestation | Garment | —————— | Pattern |

The term common to all the manifestations here represented on the left is, obviously, the ordinary French word *exécution*.[2] To designate the manifestations on the right, the term "notation" is, we know, too narrow, at least in the strict sense Goodman gives it;[3] at present, it can be accurately applied only to musical scores and (according to Goodman) the choreographic notation proposed by Rudolf Laban. The notational character of writing with respect to languages varies, no writing system in use today being perfectly phonetic; and it is a striking fact that verbal "scripts"[4] used to "note" nonverbal objects—stage directions or recipes, for example—are plagued (in this regard) by all the ambiguities and the constant slippage characteristic of "discursive language": if a stage direction calls for a "Louis XV armchair," with no mention of color, the director, who cannot use a colorless chair, chooses, say, a blue Louis XV armchair; the observer charged with noting this prop in a descriptive stage direction, since he cannot note *everything either,* writes down, more or less at random, "blue armchair," or "piece of furniture Louis XV," and we already have the beginnings of a slippage[5] that can bring us (at least) to the point of seeing a designer* TV crop up in a play by Marivaux (worse things have been seen, but for other reasons).

Not all the manifestations represented on the right are notations, then, and doubtless none of them is strictly and completely notational. Hence we need a broader term to cover all the various verbal, diagrammatic, and other means of designating an object of immanence, and also, in certain cases,[6] prescribing how they are to be realized. The most accu-

2. [Here usually translated by "realization," though, to avoid awkwardness, I have sometimes translated it as "execution" or "performance."]

3. Goodman's practical test for a notation (the notations that pass it meet a set of syntactic and semantic "requirements") is, we recall, to ask whether perfect identity is maintained between, for example, a notation and a performance, between that performance and a new notation, and so on. This test presupposes that analysis can unfailingly distinguish between properties of immanence and properties of manifestation, something which is not even always certain in music; if a performer maintains a hold for a certain length of time, how can we know, without examining the score, if this time span was prescribed or not?

4. [*Script,* an anglicism which, as Genette uses it here, means "a verbal message whose instrumental function is to (de)note a nonverbal work" (see below). This usage is based on Goodman, *Languages of Art: An Approach to a Theory of Symbols* (Indianapolis: Bobbs-Merrill, 1968), p. 199.]

5. Analogous, of course, to the one Goodman imagines, leading from the *Fifth Symphony* to *Three Blind Mice* (*Languages of Art,* p. 187).

6. "In certain cases," because, today, at least in cultures of a Western type, the inscription of a literary text very rarely serves to prescribe an oral recitation of it.

rate and convenient term seems to me to be *denotation,* because in every case the objective is to establish, using one, generally[7] conventional, means of representation or the other, the list of properties constitutive of this ideal object. And, as rigid notations are a privileged means of representation (at least in terms of efficacity) which all the others more or less successfully emulate, we can treat denotation, in general, as a broader kind of notation, and write it in this form: *(de)notation.*

The pressure of the Goodmanian semiotic system might incline us to pause for a moment to ask the following Scholastic question: if the manifestations shown on the right are denotations, may we not infer that those on the left (the realizations) are *exemplifications,* and that, if a score denotes the *Jupiter* Symphony, a performance exemplifies it? This is, in a sense, Goodman's position regarding music (alone), because he defines a musical work as the class of correct performances of a score— thus restricting the score to a purely instrumental role in the service of these performances. But we know that he does not extend definitions of this type to the other allographic arts, especially not to literary works, whose oral performances appear secondary to him;[8] he would be more likely to define a literary work as the class of its correct *inscriptions.* This dissymmetry seems to me hardly tenable even taken in and of itself, while the notion of class, which that of example inevitably refers us to, does not seem to me to account for the mode of existence of the very special kind of ideal objects we have called allographic objects of immanence. These are not classes, and none of their singular occurrences of manifestation are "examples," that is, members of a class, as I will try to show later. The answer to our question is, then, negative, or the question is meaningless.

The uniformly symmetrical positions attributed to the two modes of manifestation in the triangular schemas above may seem to run counter to ordinary usage. For some writers, like Souriau, Ingarden, or Urmson, literature would seem to be, fundamentally, an art of the spoken word, in which inscriptions, when they exist, are merely mnemonic

---

7. But not always. The list of ingredients needed to make a recipe can be provided by a photographic image.

8. "The text is not merely a means to oral readings as a score is a means to performances in music. An unrecited poem is not so forlorn as an unsung song; and most literary works are never read aloud at all." Goodman, *Languages of Art,* p. 114. Let us note in passing how the "most" strains to correct the manifest excess of the "never."

devices that facilitate oral readings.[9] However, for others, like Goodman (as I have just pointed out), the authentic form of the literary work is the written text; we may perhaps recall the pseudo-Derridean[10] piety toward writing that marked the 1970s, when, the work having been dethroned in favor of the Text, the latter was identified with Writing, opposed to Speech much as Good is opposed to Evil. The same sort of debate pits those who, like Goodman[11]—they are doubtless in the majority—regard the score simply as a means of prescribing performances, against those for whom "nothing can replace the score";[12] the latter party counts a large number of professionals. It seems to me that these functional relations (I will come back to them below) vary sufficiently, both in historical time[13] and in collective and individual cultural space, to warrant an a priori symmetrical arrangement which leaves room for local choices and developments in every direction. The ideality of a literary or musical text, or of an architectural, choreographic,

---

9. Souriau defines literature as the "art of articulated sounds"; Roman Ingarden, *The Literary Work of Art: An Investigation on the Borderlines of Ontology, Logic, and Theory of Literature* (1965), trans. George G. Grabowicz (Evanston, Ill.: Northwestern University Press, 1973), posits, as the first level of the "stratified formation of the literary work," the stratum made up of "linguistic sound formations"*; according to J. O. Urmson, "What Makes a Situation Aesthetic?" *Proceedings of the Aristotelian Society,* supplementary vol. 31 (1957) [also in Joseph Margolis, ed., *Philosophy Looks at the Arts* (New York: Scribners, 1962), pp. 13–27], literature is an art of performance in which the written text is simply a sort of score. For a critique of this position, see Richard Shusterman, "The Ontological Status of the Work of Literature," in *The Object of Literary Criticism* (Amsterdam: Rodopi, 1984), chap. 3.

10. "Pseudo," because for Derrida himself, it seems to me, writing, *qua* arche-writing, is present in both modes.

11. But also some musicians, for example René Leibowitz, who maintains that "a musical work *does not exist for anyone* until it has been performed," and that "performance alone brings it into existence, then, for the listener as well as for the performer" (*Le compositeur et son double* [Paris: Gallimard, 1971], p. 25). This formulation (the emphasis is the author's) seems to me to be excessive indeed; a musical work "exists" at least for its author, as Schönberg used to say, when he composes it. I agree that it exists only potentially for everyone else for as long as no one has seen the score, but the transition from the potential to the actual does not depend on a performance; rather, it occurs the moment the score is first read—by someone who knows how to read music, of course, and even if the purpose of music is to be *heard* by all (including those who cannot read music), and therefore performed.

12. Heard, one day, from the mouth of Betsy Jolas. Similarly, Pierre Boulez frequently describes our musical heritage as a "library"; and we often speak of the "literature" of an instrument to designate its repertory.

13. Goodman himself says that "in the case of literature, [written] texts *have* even supplanted oral performances as the primary aesthetic objects" (Goodman, *Languages of Art,* p. 121, my emphasis), which is sufficient confirmation of the fact that they have not always had this primary role, and does not rule out the possibility that they will one day lose it again.

culinary, sartorial (etc.) work, is not only what all its realizations or else all its (de)notations have in common, but also, clearly, what is common to *all its manifestations,* whether they take the form of realizations or (de)notations.[14]

The case of architecture may seem paradoxical, because this art, which today possesses systems of (de)notation powerful enough to make possible the indefinite multiplication of its realizations, never exploits this possibility, except in its aesthetically least prestigious productions (series of HLMs[15]), or in complexes consisting of several identical buildings, such as Mies van der Rohe's two Lake Shore Drive Apartments or his two Commonwealth Promenade Apartments (the initial project called for four) in Chicago, or Pei's three Silver Towers in New York. It is hard to imagine anyone constructing a replica of the Seagram Building or the Guggenheim Museum. But the fact that architectural (de)notations exist at least makes it possible to finish a work after the death of its author, like Spreckelsen's Great Arch at La Défense, or, as I have already indicated, to rebuild a demolished building exactly as it was, like the German Pavilion in Barcelona. As to the unique character of works of high fashion (actually, I am told, one realization of each is authorized *per continent,* whatever that rather hazy geographical term may mean), it stems in part from a deliberate restriction whose motives are obvious, and in part from the autographic nature of this practice—for not only does nothing prevent an art from functioning in one regime in the case of certain of its works, and in the other in the case of certain others; it is also quite possible for one and the same work to be autographic in one of its parts and allographic in another. This is obviously the case (a common one) with a pictorial work that contains a verbal inscription.

If we consider only literature, choreography, or music, we might suppose that all realizations consist in performances, and therefore in events, while all (de)notations consist in material objects, like a handwritten or printed page. But this plainly does not hold for architecture, fashion design, or cooking, where realizations consist in (more or less)

---

14. As regards literature, Hegel already maintains, surely not without exaggeration, that the fact that the verbal element is a "mere sign" makes it "a matter of indifference, in the case of poetry proper, whether we read it or hear it read"—or even whether it is translated or "transposed from poetry to prose." G. W. F. Hegel, *Aesthetics: Lectures on Fine Art* (1832), trans. T. M. Knox (Oxford: Clarendon, 1975), vol. 2, p. 964 [translation slightly modified].
15. [See Chap. 3, n. 7.]

durable objects; conversely, a (de)notation can take the form of an event, because any script (a recipe or stage directions, for example) can be presented and transmitted orally. Thus the distinction between realization and denotation by no means coincides with that between (durable) objects and (transitory) events. We can combine the two categories to indicate the (variable) way these aspects[16] are distributed between the two modes of manifestation:[17]

| Mode / Aspect | Realization | Denotation |
|---|---|---|
| Objects | Buildings<br>Gardens<br>Dishes<br>Perfumes<br>Jewels | Inscriptions<br>Scores<br>Scripts<br>Plans<br>Formulas |
| Events | Recitations of texts<br>Dance<br>Musical performances<br>Theatrical performances | Recitations of scripts |

    Let us add that no practice is irrevocably wedded to a given system of denotation. A language can be written in several different writing systems, whether simultaneously (like Serbo-Croatian, in the Latin and Cyrillic alphabets) or successively (Vietnamese, which has adopted the Latin alphabet). Musical notation has, since the Middle Ages, been caught up in a process of constant evolution: a number of alternative systems have been worked out, beginning (at least) with Jean-Jacques Rousseau and continuing on down to the twentieth century; nothing, considerations of convenience aside, stops us from converting a score into a verbal description of the "do-do-do-re-mi . . . " variety (this is known as "solfaing" or "solmization"). And one need only examine a sixteenth-century tablature for the lute to see a principle of notation, based on fingering, that differs radically from what has become our system.

16. I prefer to use this weak term to designate the difference between objects and events, which, as we have seen, is relative and gradual.
17. The practices of manifestation shown on the same line do not correspond in any way; each list has been drawn up at random.

But this description of the system *immanence-realization-(de)notation* is still skeletal, for a whole string of prescriptive choices inevitably, if sometimes implicitly, intervenes between ideal immanence and each of its perceptible manifestations; we have to run through the entire series before choosing a manifestation. If we were to spell it out, the result would take the form of a series of descriptive predicates. Suppose that I am to program the performance of a Scarlatti sonata for a concert: I have to decide between piano and clavichord; if I choose the clavichord, I have to decide between two (or more) clavichordists; that choice made, I have to decide among several particular instruments, etc. Choices made after the fact—for example, between recorded performances—are informed by the same kind of options. If I leave things to chance, the choices I have declined to make explicitly will show up, willy nilly, in a retrospective description of my randomly programmed performance: clavichord and not piano, Scott Ross and not Gustav Leonhardt, etc. The same chain of options informs, prescriptively, the choice of a score, or, descriptively, its specification. The choice between, or a description of, recitations/inscriptions of a literary work illustrates the same situation; in both cases, the initial choice is between realization and (de)notation. If you walk into a "music" store that sells music in all its forms, and ask for "the sonata *Au clair de la lune,*" without describing what you want any more precisely, the response to your request will inevitably be another question: "Record or score?" (English, always practical, dubs the second sort of music "sheet music.") One would have to make a similar choice in a store that stocked *Remembrance of Things Past* in the form of books and cassettes.

I will come back to the fact that there are, always, intermediate options between immanence and each of its singular instances of manifestation; not the least paradoxical feature of this situation is that it places, between an ideal individual *(Remembrance of Things Past)* and a material individual (my copy), a whole network of abstract and generic idealities (oral/written, manuscript/printed text, roman/italic, and so on) which, like a sieve that is indifferent to what it is used to sift, can be interposed between millions of other works and millions of other copies. But we must first justify (it is high time) our use of the descriptive term "ideal individual"; that is, we must consider the mode of existence of the allographic object of immanence in its own right.

## Ideal Individuals

Such an "object," to repeat, does not *exist* anywhere outside the mind or brain that conceives it.[18] Thus a strictly nominalist description, which is what Nelson Goodman's purports to be (negligence or politeness aside), can dispense with it by treating the allographic work as nothing more than a batch of occurrences or copies ("replicas") which, though not absolutely identical, are assumed to be artistically equivalent by cultural convention. But it remains very difficult to say what this equivalence consists in without appealing to an ideality of some sort, even if it is described in terms like "constitutive properties," "sameness of spelling,"* or the "compliance" of a realization with a (de)notation—just as it is difficult to categorize the functional equivalence of an apical and uvular *r* without falling back on the typically ideal object represented by the French phoneme /r/. We can, accordingly, describe the situation more economically by presupposing the (ideal) existence of the object of immanence, a mental construct exhaustively defined by the group of properties common to all its manifestations. The principle of Ockham's razor does not rule out all "mental constructs," but only those we can reasonably do without; this is not, in my view, the case with the one in question.

This type of object would seem to confront us with three paradoxes. All three claimed Husserl's attention—and rightly so, because the author of *Experience and Judgement* is in some sort responsible for promoting the notion of ideality (broader, to repeat, than the notion of concept) which, in my view (and in his), also applies to allographic works.[19]

The first paradox has to do with the presumably "objective," or at least communicable, nature of objects that exist only in the mind, or simply in the neurons, and so seem to be located within an individual subject. I will not make myself ridiculous by taking on this problem, known as the problem of the relations between the "noematic" and the "noetic,"

18. Menéndez Pidal speaks quite rightly, in connection with oral traditions, about a text being in a "latent" state between two vocal actualizations. Zumthor, who cites this remark, adds, with good reason, that this conception "can also be applied to mixed traditions, in which written texts are transmitted vocally" (Paul Zumthor, *La lettre et la voix* [Paris: Seuil, 1987], p. 160); in other words, it can be applied to the entire textual tradition.

19. See James M. Edie, "Husserl's Conception of the Ideality of Language," *Humanitas* 11 (1975): 201–217.

which Husserl, according to Edie, resolves "by means of his theory of transcendental consciousness." I only wish to note that it concerns all idealities, not just artistic ones. We are all the only ones to know what is "in our minds" when we think of the concept of a triangle, or, if we have learned it by heart, the text of "The Death of Lovers"; indeed, not even we "know" this when we effect, without thinking about it, an iteration or reproduction, mutatis mutandis. It seems to me that these subjective events, conscious or unconscious, can be described as so many manifestations belonging to a third mode, whose neuronal aspect is (for the moment) inaccessible to us, and whose psychic aspect takes, now the form of a silent performance (I sing *Au clair de la lune* or recite "The Death of Lovers" "in my head," and, perhaps, a bit in my throat), now that of an imaginary notation (I see a score or printed page "in my mind's eye"). These are purely personal manifestations for internal use, but they may suffice to ensure the survival of a work, and may be indispensable in the absence of all other manifestations. Indeed, it seems to me that from the moment an allographic work no longer had manifestations of *any* kind (whether realizations or denotations), it would have no immanence, since immanence is the mental projection of at least one manifestation. (The work might possibly still avail itself of that other mode of manifestation I call transcendence, which we will consider below: for example, a reproduction of a painting destroyed after the reproduction was made.) But a "mental manifestation" like knowing a literary text or musical composition by heart are, beyond a doubt, sufficient for the purpose, as we see in *Fahrenheit 451;* moreover, the limits on preserving works in this fashion are exclusively a function of the memory and survival of the individual. The story goes that Mozart, after hearing Allegri's *Miserere* only once, in the Sistine Chapel, went home and wrote down the text of this work without leaving anything out. They also say that the young Racine, tired of having all his copies of *Théagène et Chariclée* confiscated while he was at Port-Royal, finally memorized the whole of this long, not very Jansenist novel.[20] As we know, the same Racine was later in the habit of saying, "My tragedy is finished, all I must now do is write it"; and I have heard a pyrotechnist say, "I've finished my fireworks in my mind, I don't much care if they're shot off tonight or not." I will certainly

---

20. Louis Racine's *Memoires.*

not exhaust this folklore if I also report, following Adorno,[21] a remark of Schönberg's; when someone, speaking of a work of his that had not yet been performed, said it was a shame the composer had never heard it, Schönberg replied, "But I have. I heard it when I wrote it." (Indeed, this may have been the most satisfactory way of listening to his own music for Schönberg, who was one day to declare, "my music isn't modern, it's just badly played.") But let us go back to Mozart. Once again, an operation of reduction necessarily intervened between what he heard in the Sistine Chapel and the score he wrote out, for he could not have noted (and certainly was not concerned to note) *everything* he heard, but only the "constitutive properties" of the work, without the properties of the performance. The awareness he (doubtless) had of these properties was a subjective manifestation of them, but the properties themselves, capable of being transferred or converted from the performance in the Sistine Chapel to Mozart's score, clearly transcend, in that sense, Mozart's mind and brain, and are, *in that sense,* objective.

The second paradox has to do with the temporal status of allographic idealities. Husserl distinguishes two kinds. Those of the sort he calls "free" or "pure" lead, like the ideal objectivities of geometry, an atemporal or "omnitemporal" existence; the others, which he calls "bound," are subject to historical contingency, because they at least have a date of birth: this holds for "cultural" objects, that is, human products, a category which manifestly takes in artistic works.[22] If the concept of a triangle is atemporal, the concept of a wheelbarrow and the text of *The Charterhouse of Parma* patently are not.

This obvious fact does not seem quite symmetrical to me. I can see that triangular objects have always existed, at least since the beginning of the world (I decline all responsibility for describing the situation that prevailed earlier), but it seems to me that the concept of a triangle, however transcendent it may be, did not exist before a human (or some other kind of?) brain got around to thinking of it. In this sense, theological hypotheses aside, all idealities are temporal, even if they have

---

21. Theodor W. Adorno, *Quasi una fantasia* (1963), trans. Rodney Livingstone (London: Verso, 1992), p. 248.
22. [I have followed the translation by Spencer Churchill and Karl Ameriks, *Experience and Judgment: Investigations in a Genealogy of Logic,* ed. Ludwig Landgrebe (Evanston, Ill.: Northwestern University Press, 1973), p. 267.]

been in existence for widely varying lengths of time. What differentiates them, from this standpoint, is rather the temporal status of the objects they are associated with: the concept "triangle," doubtless "born" at a certain point in human history, applies to physical realities that may be described, with the above-mentioned reservation, as omnitemporal, like the (for us) visible relation among three stars in our firmament. The concept "wheelbarrow" was born at (roughly) the same time as the first wheelbarrow, and the historical character (if not the precise age) of the class of objects it defines is more or less included within its intension.[23] The text of *The Charterhouse* exhibits the same particularity, which consists not so much in being a temporal ideality as in being an ideality relative to an historical object (*The Charterhouse* itself).

But all that is born can die. Triangular objects will, perhaps, exist forever, but if the human race (and every other species capable of thinking) were one day to disappear, it seems to me that the disappearance of every organ capable of conceiving triangles would entail—whatever its present transcendence vis-à-vis its subjective actualizations—the death of the concept "triangle." The day may come when there are no more wheelbarrows, not even in a museum and college of higher technology; but the concept "wheelbarrow" will doubtless manage to survive, and, with it, the possibility that this winsome vehicle can be constructed once again. As in the previous case, however, that concept will not survive the disappearance of the species that thinks. As to the text of *The Charterhouse,* it will not survive the disappearance of all its manifestations, including the one constituted by its hypothetical last complete memorization ("an old man who dies . . . "). Of a good hundred tragedies written by Sophocles, we now "possess" only seven, a few copies of which were preserved, by a lucky accident, in an anthology. Of the others, presently "lost," the (ideal) text is neither really nor potentially present in any consciousness. Thus, for lack of an accessible manifestation, these texts are, for now, dead. Dead forever, Proust would ask? If all copies have indeed been "destroyed," that is, transformed into ashes, or any other illegible substance, then the answer is yes. If a copy of one of these manifestations, presently inaccessible and hence not productive

23. I thought I had picked a simple example, but I now realize, a bit belatedly, that there are wheelbarrows and wheelbarrows, depending on the period; let me, then, specify that I had the "modern" wheelbarrow in mind, that is, the kind with two shafts and a single wheel.

of any textual immanence, were to be unearthed some day, its text would be resurrected, on condition that a thinking individual was still, or again, capable of reading it—something that obviously presupposes several conditions. The unique copy of the Code of Hammurabi, lost for centuries and then rediscovered in 1901, contained a virtual text, which did not resume its ideal existence and its *operation* as a text until the day it was deciphered.[24] In short, there are two necessary conditions for the existence of an ideal object of immanence (whose conjunction constitutes a sufficient condition): the existence of a manifestation and that of an intelligence capable of reducing it. Its temporal duration—or intermittence—is absolutely dependent on that conjunction.

The third paradox is of an (onto)logical kind, and has to do with the fact that allographic objects of immanence are not ideal "universals," like concepts, but rather ideal individuals. The distinction between "real" (physical) objects and ideal objects does not, then, coincide with that between individuals and abstract entities: there are real individuals, like this table, or this occurrence of the word "table," and there are ideal universals, like the concept "table"; but there are also ideal individuals, or singular idealities, like the (French) word *table* or the (French) phoneme /r/.

> Phonemes, morphemes, or words are not universals at all but individuals. There is only one phoneme /p/ in the English language, and, though this one phoneme has the characteristics of "sameness" and "repeatability," and is therefore an "ideal" entity rather than an empirically real sound, it is not a general concept. . . . The same is true, mutatis mutandis, of morphemes and words. We must, therefore, following Husserl, admit *ideal individuals* (of the kind the elements of language uniquely give us) as well as *ideal universals.*[25]

Warding off, in advance, the charges that nominalists level whenever anyone admits the existence of ideal entities, Edie prudently adds:

24. On this necessity, which Nelson Goodman calls *implementation** or *activation**, see his "L'art en action," *Cahiers du Musée national de l'art moderne,* no. 41 (Fall 1992): 7–14.
25. Edie, "Husserl's Conception," p. 214. It should be noted that at the end of this article, p. 216, the author draws a parallel between the Husserlian theory of ideal individuals and the Goodmanian notion of allographic works, pointing out the "convergence which on either side stems from radically opposed positions on the nature of ideality." I do not know if Goodman (or Husserl) would much appreciate the parallel; I, for my part, find it very much to the point.

"Husserl remains innocent of Platonism for the simple fact that there is no room in his analysis for 'real' universals,"[26] that is, for the Ideas that lead a divine existence in the Platonic Heaven. The following table provides one way of representing the interrelations among these categories:

| Objects | Generic | Individual |
|---------|---------|------------|
| Ideal | A<br>The concept table | B<br>The word table |
| Real | D<br>The Platonic Idea of a table | C<br>This particular table, or this occurrence of the word "table" |

To admit only the contents of box C is the characteristic gesture of nominalism, of box D, that of Platonism, or, in medieval terms, "realism"; to admit A and C is the "conceptualist" position that absolutely everybody adopts in practice, academic disputation aside. Henceforth we will leave box D empty; what it contains seems to me at once mythical and idle. The question that remains open—despite Husserl's encouraging support—is the legitimacy of the notion of ideal individual (box B), and the possibility of applying it to allographic works.

I have filled in the three (useful) boxes of the table with examples suggested by the definition (which comes from Husserl, via Edie) of linguistic entities as singular idealities; but interposing a "word" between the concept and the physical object threatens to cloud the issue. I will, then, unify my examples as follows:

| Objects | Generic | Individual |
|---------|---------|------------|
| Ideal | A<br>The concept word | B<br>The word "table" |
| Real | | C<br>This particular occurrence of the word "table" |

The arrangement and procedure adopted here, which take the concept as their point of departure, may appear somewhat "idealist" when compared to the course ordinary experience usually takes, but the pages that follow will, I hope, justify these choices. As to the choice of linguistic objects, it is dictated, for the moment, by the fact that language provides the model par excellence of a system which obliges us to admit the notion of ideal individuals: if only extralinguistic objects were in question here, our schema would be reduced, for example, to the concept of table and the physical object "this table." What can already be seen in this second schema is that the logical relation between B and C is not of the same kind as that between A and B—we could even straightforwardly say that the former relation is *not* logical (but practical). B is in a relation of logical inclusion with respect to A (B is a particular instance or example of A), but C is not in a relation of the same sort with respect to B: C is not a particular instance, but a materialization or manifestation of B. The difference may seem slight, because it might almost as well be said that this table is a materialization of the concept table, or that this occurrence of the word "table" is a particular instance of this word. *Almost* as well, but not *very* well. A description in terms of extension ought to clarify matters. The concept word defines a class of which the (ideal) word "table" is plainly a member, but the (ideal) word "table" is not a class of which a given occurrence of the word is a member, for this occurrence—a graphic or phonic event—is no more an (ideal) word than the occurrence of a phoneme is a phoneme; the latter occurrence is a phonetic act whose object is to materialize an ideal phonematic entity. In other words, the logical series of nested categories which begins with the class of phonemes and subsumes (for example) the subclass of French phonemes (etc.), ends with the phoneme /r/, which contains no particular instance still belonging to the class of phonemes, because an occurrence of a phoneme is *not* a phoneme. I have chosen to fill in my table with a series (the *concept word—word—occurrence of a word*) that is more frequently encountered and so more accessible than the more technical series, "the concept phoneme—phoneme—occurrence of a phoneme." However, it turns out to be *too* accessible, that is, equivocal, because the word "word," like almost all everyday (nontechnical) words, refers to at least two very different things, while obscuring the difference between them: either word-occurrences ("there are ten thousand words in this article") or ideal *terms* of which there can be occurrences ("the word 'table' comes up ten times in this article"). But the "word 'table'" in my schema was patently meant to be an ideal term. I therefore propose a new, less ambiguous version of this schema,

| Objects | Generic | Individual |
|---------|---------|------------|
| Ideal | A<br>The class of all terms | B<br>The term "table" |
| Real | | C<br>This particular occurrence of<br>the term "table" |

which should make it plain that an occurrence (or manifestation) of a term is not a term, and therefore not a member of the class of terms. Again, a series of logically nesting categories (which might, for example, include, between the genus "term" and the French term *table*, the species "French terms," the family "grammatically feminine French terms," and so on) terminates in an object which, because its extension is logically indivisible, no longer forms a class containing other individuals of the same kind, but is clearly an ideal, logically ultimate, and indivisible individual,[27] even if can be materialized by an indefinite number of occurrences or instances of manifestation. These last will also be individuals—material or physical, in this case.

The terminological category that most aptly designates this opposition is, of course, the Peircian pair type/token*, the usual French translation of which is *type/occurrence,* or (when we refer specifically to

---

27. "Given a series of terms arranged in a hierarchy of genuses and species subordinated one to the other, the entity represented by the last term in the series is called an individual; it does not designate a general concept and admits of no logical division." (André Lalande, *Vocabulaire technique et critique de la philosophie,* 10th ed. [Paris: PUF, 1988], s.v. "Individual.")

manifestations effected by physical objects) *type/exemplaire*.[28] But the word "occurrence" can be a bit misleading here (unless it is employed in an expressly restricted sense), for it can evoke (as it seems to in Goodman) the idea of membership in a class. Tokens, linguistic or otherwise, are merely manifestations, that is, realizations in the broad sense. Of course, we can again say that to make a table is to realize the concept table, but this is certainly not the best way of putting the matter: the concept table (the class of tables) *logically* includes all tables; the phoneme /r/ does not logically include its manifestations, which, to repeat, are *not* phonemes, but sounds. As for the word *exemplaire* [copy or exemplar], it presents the added inconvenience of being easy to confuse with the word *exemple* [example]; I will come back to this question.[29] Thus it seems to me that the most reasonable translation of "token" is, emphatically, *"manifesta-tion"*[30]— whence, when called for, the term "occurrence (or instance) of manifestation."

It will doubtless have been understood that allographic objects of immanence are also, in my view, types\*, while their objects of mani-festation are tokens\*, and thus occurrences or instances of manifesta-tion. To return to this subject without losing sight of the more general problematic of singular idealities, I propose two new ways (the last two) of filling in our table:

| Objects | Generic | Individual |
|---------|---------|------------|
| Ideal | A<br>Poems | B<br>"The Death of Lovers" |
| Real | | C<br>This particular copy of<br>"The Death of Lovers" |

28. Be it recalled that Goodman rejects this category as "informal parlance," preferring to treat these "tokens"\* as "replicas of one another"; but he has just defined the type as "the universal or class of which marks are instances or members" (*Languages of Art*, p. 131). This definition seems to me—I have already indicated this, and will come back to the point—totally wrong. Making it a point of honor to be as nominalist as possible here reveals itself to be a mistaken strategy.

29. [The same may be said, though for somewhat different reasons, about English "instance" and "example."]

30. [It does not follow that the best translation of French *manifestation* is "token," in part

or again:

| Objects | Generic | Individual |
|---------|---------|------------|
| Ideal | A<br>Lieder | B<br>*Der Tod und das Mädchen* |
| Real |  | C<br>This particular performance of<br>*Der Tod und das Mädchen* |

It can, I hope, be clearly seen that if "The Death of Lovers" undoubtedly belongs to the class of poems, and *Der Tod und das Mädchen* to that of lieder (for to say "poem" or "lied" is to say poem-type or lied-type), singular copies of the first or singular performances of the second do not belong to these two classes (for the same reason), and cannot be referred to as "poems" or "lieder" except by metonymy.[31] Again, a logical series of nested categories such as "literary works—poems—sonnets—sonnets by Baudelaire—'The Death of Lovers,'" or "musical compositions—lieder—lieder by Schubert—*Der Tod und das Mädchen*," necessarily culminates in the last-named objects, "under" which there are no more "literary works" or "musical compositions," but copies (or performances) of literary works or performances (or copies) of musical works. As these do not (logically) belong to the class "literary works" or "musical works," they cannot *belong to* the subclass which would be (but is not) constituted by "The Death of Lovers" or *Der Tod und das Mädchen*. Something cannot, indeed, belong to a subclass without belonging to its class, or to a species without belonging to its genus: to be a dachshund, it is necessary to be a dog. Nothing, *in this sense,* belongs to these works; that is precisely what defines them, despite their ideality, as individuals. I say "despite," because this statement runs counter (in my case, at any rate) to the spontaneous belief that there are only material individuals, or that what is not a material

---

because Genette often uses *manifestation* to mean something like "the process of being manifested"; I have therefore frequently translated French *manifestation* as "manifestation."]
31. See Stevenson, "On 'What Is a Poem.'" Stevenson is more inclined to admit this double sense of the word.

object can only be an "abstraction." I do not know (and do not much care) if Husserl was the first philosopher to admit the existence of singular idealities, but, as we have seen, the logical definition of the term "individual" in Lalande's good old *Vocabulary* by no means excludes that possibility—which is to say that it implies it. To the definition we have already cited, Lalande adds: "We can describe the same property by saying that an individual is a logical subject that admits of predicates, but cannot itself be the predicate of any other logical subject." Indeed, we can literally say that a sonnet is a poem and that "The Death of Lovers" is a sonnet, but we cannot say, except by metonymy,[32] "this is a 'Death of Lovers,'" while pointing to a copy of the poem. A copy of "The Death of Lovers" is not a "Death of Lovers" because a copy of a poem is not a poem. Individuals are the logically ultimate objects in their genus; "The Death of Lovers" is an (ideal) individual because it is an ultimate object in the genus "poems." "Beyond it," there begins another genus (another class), the genus "copies of poems."[33]

In other words, despite the kinship between the two terms, an instance (of manifestation) *is not an example;* or, more precisely, an instance is not an example *of its type.* If a type is an example of the class of types to which it belongs ("The Death of Lovers" is an example of a poem), it cannot, qua individual, have examples in its turn any more than a physical individual can (this table does not have examples). It has, rather, instances of manifestation (physical individuals, like this table or the *Mona Lisa,* have neither examples—because they are already individuals—nor instances—because they are already physical[34]). I say "is not an example of its type," because an instance or copy can be an example of many things—but not of its type. Thus this copy of *The Flowers of Evil* is an example of a book, an example of a parallelepiped, an example of an object weighing fourteen ounces, and so on; in particular, it is an example (that is, a member of the class) of copies of *The Flowers of Evil.*

32. The existence of metonymies that substitute type for copy, which are, like all figures of speech, (tolerated) violations of logic, can lead to manifestly absurd statements, such as: "Wilhelm Kempff played 32,000 Beethoven sonatas in his lifetime." The absurdity of *"The Charterhouse of Parma* is in the living room" is less evident, yet is, in fact, of the same kind.
33. This class too includes its nested subclasses: copies of a given edition, impression, etc.
34. The same clearly holds for human beings, who are, among other things, physical individuals; but this point would take us a bit beyond the scope of our subject.

In sum, and to wrap up our discussion of this hot potato: if, as the point of departure for a series of nested classes, we take the class, not of poems, but of copies of poems, followed by the subclass of copies of sonnets, and then the subsubclass of copies of sonnets by Baudelaire, the logical "hierarchy," as Lalande says, could ultimately reach down to include *this* particular copy of "The Death of Lovers."[35] But, in this case, it is "The Death of Lovers" that would be excluded from the chain, for this poem (type) does not belong to the class of its copies, nor, incidentally, to the class of copies of anything at all. It should be clear, then, why I have arranged my table as I have: since the choice of the initial class determines the entire trajectory, taking the class "copies" as our point of departure means that we can descend as far as this particular (or some other) copy; starting out from the class "poems" means that we can descend no further than this particular poem (type). The term "type" is thus a way (the most convenient, on condition that we agree on its definition[36]) of designating ideal individuals.

There are, however, situations in which an allographic work does not consist in *one* individual type, but in *several*—which differ by definition, given that "several" identical idealities would amount to only one. This is the case, more common than might be supposed, whenever a work has several "versions" that are nonetheless considered to be versions *of the same work:* for example, *The Song of Roland, The Temptation of Saint Anthony,* or *Petrushka.* These cases are evidently recalcitrant to the nominalist principle Goodman posits for literature, according to which a work *is* its text, inasmuch as the existence of a multiplicity of texts (or of scores) requires us to dissociate somewhat, and therefore to distinguish, the work and "its" (that is, here, any one of its) object(s) of immanence. This form of transcendence will claim our attention below, but we need to note straightaway that it does not constitute an objection

35. This hypothesis is in no wise farfetched; a warehouseman, and, in certain respects, a bookseller or a librarian, deals with copies rather than works. If we are looking for a copy of *The Charterhouse of Parma,* we have to look for it among (for example) the copies of novels by Stendhal. Professionals make a routine distinction between "titles" (types) and "volumes" (copies or instances): "I have 300,000 volumes representing 30,000 titles in stock." In literary terms, *The Charterhouse* is an individual object, but in (metonymical) warehouse terms, it forms a class, of, for example, ten volumes.
36. "Model" is one of its competitors in other fields; in "the 2CV [a make of Citroën] is in the garage," "the 2CV" refers to an instance; in "a 2CV doesn't have a radiator," "a 2CV" refers to a model, that is, an industrial type.

to *our* principle, according to which an allographic object of immanence, or *type,* is always an ideal individual: what is not an individual in this case, but clearly a *class* (of types), is not the object of immanence "text of the Oxford manuscript," "1849 version of *The Temptation of Saint Anthony,*" or "1911 version of *Petrushka,*" but the (plural) work *Song of Roland, Temptation,* or *Petrushka,* a class of literary or musical texts of which each version, since it is a text, is a member or example (but not a copy). A distributive expression like "a *Charterhouse of Parma*" cannot be taken literally as designating a copy of this work with a text that is (virtually) unique, but "a *Song of Roland*" is a perfectly appropriate way of designating one of the *texts* of *The Song of Roland.* These works, of which each is a class of types, may be termed, in line with Stevenson's proposal, *megatypes*—or, better, if one is willing to hazard such a barbarism, *archetypes.* I will not make undue use of the latter term.

These pluralities of immanence—which must not be confused with multiplicities of manifestation—are not peculiar to the allographic regime: multiple autographic works like *The Thinker* or *Melancholia* also immanate, as we have seen, in several objects, obtained by imprint, while plural autographic works, like *Saying Grace,* immanate in several objects obtained when a work is copied, by the original artist or someone else. What *is* peculiar to allographic works is the capacity some have of possessing several objects of immanence, *all of them ideal.* This is why the descriptive term "archetypes" must be reserved for them: for *The Thinker,* which does not immanate in types, cannot (at least not literally) be described as an archetype. If there is an "arche-" in this case, it is rather an arche-sculpture.

## The Principle of Individuation

The definition of the object of immanence as an ideal, logically ultimate individual type, beyond which all additional specifications can only be features of manifestation, can, I trust, be taken for granted from now on. What is less firmly established is the *principle of individuation* of types, or, in other words, the point at which the logical hierarchy of classes and subclasses, genera and species, terminates in the case of each particular series. This principle seems to me to vary with the practices involved, that is, both the arts involved and also the usages or conventions adopted for each of them in a given state of a culture.

Thus matters are quite simple in the case of literature, because the ultimate level is clearly defined by the verbal (lexical) chain that determines a text. Take a formal schema like the rhyme scheme *a b b a, a b b a, c c, d e e d,* (or *d e d e*): it determines what is traditionally called a genre, that of the sonnet, which can comprise an infinite number of different individual types. An additional condition, such as *having lines of twelve feet,* determines the species of sonnets in hexameter, without further defining an individual type. A grammatical schema can restrict the specific field still further, without reaching the level of the individual. Take, as an instance of an opening line of this type, the schema *verb in the imperative—adjective—exclamation—feminine possessive adjective—feminine noun—coordinating conjunction—reflexive imperative—comparative adverb—adjective;* this schema is satisfied (and, now, individuated), by the first line of "Meditation,"

> Sois sage, ô ma Douleur, et tiens-toi plus tranquille,
> [Be good, my Sorrow, quiet your despair,][37]

but also by an Oulipoidal[38] variation like

> Sois sale, ô ma douzaine, et tords-toi plus transie,
> [Nonsense verse: Be dirty, o my dozen, and twist yourself more
> frozen].

By the same token, a thematic schema like that of the classical detective novel ("someone commits a murder, a detective conducts an investigation and finally discovers the guilty party") admits of an indefinite number of specifications, which come to an end only with the definition of a singular verbal string, such as the text of *Ten Little Indians.* We can, then, say that a text's principle of individuation is provided by the determination of the lexical string, even if the act of production

37. [Charles Baudelaire, *"Recueillement," Les fleurs du mal* in *Œuvres,* vol. 1 (Paris: Pléiade, Gallimard, 1975), p. 110 [tr. "Meditation," *The Flowers of Evil,* trans. and ed. James McGowan (London: Oxford University Press, 1993), p. 347].
38. [See Chap. 7, n. 4.]

does not usually follow the aforementioned procedure of making successive specifications.[39] Once this string is established, all additional specifications, such as "recited with the accent of the city of Agen," or "set in Garamond on an 8-point body," can only be "contingent properties," or features of manifestation. It might seem that this rigid principle could be made more flexible in at least one way, which would transform this type into an archetype: that is, if we maintain that "Meditation" or *Ten Little Indians* is still itself after it has been translated into another language, so that it can consist in several types (and constitute a class of types). But such a position, which I will examine again later, seems to me untenable: the archetype, in this case, is not the text, but the *work*, regarded (if we agree to regard it thus) as something that can consist in several texts in several languages. Every one of these texts, or lexical strings, remains a logically ultimate individual type. To be sure, the level of individualization can be set exceptionally low, as when an author specifies a lettering font or the color he wants his work printed in. In these rare instances, not always respected in posthumous editions (I will come back to this too), the type is defined at a sublinguistic level.

In music, the multiplicity of aural parameters ordinarily renders the conventions governing individuation more supple and less stable. A syntagmatic ("formal") schema like A (A') B A, found in a large number of melodies, obviously only determines a genre (that of the lied, or the jazz "standard"). An harmonic specification like "A on the tonic, B on the dominant" barely determines a species, so hard is it to avoid this arrangement in the standard tonal system. Specifying a key determines a species like that of the "lieder in F" or "lieder in G." What can determine an individual type is, for example, the A-phrase of *Au clair de la lune*, defined by a succession of intervals, *tonic—tonic—tonic—second—third—second—tonic—third—second—second—tonic*, which may be further specified by relative values of duration (four quarter-notes, two half-notes, four quarter-notes, a whole note).[40] There is more room for choice when it comes to specification by key, in this case C major:

39. It *can* follow it, as in the "exquisite corpse" of the Surrealists, where the filling in, and thus the individuation, of a schema such as *noun–adjective–verb–noun–adjective* is left to chance.
40. Generally speaking, it is definitions of this kind that serve as the basis for copyrights, which is why a jazz musician like Charlie Parker often borrowed only the harmonic structure of standard themes, while changing their titles. These harmonic structures can be individualized in many different ways, and (perhaps for this reason) cannot be copyrighted. But,

*Au clair de la lune* in G major (or in C minor, etc.) would of course still be recognizable, and would be considered a "transposition" only if the definition used were much stricter than the one ordinarily applied to popular songs. The key of works in the "standard repertory" of classical music is usually specified: it is hard to imagine playing the *Jupiter* Symphony in G or A. However, it is traditionally considered acceptable to transpose vocal works in order to adapt them to various tessituras: a baritone does not sing a lied in the same key as a tenor, and we rarely take the trouble to find out what key the original score was in. (I will mention a few exceptions below.) Even in the case of instrumental music, the level of specification of the type can vary: everybody knows that Johann Sebastian Bach, who composed toccatas and partitas for *clavichord* (so that playing them on the piano already involves transcription of a sort), leaves the choice of instrument open in his *Well-Tempered Clavier,* and allows for even wider choice in *The Art of Fugue.* To leave room for such options is to raise the level of individuation, but nothing stops us from perversely setting it lower than usual by composing a sonato for upright piano. Let us also not forget that the tempos of performances are prescribed in all kinds of ways (or not at all), metronome markings aside; and, even when there are metronome markings, one needs to know how to read a metronomic scale, a skill some say Beethoven lacked. It is also well known that standard concert pitch is not so stable as to withstand every trial.

The musical "individual" is thus defined with widely varying degrees of precision, as best one can and/or as one feels it must be defined.[41] But the fact remains that the performer, for his part, must (cannot *not*) individualize his performance, and generally well beyond what is indicated: no one can prescribe (or even, sometimes, define) the timbre of a voice. Conversely, no pianist can play the *Hammerklavier* Sonata on a piano in general, or even on a Steinway in general; he must play it on *this particular* Steinway or *that one.* And, by definition, a performance

---

with a little ear and training, one can learn to recognize *Cherokee* under *KoKo,* or *I Got Rhythm* under *Constellation.*

41. Similarly, an architect can specify "marble flagstones," or "flagstones made of marble from Carrara"; "curtain wall of smoked glass," or "curtain wall of smoked glass of such and such a thickness and make," etc. Each of these choices of specification shifts the level of the type to a different point between the "hierarchy" of generic inclusions and that of the options of manifestation.

cannot be a performance of a generic object; we do not play a sonata in general, but rather *this particular* sonata; we do not recite (or print) a poem in general, but rather *this particular* poem, and we play, recite, or print them in *this particular* way, which can never be prescribed down to the last detail. This state of affairs obtains in all the allographic arts. In cooking, for example, nobody makes the generic definition of cassoulet. One rather follows the recipe for a *particular* cassoulet—the cassoulet of the Landes or Toulouse, of Castelnaudary or Pierre Perret—and, what is more, one uses a specific ingredient to make it (*this* piece of *this* duck), which no recipe can prescribe. The same applies, of course, to any real practice. If you go to the fruit and vegetable store and ask for a pound of fruit, saying no more than that to the man behind the counter, he will have to choose for you (blindly, if necessary) between pears and grapes. Ask him for a pound of pears, and he will probably have to choose between Williams and Comice. Specify Comice, and he will sell you the four on the left, not the four on the right. If you are of a very suspicious bent, pick your pears out yourself one by one; but this logic leads, in the end, to the conclusion that we need to do everything for ourselves, which brings us back round to the autographic regime and Michelangelo doing his shopping at Carrara, like Françoise doing hers in Roussainville-le-Pin. Allographic "emancipation" is not be had without a minimum of personal initiative, on the one hand, and trust and delegation of tasks, on the other.

## Establishing a Text

Reduction, the necessary and sufficient condition for the constitution of an allographic object of immanence, by no means guarantees the constitution of a *correct* object of immanence. If its point of departure, which is necessarily a manifestation, is an erroneous manifestation (or several identically erroneous manifestations), the type extracted by reduction will also be erroneous. To attain (if possible) a correct type, we need to have a correct manifestation at our disposal, whether it is given (for example, a unique autograph manuscript, which is, in principle and by definition, always correct), selected (for example, the last edition emended by the author) or conjectured (for example, the conjectural "archetype" of a stemma of pre-Gutenbergian manuscripts, that is, of allographic copies of an edition). All these essential operations of examination, comparison, criticism, and reconstitution come together in the operation known as *establishing* a text or score, or, more generally, an ideal object of immanence. This necessity is characteristic of allographic works; autographic works need "only" be authenticated, that is, traced back with certainty to an act of their author's.[42]

This is of course not the place to discuss, in the wake of so many others, the (variable) methods for establishing literary or musical texts. Let me simply recall that the cardinal principle here is the quest for a copy, real or conjectural, that conforms as closely as possible to what one believes was the author's "intention." The singular here is plainly either very naive or very reductive, for an author may have *several* intentions, at least successively, and the privilege generally accorded the latest is not always absolutely justified. Thus certain editors are known to prefer the text of an original manuscript to that of the first edition, even when the latter has been emended by the author,[43] or else to prefer a first edition to the last emended edition.[44] But, since this is not the universal choice, divergences in editorial policy can give rise to several coexisting versions with successive origins, and thus, once again, to plural works, like Senancour's *Oberman(n)*, which we will come back to when we consider transcendence.[45]

42. Authentication can be one of the elements involved in establishing a text or score: one cannot rely on a manuscript unless it is certain that it is an autograph, or has been revised by the author. This necessary condition is not always sufficient, however; certain obvious slips (for example, if Flaubert once writes "Ema" for "Emma") are as a rule corrected by even the most punctilious editors, though they will signal the emendation in a note. Again, technical constraints, later removed, can determine choices we are certain were not entirely deliberate. Thus the insuffcent length of the keyboards of his time sometimes forced Beethoven to contract piano runs he would have preferred to extend; the keyboards of modern pianos authorize performances that do full justice to their logical development, and may even entitle us to make late "corrections" of the original scores.
43. For example, Bernard Masson's edition of *Lorenzaccio,* Imprimerie nationale, 1978.
44. As with Maurice Cauchie's edition of *Le Cid,* Textes Français Modernes, 1946, or Georges Condominas's edition of *La vie de Rancé,* GF, 1991. The motivation for these heterodox choices is usually a feeling that late corrections made by an author who has "seen reason" have resulted in an unfortunate banalization of the text.
45. A (minor) example of a "final intention" which it is quite tempting to correct by going back to an earlier version: in the manuscript of *Cities of the Plain,* Proust has Madame Verdurin say, "Je ne sais pas ce qui peut vous attirer à Rivebelle, c'est infesté de rastaquouères" [I can't imagine what you find attractive in Rivebelle, it's infested with foreign riffraff]

In the case of medieval manuscripts, which are allographic manuscript editions[46] marked by the divergences that inevitably creep into successive transcriptions (whether direct, or produced by dictation to a group in the scriptorium), the sometimes overly sanguine assumption of classical philology was that it was possible to establish a genealogical stemma pointing back to an archetype (real or conjectural), that is, a first copy regarded as being, by definition, the closest to the author's intentions. This doctrine is appropriate to all the texts we have inherited from Antiquity, but it is poorly adapted to medieval (especially poetic) vernacular works, often handed down in transcriptions based on an oral tradition that left room for improvisation. Thus we have had to retreat, and to accept, here too (here above all), greater textual plurality.[47]

I have said that the same holds for objects of allographic immanence in general (scores, building plans, fashion sketches, etc.), which obviously pose problems of the same sort. I will now add that a realization, as long as we have some trace of it (a building, a dress, a recording of a performance by the composer or poet himself), can legitimately enter into competition with the existing (de)notations (if, for example, a performance given by the composer after the score is written out bears witness to undeniable, deliberate "emendations"). It can even replace them, if the only record of a musical work for which no score at all exists is a performance by the composer. In the latter case, we are again

---

[*Sodome et Gomorrhe* (1922), in *À la recherche du temps perdu,* vol. 3 (Paris: Pléiade, Gallimard, 1988), p. 360 (tr. *Cities of the Plain,* in *Remembrance of Things Past,* vol. 2, trans. C. K. Scott Moncrieff and Terence Kilmartin [New York: Random House, 1981], p. 1002)]. The typist was unable to decipher the last word, and left a blank. As he was proofreading the typescript, Proust spotted this gap; apparently because he no longer recalled what he had written, and probably without consulting his manuscript, he filled the blank in with a banal *(scriptio facilior) moustiques* [mosquitoes]. The editors of posthumous editions are divided as to which of the two readings to adopt, the "tempting" (and conjectural) or the orthodox one, which retains what Proust *last* wrote. As to the strange "vertebrae" on Aunt Léonie's forehead, attested as early as the sketches, it seems we will simply have to resign ourselves to them. [*Du côté de chez Swann* (1913), in *À la recherche du temps perdu,* vol. 1 (Paris: Pléiade, Gallimard, 1988), p. 52 (tr. *Swann's Way,* in *Remembrance of Things Past,* vol. 1, trans. C. K. Scott Moncrieff and Terence Kilmartin [New York: Random House, 1981], p. 56). The anglophone translators plumped for "bones" rather than "vertebrae."]

46. This means, of course, the copies made to multiply texts before the invention of printing.

47. See, among other works, Paul Zumthor, *Essai de poétique médiévale* (Paris: Seuil, 1972) [tr. *Toward a Medieval Poetics,* trans. Philip Bennett (Minneapolis: University of Minnesota Press, 1992)] and *La lettre et la voix* (Paris: Seuil, 1987); Bernard Cerquiglini, *Éloge de la variante: Histoire critique de la philologie* (Paris: Seuil, 1989).

brought back to the autographic regime (the regime, usually, of jazz), which may be *multiple* by virtue (the virtue is relative) of recording. But there is not always a tape recorder within easy reach of the stage.

## Transfers and Conversions

A text (and, more generally, an allographic object) that has only one instance of manifestation (for example, an authenticated autograph manuscript) poses virtually no problems of establishment (except, as already noted, for the correction of possible slips, or in cases where the author was obviously not at liberty to do as he wished); and, plainly, this unique instance can serve as the direct basis for an indefinite number of individual or collective receptions, unless it wears out—like a letter addressed to the whole family and passed from hand to hand. However, exploiting its (potentially) allographic character—that is, the correct transmission of its text to new occurrences of manifestation—presupposes a number of operations we need to examine a little more closely. As indicated by this triangular schema,

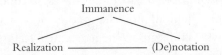

presented earlier, these operations of remanifestation necessarily consist either in (new) realizations or in (new) denotations. I will call these transmissions, depending on whether they occur within a mode or from one mode to another, (intramodal) *transfers* or (intermodal) *conversions*. In both cases, the aim is obviously to transmit the object of immanence, in its entirety, from one manifestation to another; in both cases, the initial copy or occurrence acts as a *model* for the production of subsequent ones. But here too the model acts, now as a purely mechanical (or photonic) *matrix,* now as a *signal* that must be understood before it can be interpreted. I will again use the term *imprint* for the former kind of model, and *copy* for the latter; but there are, as we know, copies and copies, and this obliges us to introduce a third term.

The panoply of methods for transmitting a written text by transfer provides a rather convenient paradigm for all other methods of transmission. The most mechanistic, requiring no participation of the intelligence in the process itself, consists in taking an imprint. The good old photocopy furnishes the readiest illustration; here, more is reproduced than just the text, since many (how many varies with the type of machine) of the model's properties of manifestation are preserved (at a minimum, the writing or typeface, as well as the layout). The second procedure, which might be labeled *facsimile copying,* is what I will here call *copying* tout court: a skilled technician sets out to reproduce, as faithfully as possible, all the textual and paratextual characteristics of the model—including, if possible, the nature of its support. This is how forgers proceed. The product of such labor could be described as a pseudo-imprint or quasi-imprint: it possesses (at a minimum) all the properties of imprints, though these have been arrived at by a completely different route. I will not say that there is no participation of the intelligence here (to say skill is to say intelligence), but the intelligence involved is not knowledge of the text as such: a good calligrapher can counterfeit a manuscript without knowing the language it is written in, or even without knowing how to read the writing (or any other writing); a good typographer can, under the same conditions, counterfeit a printed page. The third procedure is the only one to transmit *nothing but* the text, without regard to the paratextual features of the model; it is thus the only one to utilize the text alone, qua signal, after it has been extracted by reduction from the model. For the moment, it is also the only one which calls for a certain linguistic competence: to transcribe a text in blackletter into modern English longhand, we must at least know how to transliterate. I have called this third type of transfer transcription.[48] The product of the first two types may be described as (more or less) "faithful"; those of the third are merely *correct,* that is, merely compliant with the object of immanence, the text.[49]

48. Some kinds of transcription (from manuscript to print), utilized in "diplomatic" editions or genetic studies, also take pains to preserve, to the greatest extent possible, the spatial arrangement of the manuscript, which is regarded as meaningful.

49. As an accessible example of facsimile editing, we may cite the edition of Valéry's *Cahiers* [notebooks] published by Les Presses du CNRS between 1957 and 1961 (though it is faithful only in a highly approximate sense); as an example of typographic transcription, the edition of the *Cahiers 1894–1914* currently being prepared for Gallimard by Nicole

These are the three most widely practiced types of transfer, even if improvements in the first must gradually lead the second to its grave.[50] We can imagine a fourth type, which would not be at all profitable, and thus could be pursued only as a technical exercise. Suppose we wish to produce an exact copy of a handwritten or printed page. We provide a technician with the text (orally, or in a graphic form different from that of the original) and inform him of all the paratextual characteristics of the page(s) to be reconstituted: their layout and dimensions, as well as their typographical (roman or italic, Garamond or Didot, etc.) or calligraphic features (cursive/uncial/blackletter/modern English longhand/roundhand/slanting roundhand, etc.). If all the instructions are correctly given and carried out, the result will be, at least in the case of the typographic text, a very decent facsimile. In fact, this is essentially the task we expect a computer to perform, so that this procedure could be described as the *treatment* of texts[51] par excellence—with the difference that, first, computers do not yet have calligraphic fonts at their disposal, and, second, that we ordinarily utilize a computer, not to reproduce already realized models, but to realize an ideal model communicated in the form of commands.

At a more fanciful, or even fantastic level, we also need to mention the hypothesis, often put forward in jest, that a given text (for example, the text of *Don Quixote*) might be reproduced purely at random: a drunken compositor, an inspired or infinitely patient monkey at his typewriter, etc.; we should also cite, of course, the Borgesian hypothesis of a Ménardian remake*. Contrary to Borges, Goodman maintains[52]

---

Celeyrette-Pietri and Judith Robinson-Valéry, which, in fact, is more respectful of the spatial arrangement of the text; and as examples of diplomatic editing carried out as scrupulously as possible, the editions of *Un cœur simple* and *Hérodias* by Giovanni Bonaccorso (Les Belles Lettres, 1983, and Nizet, 1992).

50. We should note that printing in its classical form (together with word-processing and the computer print-out) exemplifies the two principal forms of transfer simultaneously, or rather successively: typesetting is an example of transcription, printing of imprint. Typewriting brings both into play at the same time.

51. [The French for "word-processing" is *traitement de texte,* which means, literally, "text-treating."]

52. Nelson Goodman, *Of Mind and Other Matters* (Cambridge: Harvard University Press, 1984), p. 141; Nelson Goodman and Catherine Elgin, *Reconceptions in Philosophy and Other Arts and Sciences* (London: Routledge, 1988), p. 62. Cf. Jorge Luis Borges, *Labyrinths: Selected Stories and Other Writings,* ed. Donald A. Yates and James E. Irby, trans. James E. Irby et al. (N.p.: New Directions, 1964).

that, in such a case, we would quite simply be dealing with the real *Don Quixote*. But, as we will see, the disagreement concerns not textual, but only *operal*[53] identity (which will claim our attention later): Borges clearly agrees with Goodman (and everyone else) that the *text* produced by Ménard is that of *Don Quixote;* this suggests a sixth method, or, at any rate, process to us, one which, this time, is the fruit of neither an objectively random occurrence, nor (the Borgesian hypothesis categorically rules this out) simple memorization (after the monkey, the elephant), but, rather, a sort of willed palingenesis: Ménard *transforms himself into* Cervantes.

The forms of writing reproducible by imprint or transcription are, let us note further, not limited to the ordinary writing systems (phonetic or logogrammatic) in use today. They also include derivative procedures, such as stenography or stenotypy (derived from spoken language), the "alphabets" of Braille or Morse code (derived from written language), and, doubtless, others I am ignorant of, but which I suspect exist. Nor should we link writing too closely to visual perception (or spoken language to hearing). Braille, by definition, does not involve visual perception, while we can *spell out* a text using the "names" of its letters without carrying out a conversion of it (to spell is not to read, to solfa is not necessarily to sing): a deaf person can read the spoken word on a speaker's lips ("read my lips"*), while the language of the deaf and dumb makes gestures out of linguistic elements that are, indiscernibly, letters or phonemes.

It goes without saying, I hope, that all these methods of transfer from one (de)notation to another also apply to musical scores, architectural plans, the sketches of fashion designers, choreographic notations—and, a fortiori, to the various kinds of "scripts": scenographies, recipes, and so on. Today, analogous methods can be applied to musical performances or oral recitations: phonographic imprints (digital or not, be it noted in passing), faithful imitations, or, simply, correct iterations of performances that retain only features of immanence—the acoustic equivalent of transcription. Thanks to audiovisual recording, these methods have been extrapolated to other allographic practices as well, such as theater or choreography. The only limits here, it seems to me, stem

53. [*Opéral*, a neologism derived from opus and operate. Genette glosses this word in Chap. 13, n. 42]

from the practical difficulties confronting anyone who wishes to take an imprint of a building, or the (absolute?) impossibility of taking an imprint of a flavor or aroma. In all these cases, reconstitution based on (de)notation is, evidently, the most convenient procedure. But, it will be objected, such a (de)notation must first exist. The response is that, when it does not exist beforehand, it must be established after the fact, as Mozart established one for Allegri's *Miserere*. Doubtless it is harder to "read off" the plan of a building this way, or the plan of a choreography or script of a stage production, but this is only a question of competence; they say that a gastronomic critic (Patricia Wells, perhaps) boasts she can reconstruct the recipe of virtually any dish submitted to her expert appraisal. It is, in any event, certain that these difficulties are not a function of the type of art under consideration, but rather of the relative complexity of each work: although architectural or musical notations are as a rule stricter than the one used in cooking, it is easier to reconstruct the recipe for radishes-and-butter[54] than the plan of the Amiens Cathedral or the score of *Tristan und Isolde*. But it is plain that, in evoking possibilities of this kind, we have left the domain of transfers and crossed over into that of conversions.

By conversion, I mean any transmission of an allographic object of immanence from one mode of manifestation to another. Conversion from a (de)notation to a realization consists in what is commonly called *reading;* from a realization to a (de)notation, in what is called, no less commonly, *dictation.* The reading of a (de)notation—for instance, an inscription of a text or a musical or choreographic score—generally takes place in the absence of its author, but rarely against his will: if you do not want to be read, your best bet is not to write. Dictation, in contrast, can take place against the author's will, despite the usual pedagogical connotations of the term: this was, for a long time, the case with pirate editions of plays, known as "memorial reconstructions."[55] "Even at a time when, thanks to printing, books were very widely diffused, Lope de Vega was obliged to ask the state authorities to punish a troublesome group of people . . . whose trade consisted in 'stealing' comedies (three thousand lines or more long) from their authors; after listening to them only

54. [Raw radishes dipped in butter, and, in the more complex versions of this dish, placed on bits of bread.]
55. [The French equivalent is *à la voix des acteurs,* "from the actors' voices."]

twice, they would write them down, replacing lines they could not quite recall with bad verse."[56] This is how, as late as 1784, the first, obviously illegitimate edition of the *Marriage of Figaro* was produced; and everyone knows how certain texts by Aristotle, Hegel's *Aesthetics,* or Saussure's *Course in General Linguistics* have come down to us. This method can, naturally, be applied to any performance whatsoever—though the open or clandestine use of tape recorders, portable video cameras, and so on makes it superfluous today.

Simple dictation is rarer than the widespread use of the word would suggest: it is limited to the immediate (de)notation of an improvised performance. Dictation in the prevailing sense proceeds from a *double conversion:* indirect transfer from one inscription to another by way of an oral reading, that is, a realization. This, as I have already noted, is how medieval "copies" were most often produced, in the scriptorium. But the least transcription involves, more or less consciously, a (twofold) operation of the same sort: silent reading and internal dication. Not all these indirect transfers presuppose, however, passage by way of the ear: a deaf man can write out a discourse he has read "off the lips" of a speaker, while a deaf (but competent) musician could, simply by watching the gestures of a performer, write out an improvised performance or an interpretation he has not heard. It is obvious, at any rate, that a pianist (for example), after being shown a silent video recording of a performance on the piano, would have no trouble identifying the piece played if he was familiar with it, or in perceiving many features of it if he was encountering it for the first time—to say nothing of the features of the performance itself.

All of these obviously far-fetched hypotheses might seem pointless. But, from a theoretical standpoint, it is essential to notice at least this: conversions, and a fortiori indirect transfers by double conversion, presuppose a reduction (conscious or not) to the type. Indeed, the simplifications or shortcuts of ordinary language notwithstanding, it is inexact to say that a pianist "performs a score" or that a secretary "writes down the speech" *[performance]* given by a speaker. What the pianist performs is the *musical text* written out in a score whose particular extramusical, graphic features matter little to him; what the sec-

56. Ramon Menéndez Pidal, *La chanson de Roland et la tradition épique des Francs,* trans. I. M. Cluzel (Paris: Picard, 1960), p. 57.

retary writes down is the *verbal text* of a speech whose paratextual features (rate of delivery, timbre, accent, etc.) do not, as a rule, matter much
more to her. A performance does not realize a (de)notation, but its ideal
object of immanence. To put it more synthetically (if tautologically):
a manifestation can only manifest an immanence.

## Inconvertibilities

The allographic work, to repeat, exhibits the paradox (and practical
inconvenience) of being entirely itself only in the ideal object it immanates in; but this object, because it is ideal, is physically imperceptible,
so that there exists, even for the mind, nothing more than a vanishing
point that can be defined but not observed (for instance, "that which
a score and a performance of the *Jupiter* Symphony have in common"[57]). The same holds, of course, for all idealities, and especially for
abstractions, but the situation is more problematic in the case of artistic ideality, whose cardinal function is aesthetic, and therefore, in theory, "perceptual" in one way or another (we will encounter this point
again). Allographic works can fulfill this function only by way of their
manifestations; moreover, it is always bound up with other functions
that only one particular mode of manifestation can fulfill, or else fulfills
better than any other. We will later examine this question for its own
sake, but here we need, at least, to observe that most works, in all regimes, have practical (nonaesthetic) functions that can be fulfilled only
when the works are realized: even if their (de)notations are enough to
define an artistic achievement, building plans cannot be lived in, sewing
patterns can hardly be worn, and recipes are not very nourishing. Now,
as the example of architecture plainly shows, it is not always easy or pertinent to separate the aesthetic from the practical function: the first often
results from successfully fulfilling the second. Literature is doubtless an
extreme case, not, to be sure, of the absence of a practical function, but
rather of the ability to carry it out equally well in both its modes of

57. Strictly speaking, we should restrict this convenient, but too generous, formulation still
further, for the score and the performance also have in common that fact that they are both
physical objects (or events): the object of immanence is thus only *part* of what they have
in common.

manifestation. Precisely because "language acts" are acts of *language,* which of the two channels they pass through is largely a matter of indifference: for an honest man, an oral promise has the force of a signed contract. Yet certain functions of persuasion, for example, are still reinforced by the presence and "action" of a speaker. As Aeschines said of his adversary Demosthenes, admiringly, "You have to see the beast." The absence of a practical function is best illustrated by music, but not absolutely: the fanfare galvanizes the battalion, and we do not dance to scores. In contrast, (de)notation, as its name indicates, is almost always the more appropriate means for analyzing or acquiring deeper knowledge of a work: no mere audition is as valuable, from this point of view, as the study of a score or written page for anyone who knows how to "read" it (notwithstanding the advantages of listening to oneself declaim a passage, a technique dear to Flaubert, who perhaps relied a bit too heavily on it, or may sometimes not have had a good enough ear). This is no small reservation; it reminds us that this sharing out of functions depends not only on the types of work involved, but also on the competence of the audience, or even the sharpness of their senses: an ordinary score is of no use to the blind, nor a record to the deaf. But the aesthetic relation is doubtless sustained and enhanced by the study of works, and comes into play no matter what the form. We have learned to "hear the sounds" of a poem even on a silent reading of its text; Ravel appreciated the orchestral refinements of Rimski-Korsakov on reading the score; and a gourmet being fed intravenously can still savor, in his fashion, the subtlety of a recipe—at least if he already has the requisite knowledge and can remember the flavors involved, for Locke's objection still holds: no one can truly appreciate the taste of a pineapple by report.

There are, then, limits, in both directions, to the *convertibility* of manifestations. Some derive from technical impossibilities: certain scores are "unplayable" under the conditions they prescribe (an eleventh chord for the right hand, an A6 for a human voice), though what is noted in them, unproblematically, is a musical object that is entirely conceivable in its ideality. An architectural plan may be impossible to realize because it defies the laws of equilibrium or of the resistance of materials. In the days when we still had seasons, a simple and yet enticing recipe, like asparagus with grapes or pheasant with cherries, could remain a dead letter; and, while we are on the subject of letters, there is nothing to prevent us from writing an unpronounceable name, like that of Calvino's character *Qfwfq*. This is, after all, the fate reserved for a good many punctuation marks, whose manifestation, oral or otherwise, calls for various sorts of subterfuge, like the expression "in parentheses," or the gesture, apparently imported from the United States, which consists in wiggling one's index and middle fingers to either side of one's head in order to mime quotation marks. Conversely, certain cries that can enter into an oral performance cannot be represented in written form; the same holds for sounds characteristic of "concrete music" or of certain jazz performances (breathing effects in the case of saxophonists like Ben Webster or Dexter Gordon[58]), which cannot be scored.

Other instances of inconvertibility arise from a lack of correlation between intramodal options: no feature of recitation corresponds "naturally" to the differences between roman and italic, and even less to that between Times and Didot; no notation differentiates between the tone color of a flute and that of a violin, etc. We usually either circumvent these impossibilites with supplementary indications, such as verbal specifications of the instruments required, or else treat them as "contingent," like choices as to layout or typeface in literature, which we rarely attempt to "translate" in reciting a text. But there are notable exceptions to this rule: some are generic (writing poetry in separate lines, each of which begins with a capital letter), others are idiosyncratic (e. e. cummings's rejection of capital letters), and most are peculiar to one or another particular work. The "concrete" poems of Antiquity (Theocritus's *Syrinx,* with lines each shorter than the last, like the pipes of Pan's flute) or the Middle Ages,[59] the graphic whimsy of *Tristram Shandy,* Thackeray's choice of Queen Anne typeface for *Henry Esmond* (a thematic, stylistic, *and typographic* parody of an eighteenth-century novel), the configurations of letters in Mallarme's "A Throw of the Dice," Apollinaire's calligrammes, the play with the colors of the ink in Butor's *Boomerang* or Caillois's *Esthétique généralisée,* the effects contemporary poetry achieves through the use of white spaces, all constitute so many paratextual elements that cannot be transmitted in a recitation but are

58. The "breathy sound," "white noise" with no set pitch, is produced by a vibration of the reed too weak to result in a true note.
59. Paul Zumthor, *Langue, texte, énigme* (Paris: Seuil, 1975), pp. 25–35.

in principle intrinsic to the work,[60] setting its threshold of ideality far below the strictly linguistic level. Moreover, they can just as well be described as characteristic of *mixed* works, since they simultaneously call on the resources of language and on those (figurative, decorative, connotational) of the graphic arts, as the term "calligramme" indicates all by itself. Classical Chinese poetry (though it was meant to be recited orally, or even sung) did not, we know, forego the added grace of this mixture of modes. The opposite kind of inconvertibility (features of recitation that cannot be written down) is rarer today, because the oral mode is gradually disappearing, but it may take on renewed importance with the rapid increase in the number of recordings of writers reading their own works, so that future critical editions will perhaps have to collate certain manuscripts with certain cassettes.

Graphic effects in musical scores are by no means unheard of; from the Middle Ages to Éric Satie (and beyond), there is no dearth of examples of "music for the eye," "concrete" scores whose visual features sometimes have their audible counterparts[61] (scales or arpeggios that look like roller coasters), though this is not always the case. After all, even equations as venerable as the one that involves translating certain names into notes (B A C H = B-flat A C B) are a dead letter for those who do not know the German do-re-mi.[62] I imagine, again, that many properly graphic aspects of architectural plans are inevitably lost when the plans are executed, and I am quite certain that the same holds

60. But, as I have said, they are not always respected by publishers, especially of posthumous editions, as is shown by the fate usually meted out today to Thackeray's typographic prescriptions.

61. On condition, however, that we admit a relation of analogy between high-pitched/low-pitched and high/low or right/left; but there is no firm basis for this analogy, which Berlioz, for example, thought was absurd: "For why should the sound produced by a string vibrating 32 [sic] times a second be closer to the center of the earth than the sound produced by another string vibrating 800 times? How can the right-hand side of the keyboard of an organ or piano be the 'top' or 'high' part of the keyboard, as it is usually called? Keyboards are horizontal." Hector Berlioz, *À travers chants* (1862) (Paris: Gründ, 1971), p. 241 [tr. *The Art of Music and Other Essays,* trans. and ed. Elizabeth Csicsery-Rónay (Bloomington: Indiana University Press, 1994), p. 150]. Moreover, even on a staff, a scale is literally "rising" or "falling" only if we hold the score in a vertical position.

62. [In French, the eight notes of the scale are ordinarily designated *do* (or *ut*) *re mi fa sol la si* (or *ti*) *do, do* or *ut* being the equivalent of C in the Anglo-American system; thus Beethoven's Fifth Symphony is said to be in *ut mineur*. The German system is much like the Anglo-American, with a few exceptions; for example, Anglo-American B-natural is German *H,* German *B* is Anglo-American B-flat.]

for various stylistic effects of certain recipes, like Ragueneau's recipe for almond tarts in *Cyrano de Bergerac*.

## Texts and Scripts

This last example evokes, in its way, a delicate problem we need to examine more closely. I have drawn parallels between certain cases of inconvertibility from denotation to realization, and vice versa; the illustration from literature was that of the reciprocal inconvertibility between inscriptions and recitations. But Ragueneau's recipe does not involve an (inadequate) relation between written and oral forms, since a "stylistic" feature for the most part transcends this distinction, as is clearly the case here: the recipe for almond tarts is in verse in both its oral and written forms. What *is* involved is the impossibility of transferring this feature of the (oral and written) recipe to its realization, the tarts that emerge from the oven. Thus the parallel masks a dissymmetry which can be described in these terms: in literature, (de)notation is an inscription and realization is a recitation; in cooking, (de)notation is a verbal statement, indifferently (despite the etymology of the word "script") oral or written, and its realization is a meal served on a dish. This dissymmetry obviously stems from the fact that the literary object of immanence is a text, that is, a verbal object, while the culinary object of immanence is a "dish," that is, an object which is by no means verbal,[63] like a stage production or other type of work (de)noted by a script. Or, to put it differently, the status of a text and that of a script differ at least in the sense that the text is an object of immanence, the script merely a means of (de)notation that we could in certain cases, and perhaps advantageously, replace with another type of notational device: it would doubtless not be impossible to invent a code for culinary or scenographic notation that would eliminate the "discursive language" of recipes and stage directions. Not only does language not function in the same way in both cases—in scripts, it is transitive and instrumental, in literary texts, it is intransitive and operal ("artistic")—but it also does not function at the same level, operating at the level of manifestation in scripts, at that

63. In fact, what is at issue here is, rather, what is elsewhere known as a "concept," a somewhat paradoxical aesthetic object that we will consider in a moment.

of immanence in texts. Furthermore, since a script (like a text, and, indeed, any verbal object) is an ideality, it in fact only constitutes a potential manifestation, which is in its turn actualized only in real manifestations, oral or written.[64] This following schema offers a way of representing this dissymmetry:

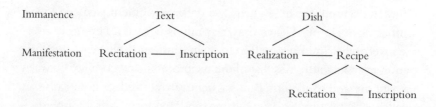

Immanence           Text                     Dish

Manifestation  Recitation —— Inscription   Realization —— Recipe

                                               Recitation —— Inscription

The distinction between text and script enables us to diminish somewhat the effects of the difference between strict notation and verbal denotation. Generally speaking, I am not certain that a verbal description is incapable of determining, say, a musical object as rigorously as a score. If it is true that (standard) musical notation *has* to specify the pitch and value of a note, whereas language *may* content itself with saying "A," this kind of specification is, conversely, by no means *precluded* in language, which can always spell out, "A3, sixteenth-note."[65] Thus the superiority of the notation is rather a matter of its convenience and concision—and, secondarily, its translinguistic universality—which, as we have seen, does not prevent or dispense it from recurring to auxiliary verbal notations. Above all, it must be observed that the relative weaknesses due to the semantic "density" and ambiguities of language do not deny notational rigor only to scripts, whose task is to (de)note nonverbal objects by means of language. However, writing, phonetic or otherwise, does not suffer any more than the spoken word from such weaknesses vis-à-vis one object of immanence (the text), which, aside from the few marginal features just mentioned, is essentially verbal in nature—and for good reason, since this object is nothing other than the set of verbal properties of an oral or written manifestation. Thus the imperfection of language as a system of (de)notation does not imperil the allographic regime of lit-

64. Of course, this ideality of scripts is barely apparent to the person who utilizes them, for example, for he only deals with actually manifested recipes and realizations. But converting one to the other clearly presupposes, here as elsewhere, reducing them, consciously or not, to a type (what the recipe and its realization have in common).

65. Moreover, Goodman acknowledges this possibility (*Languages of Art,* p. 199).

erature (which, be it recalled, can also function in a regime that is at least partially autographic: that of bards, minstrels, or wandering "griots"). It *is* true that the relation between immanence and manifestation is not of exactly the same kind when we receive a verbal object as a text and when we receive it as a script. But it is not certain that this distinction is completely irrelevant to literary works.

Indeed, a structural description that accounts for an established opposition—between, for example, the status of a sonnet by Ronsard and a recipe by Robuchon—by characterizing it in excessively rigid fashion (as the above schema does), can easily gloss over its relative, conditional character. As Ragueneau's performance clearly shows, a script may also function as a text and constitute itself as a literary work. The Ragueneau case displays a marked feature of literariness whose effectiveness it would be very hard to dispute: its verse form. Less conventional stylistic traits might leave the reader free to make his own appraisal of an (in some sort) indeterminate literariness; the same utterance (for instance, this introduction to a recipe, which I am not making up: "Ayez une belle courge ..." [Have a lovely gourd ready ..."]) might be received by some as a mere script, by others as an "intransitive" text, whose relation to any conceivable realization would be insignificant. But there is nothing to prevent a verbal object from being simultaneously[66] transitive and intransitive, instrument and monument. Beckett's *Acts without Words* provides a good illustration: it is a simple set of stage directions for a future stage production, and, at the same time, a narrative text to be appreciated in its own right.

Conversely, for the text of a literary work to function as a script, it is not enough for it to function transitively, like an informative or directive language act. Reading *Robinson Crusoe* as a guide to survival in the wilderness or *Remembrance of Things Past* as a treatise on the sociology of high society does not make their texts over into scripts, because a script is not just any instrumental verbal message (however transitive their function, neither *On the Crown* nor "E=mc²" are scripts), but a verbal message whose instrumental function is to (de)note a nonverbal *work*—and the way one should conduct oneself on a desert island or in Parisian high society is not usually considered to be, in and of itself, a work of art. What best evokes the converse of the script-become-text

---

66. Or perhaps successively, in more or less rapid oscillation, as in a perception of Jastrow's duck-rabbit or Necker's cube that flips back and forth between the two possibilities.

we are trying to pinpoint is Aristotle's remark to the effect that the story of Oedipus is tragic whichever the mode, dramatic or narrative, it is represented in.[67] On this by no means far-fetched hypothesis, or any analogous one, it is clear that the object, indifferently (de)noted by one means or another, is the chain of events leading up to (for example) the tragic ending, so that the artistic achievement which here defines the work consists in the invention of this story. If what is involved is a story that is both true and is also regarded as such,[68] it will be received as an "involuntary work," furnished by reality, which is "stranger than fiction," and therefore as a kind of natural aesthetic object. For a strictly fictionalist poetics, the text of a play or narrative is thus simply the (de)notation, here verbal, of a work consisting in the invention, or "fiction," of a fact that is remarkable in and of itself, regardless of its mode of transmission. But that is plainly to treat a text as a script.

Neither Aristotle nor anyone else, to the best of my knowledge, advocates such a poetics in so extreme a form, but the foregoing remark has the merit of showing that literature considered as an art (leaving its other functions aside) is not purely and simply assimilable to the art of *arranging* words and sentences—in other words, it shows that literary works are not *solely* verbal works: thematic invention in all its forms plays an equally important role, or, at a minimum, also has a role to play, in eminently variable proportions. We know how much importance a James or a Borges attached to a "good scenario."

This instability in the relationship between the transitive and intransitive aspects of a (de)notation is to be found in all the other allographic arts as well, even if what is at stake is not always equally obvious. Goodman clearly states that an architectural plan can take the form of a sketch, as long as it can be utilized in terms of an articulated system, that is, by reducing it to its pertinent features.[69] Conversely, a diagrammatic

---

67. Aristotle, *De Poetica (Poetics)*, (1453b) [trans. Ingram Bywater, in Richard McKeon, ed., *The Basic Works of Aristotle* (New York: Random House, 1941), p. 1466].
68. As is, doubtless, for Aristotle, the story of Mitys' murderer, killed when his victim's statue fell on him—a "matter of chance that seemed to have happened by design," which always produces "the most beautiful stories." Ibid., 1452a. [Genette's translation of Aristotle differs somewhat from Bywater's, which says that "matters of chance seem most marvellous if there is an appearance of design as it were in them" (ibid., p. 1465).]
69. *Languages of Art*, p. 219.

plan can be received as an artistic drawing; we know what aesthetic (and not just aesthetic) value the plans of a Frank Lloyd Wright have for many admirers. The same holds for musical scores, which can be appreciated as works of graphic art, whether in manuscript or printed form. In all these cases and many others as well, the "symptom" of transitive use lies in the possibility of effecting a reduction, which signals (that we should conclude) that the true work resides elsewhere, and that what we have before our eyes (or ear, etc.) is a mere manifestation. The symptom of intransitive use, which Goodman calls saturation*, resides in the impossibility—the psychological or cultural impossibility, at any rate— of carrying out such an operation, which is, in such cases, checked by our sense that nothing is "contingent" and that every detail counts, down to the texture of the paper or the voice. If it were not for the weight of established traditions, the least *clinamen* could abruptly shift our attention from one regime to the other. The same line, the same chaotic drawing can be received as a work or the sign of a work.

On 10 January 1934, in Paris, Picasso wrote by hand, using India ink, on eleven sheets of Arches paper, in eleven different ways, one after the other, the sentence "Il neige au soleil" ["it is snowing in the sun"]. Citing this sentence in this fashion, I retain, by necessity or choice, only its textual, and therefore allographic, aspect. Of the other, purely graphic aspect, which any one of these eleven inscriptions illustrates, I could doubtless transmit "the essentials," by saying, in the form of a script, with some simplification, that, here, the words *Il neige au* are written inside the "o" of *soleil*. Obviously, this would again be the result of a reduction; I would thus be treating this graphic effect as an allographic object capable of (among other things) being (de)noted in this way, and therefore amenable to countless correct, yet different, realizations. If I wish to begin to respect its autographic regime, I must, at a minimum, show you a photographic imprint like the one on the next page.

But this is, manifestly, only a "reproduction"; the illustration gives you a physical perception of what Picasso produced, but this perception is indirect and therefore partial: the nuances of the colors and texture of the paper, if nothing else, are missing from it. If you want "the thing itself" in the uniqueness of its autographic immanence, you will at least have to go to the Hôtel Salé [which houses the Paris Picasso Museum]. But I see that I should have begun this progression with the

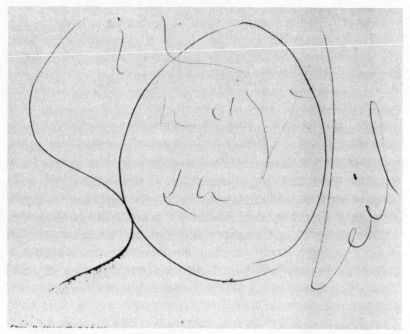

Source: *Catalogue des collections,* Musée Picasso (5, rue de Thorigny, 75003 Paris), Vol. 2, n° 1008–1018 (MP 1120–1130). ©1996 Estate of Pablo Picasso/Artists Rights Society (ARS) New York.

most radically allographic state[70] of the object: the state which would consider the sentence "Il neige au soleil," not as a text, an intransitive verbal object enclosed in its Jakobsonian "poetic function," a play of sounds or written marks (*ei—ei*), etc., but as a script charged with recording the following probable fiction, which no weather report confirms: that on 10 January 1934, it was snowing in the sun in Paris. I do not think anyone can doubt that the sentence is *both* the one *and* the other. This "sustained hesitation" between form and meaning, message and context, can thus, at one pole, go so far as to reduce the "contents," but perhaps also the form of a work, literary or otherwise, to an idea (snowing in the sun)—or, as one says nowadays when speaking of anything at all, to its *concept.*

70. Radically, because it locates the object of immanence, as was noted above, *beyond* the words which transmit it. In this sense, of course, cooking is more allographic than literature, and fiction more allographic than poetry, for one cannot deny that the culinary object is more distinct from its recipe than is a text from its oral or written manifestations, or that the plot of *Tom Jones* is at a greater distance from its legible trace that is the plot (?) of "A Throw of the Dice." But this way of putting the matter is doubtless rather metaphorical.

# The Conceptual State

I T REMAINS, THEN, TO DEFINE THE REGIME OF IMMANENCE OF A VERY special sort of work, which has appeared (or rather, as we will see, been *institutionalized*) only very recently, and which we call, using an adjective that is even more recent, *conceptual*. I am going to put in this category forms of art lying well outside the domain officially covered by the term. In due course, I hope to justify this extension, which, moreover, I am not the first to make.

## From Object to Act

I will start out from a particular case, chosen for its simplicity, and, secondarily, its celebrity—a "pure" ready-made (by this rather unorthodox adjective, I mean a ready-made that has not been assisted or corrected like the *Mona Lisa* with a moustache, detached from a more complex set of objects like *Bicycle Wheel,* or affected, like the snowshovel christened *In Advance of the Broken Arm* or even the urinal *Fountain,* by being given a more or less ingenious, ironic, or enigmatic title):[1] the bottlerack

---

1. And, a fortiori, not *artificially reconstituted,* like Warhol's *Brillo Boxes* of 1964, even if the "conceptual" effect of this work is not very different from that of Duchamp's ready-mades,

Duchamp proposed to the public in 1914 under the literal title *Bottle-rack*.[2] There are basically two ways of accounting for such an object; they do not at all have the same significance, metonymy aside. The first, illustrated by Arthur Danto, among others, says that this bottlerack *constitutes* the work in question, or that the work *consists* in the bottlerack.[3] The second, put forward more frequently, but also more evasively, says that, in this case, Duchamp's work consists not in this commercially available bottlerack, but rather in the act, or, more expressively, *gesture [geste],* as we still say, of proposing it as a work of art.[4] In order better to see the distinction here, let us assume that this proposition took the form of an explicit declaration, such as "I propose this bottle-rack as a work of art."[5] On the first theory, we accept the declaration and define

which are simply (or not so simply) *borrowed* from the domain of current industrial production. The (ideological) difference hinges on the accent Warhol puts on the commercial or promotional aspect of his objects—in a word, on business\*, which was of much less interest to his illustrious predecessor.

2. "Proposed to the public" does not, in this case, mean "put on public exhibition." *Bottlerack* was picked out, christened, and doubtless shown to a few people in 1914, like other works, beginning with the 1913 *Bicycle Wheel.* The first ready-mades to be exhibited (it is not known which these were) were apparently shown at the Bourgeois Galleries in New York in 1916. *Fountain,* we know, was submitted to the *Salon* of the Society of Independent Artists in April 1917 (it was not officially refused, but discreetly spirited away).

3. Arthur C. Danto, *The Transfiguration of the Commonplace: A Philosophy of Art* (Cambridge: Harvard University Press, 1981), pp. 93–95. Danto's favorite example is *Fountain,* but his interpretation can of course be carried over from one ready-made to another. Moreover, it complies with the classical definition given in the *Dictionnaire abrégé du surréalisme* (1938): "everyday object invested with the dignity of an object of art by the simple choice of the artist."

4. See, for example, Ted Cohen, "The Possibility of Art," in Joseph Margolis, ed., *Philosophy Looks at the Arts,* 3d ed. (Philadelphia: Temple University Press, 1987), p. 196. Arthur C. Danto, *The Philosophical Disenfranchisement of Art* (New York: Columbia University Press, 1986), p. 34, cites this interpretation in order to reject it in rather sophistic fashion: "Professor Ted Cohen has claimed that the work is not the urinal at all, but the gesture of exhibiting it: and gestures are of just the wrong type to have surfaces, gleaming or dull." It is not, however, Cohen who pays attention to the "characteristics" of the surface of *Fountain,* but, among others, Dickie (see below, n. 9); there is thus no contradiction in what Cohen says, but there *is* disagreement between those for whom the ready-made is a kind of "sculpture" and those for whom it *tends,* rather, to be a happening\*. Timothy Binkley, "'Piece': Contra Aesthetics," *Journal of Aesthetics and Art Criticism* 35 (1977): 265–277, admits that the work, in the case of a ready-made, consists more in a *fact* and (as we will see) an *idea* than an object, but takes the existence of works of this kind as the basis for an "anti-aesthetic" conclusion close to Danto's—which, however, is marked by certain qualifications, or ambiguities, that we will encounter again one day.

5. Obviously, what is at stake in this case is not the enunciation of the judgment that this bottlerack (and others like it) deserves, on leaving the factory, to be considered a work of

the object, the bottlerack, as (having become) a work; on the second, we regard the bottlerack as no more than an occasion or support, and define the proposition itself as a work.

Of these two interpretations, I adopt and will defend the second; but I want to specify that the artistic value which may be attributed to the act of proposing depends largely on the nature of the object proposed, even if it is granted that to exhibit a radiator or boiler could take on much the same value. That the work consists in the act does not entirely neutralize the specificity of the object: the proverb notwithstanding, to steal an egg is not to steal an ox,[6] and to exhibit a boiler is not to exhibit a bottlerack.

The choice we make between these two positions has crucial consequences at the level of *aesthetic* theory (in the proper sense of the word). If we argue that the bottlerack "by" Duchamp is an artwork, while granting that this object, like ready-mades in general, was not promoted for aesthetic reasons, as Duchamp himself confirms,[7] we can infer, as Danto and Binkley more or less do, that the artistic is not always bound up with, and therefore is not necessarily bound up with, the aesthetic. If we say that the work here consists, not in this particular object, but in the act of proposing it, we leave open the possibility that there is an aesthetic quality, not to the object, certainly, but to the

---

art, as we say of a model of Bugatti's that it is a work of art (by Ettore Bugatti); at stake is a "declaration" in the Searlian sense, which claims to *confer,* performatively, the status of a *work by Duchamp* on this industrial object. Of course, to exhibit a bottlerack without comment is a more striking sort of practical declaration, because it is wordless, than an explicit verbal statement. *Saying* is sometimes the equivalent of *doing,* but *doing without saying* always does (and says) more. [The title of the French translation of Austin's *How to Do Things with Words* is *Quand dire, c'est faire* (when to say is to do).]

6. [The proverb runs, *qui vole un œuf vole un bœuf* (literally, "who steals an egg steals an ox") and means, roughly, that petty thievery begets grand larceny.]

7. For example: "The choice of these Readymades was never dictated by aesthetic delectation. The choice was based on a reaction of *visual indifference,* without any reference to good or bad taste" (see Anne d'Harnoncourt and Kynaston McShine, eds., *Marcel Duchamp: Catalogue of the Exhibition of 1973* [New York and Philadelphia, Museum of Modern Art and the Philadelphia Museum of Art, 1973], p. 89 [translation modified]); or again, "When I discovered the 'ready-mades' I intended to discourage the aesthetic hullabaloo. But in Neo-Dada they are using the ready-mades to discover their 'aesthetic value'!! I threw the bottle rack and the urinal in their faces as a challenge and now they admire them as something aesthetically beautiful." Cited in Irving Sandler, *American Art of the 1960s* (New York: Harper and Row, 1988), p. 52. I am not certain that "neo-Dada" really adopted this attitude, which obviously runs counter to the artist's intention. It is not without precedent, however; we will come across one or two.

act. Thus we also leave open the possibility that there is a pertinent relation between the artistic and the aesthetic—on the sole condition that
the aesthetic is defined broadly enough to embrace more than just *physically* perceptible properties. This broad definition seems to me to be in
any event necessary, if we wish to assume that a literary work, for example, has an aesthetic character, which is the very least we would wish to
assume. In other words, the fact that the ready-mades are antiaesthetic
or an-aesthetic in intent (which seems to me hardly open to doubt)
does not at all mean that we cannot, at a "figurative" level *[au second
degré]*, treat this intent itself (and not the object it bears on) as aesthetic.[8]
But I will put off dealing with this question in order to concentrate on
that of the regime of immanence; the definition of it just posited ("the
work is not the urinal at all, but the gesture of exhibiting it"), which is,
moreover, provisional, must still be justified.

This definition would seem to be contravened by the fact that Duchamp's ready-mades (and many objects of more recent date that seem
to me to have similar status) are today exhibited in various museums and
galleries, several decades after being "proposed"; thus they are brought
before the attention of a public which, knowing perhaps nothing of the
artist's founding gesture, may contemplate them for themselves, as works
of art. There is no legislating judgments of taste, and an art lover who
finds aesthetic qualities in a bottlerack (which certainly possesses them),
as others compare *Fountain* to a Brancusi, Arp, or Moore,[9] has, of course,
a perfect right to do so. In that case, however, the object—bottlerack or
urinal—should be attributed to its true creator, who, inasmuch as he (not

8. This is, moreover, what I think Danto himself unwittingly does when he says (*The Transfiguration of the Commonplace*, pp. 93–94) that *Fountain* is "daring, impudent, irreverent, witty,
and clever"; these are all adjectives that cannot be used to describe this urinal any more
than its commercially available "replicas," but that can indeed be applied to the provocation
(the act of "defiance") of which it is the support.

9. Danto, in *The Transfiguration of the Commonplace*, p. 93, and in *The Philosophical Disenfranchisement of Art*, p. 33, cites a statement to this effect by George Dickie (*Art and the Aesthetic:
An Institutional Analysis* [Ithaca: Cornell University Press, 1974], p. 42) that sounds a bit paradoxical coming from an advocate of an "institutional theory," which, in principle, puts the
accent on the sociocultural (rather than aesthetic) factors shaping the reception of works.
A number of others, among them Jean Clair (*Catalogue de l'exposition Duchamp au MNAM*,
1977, p. 90), have drawn the same parallel—which Danto, of course, does not endorse,
though he happily works his own tongue-in-cheek* variations on this undeniably tempting theme, declaring in *The Philosophical Disenfranchisement of Art*, p. 34, that he considers
*Fountain* to be "a contribution to the history of sculpture," rather than the happening*
Cohen (and I) see it as.

Duchamp) is responsible for its aesthetic qualities, should be given credit for his work, as happens whenever a coffeepot or toaster is exhibited at the Metropolitan Museum of Modern Art for the quality of its design* and the greater glory of its designer*. We cannot, without lapsing into inconsistency, simultaneously exhibit *Bottlerack* for its properties as an object, attribute it to someone who had nothing to do with bringing these properties into existence, and loftily declare that we are indifferent to them. But we do not, in fact, exhibit it in this spirit, though we do accept the risk of misunderstanding, which is in any case inevitable; we exhibit it to (as it were) perpetuate the act of proposing it, which the art-world thus makes its own. "Duchamp once defied us to exhibit the kind of bottlerack that is commercially available, and we now face up to the challenge, the reasons for which we have (since) understood"—reasons which, as informed art lovers know, are not of an aesthetic nature, in the ordinary, "straight" *[au premier degré]* sense: that is, they do not stem from any interest in the *form* of this bottlerack. Or, rather, of *these* bottleracks, because this ready-made is to be found, I believe, simultaneously and therefore in at least two exemplars, in the Philadelphia Museum of Art and a collection in Milan.[10] This fact undermines, be it said in passing, the interpretation advanced by Danto, for whom, of *two* physically indiscernible objects, only *one* has become an artwork.[11] In fact, as the art-world has very well understood, any bottlerack in the same series would do. And adding "in the same series" may well be a concession to the fetishism of the collector. The relevant description is most probably simply "any bottlerack at all," or even "anything at all as long as . . . ." We have yet to specify what that necessary and sufficient condition is.

10. Galleria Schwartz. Neither of them is the original, which is now lost. In theory, the ready-mades are by no means intended as unique pieces. Only three (in Philadelphia) are originals; in 1964, Arturo Schwartz, with Duchamp's approval, made eight copies of thirteen of them (there are some fifty in all).

11. "[The Institutional Theory of Art as put forward by Dickie] leaves unexplained . . . why that particular urinal should have sustained so impressive a promotion, while other urinals, like it in every obvious respect, should remain in an ontologically degraded category. It leaves us still with objects otherwise indiscernible, one of which is an artwork and one of which is not" (*The Transfiguration of the Commonplace,* pp. 5–6). The argument about indiscernible *pairs* is everywhere in Danto, but the fact that *Fountain* or *Bottlerack* today immanates in several instances, none of them the original (as Danto himself indicates, *The Philosophical Disenfranchisement of Art,* p. 14) means, at a minimum, that the extremely mysterious ontological promotion claimed for the object has been parceled out: *several* urinals have remained urinals (etc.), and *several others* have become ready-mades.

The positive reason for refusing to ascribe the artistic value of the ready-made to the object as such is clearly set forth by Binkley in a discussion of yet another ready-made, one which is heavily "assisted": the all too famous *Mona Lisa* with a moustache, entitled, as everyone knows— and this does not help matters any—L.H.O.O.Q.[12] It is

> a reproduction of the Mona Lisa with a moustache, goatee, and letters added. [This description contains] no amorphous "such- and-such" standing for the most important thing. The description tells you what the work of art is; you now know the piece with- out actually having seen it (or a reproduction of it). When you do see the artwork . . . you learn nothing of artistic consequence which you don't already know from the description Duchamp gives, and for this reason it would be pointless to spend time at- tending to the piece as a connoisseur would savor a Rembrandt . . . . (In fact, the piece might be better or more easily known by description than by perception.)[13]

If we accept both this observation and the Goodmanian principle according to which works of art demand that we pay infinite atten- tion to their slightest details, it rather clearly follows that the object *L.H.O.O.Q.* (and, more generally, all ready-made objects) does not, *in itself,* constitute a work of art. The hastiest conclusion, which doubtless has its partisans, would obviously be that there is nothing at all resem- bling a work in question here, and that Duchamp, at least as far as his ready-mades go, was merely a merry prankster. There would be noth- ing to object to this, were it not for the fact that it has, perhaps, yet to be proven that playing pranks, merry or otherwise, is not in any sense an artistic practice, something it would no doubt not be very easy to prove. One can skirt the dilemma by simply refusing to pin any label whatsoever on Duchamp's act, but I am not certain that that would qualify as an honorable defeat. In short, this attitude certainly exists, but its legitimacy or coherence seems dubious to me, and, in any case, the whole history of (the world of) art in the twentieth century shows that it is not universally shared. What needs to be accounted for is the oppo- site or at any rate different position of those (myself among them) for

12. [If one pronounces the French names of these letters rapidly, the result sounds almost exactly like "Elle a chaud au cul," which means "her ass is hot," or, roughly, "she's hot to trot."]
13. Binkley, "'Piece': Contra Aesthetics," p. 266.

whom the ready-made is well and truly, if not the object of, at least the *occasion for,* an aesthetic relation.

"Occasion" is as vague as can be, and deliberately so, because my thesis is that the object of this relation is not the exhibited object itself. But, as there is nothing to this whole business beyond what is described in the sentence "Duchamp exhibits (as a work) an ordinary commercial bottlerack," it is clear that, if the artistic object here is not the bottlerack, it can only reside in what is described by the verb "to exhibit." To be quite scrupulous, we also need to examine, before rejecting it, the hypothesis that the entire artistic force of the thing is contained in the subject of the sentence, that is, Duchamp himself. This hypothesis, associated, in sum, with what has been called the "institutional theory" of art,[14] comes down to saying that the bottlerack is taken for a work of art solely because it is exhibited by an already recognized artist. Plainly, there is something of this in the reception generally accorded ready-mades: a bottlerack proposed by a complete unknown stands an excellent chance of never turning up in any exhibition whatsoever, and, even if it did, the event would not be likely to create much of a stir. But it should be possible to distinguish the aesthetic significance of an event from its professional reception and the echo it finds in the media. Even after these secondary aspects have been allowed for, it is doubtless still true that the two events "Duchamp exhibits a bottlerack," and "John Doe exhibits a bottle rack" do not have exactly the same significance, no more than do "John Doe dies of a heart attack" and "the President dies of a heart attack," or "Cousin Emily joins the Carmelites" and "La Cicciolina joins the Carmelites"; but it is also true that one of the elements of these complex sets holds constant, whatever its subject. To exhibit a bottlerack is, to be sure, an unspectacular, rather minimalist act, but putting a moustache on the *Mona Lisa* is an act striking enough for its significance to capture our attention independently of its author's personality. Conversely, an explanation that turns solely on the factor "Duchamp" is hardly capable of distinguishing the value of a ready-made (assuming that they all have the same value) from that of any other type of production by the same artist, or, indeed, from that of any of his other acts: if something need only be "made by Duchamp" to be art,

14. See, among others, George Dickie: *Art and the Aesthetic;* and "Defining Art II," in Matthew Lippman, *Contemporary Aesthetics* (Boston: Allyn and Bacon, 1973).

the fact of exhibiting it becomes contingent, as does the object exhib-ited, and this conclusion seems to me untenable. I grant, then, that the personality of the author, or, rather, his status, counts (to a *certain* extent), but not to the exclusion of the two other elements that go to make up the event: the act of exhibiting and the object exhibited. It seems to me obvious that the event we are here considering is, indissociably, "Duchamp exhibits a bottlerack." If it is John Doe and not Duchamp, or a corkscrew and not a bottlerack, or "keeps in his cellar" and not "exhibits," the event is different in all three cases, by virtue of the change in the subject, object, or action. For the moment, I wish to maintain only this: if the ready-made is a work of art, this cannot be solely due to any one of the factors that make it up, but must rather be a func-tion of the event considered as a whole.

## From the Act to the Idea

Shifting the operal factor from the object proposed to the (total) act of proposing it is not, however, enough to define the mode of existence of ready-mades correctly; to stop there would be tantamount to rang-ing ready-mades alongside (autographic) arts of performance like the dance, or the execution (or improvisation) of music. But a performance is an act which—like any work, autographic or allographic—requires us to pay scrupulous attention to its tiniest detail; it therefore presup-poses a perceptual relation *in praesentia,* or, at least, by way of a faithful recorded reproduction. This is the sense in which a dance step or musi-cal performance is an aesthetic object and artistic achievement: it is not enough to *know* that "Nijinski danced *The Afternoon of a Faun* or that "Pollini interpreted the *Hammerklavier* Sonata." In contrast, fully to ap-preciate Duchamp's work, it is no more necessary, useful, and pertinent to have witnessed all the physical, verbal, administrative, and other acts by dint of which Duchamp one day submitted this bottlerack, or some other object, to the judgment of the artworld, than it is necessary, use-ful, and pertinent to lose oneself in rapt or painstaking contemplation of the work itself. That the object eventually ended up in a gallery and is today kept in one or more museums is all that matters. Not even an ephemeral and, consequently, evential conceptual work, like Claes Oldenburg's *Invisible Sculpture,*[15] can be defined as a performance, for the spectators who saw this happening live were no better placed to perceive its significance than were those who learned about it in the press, or, later, from books on art history; furthermore, their reception of it would doubtless have been wide of the mark if they had devoted detailed attention to it, watching it as one watches a ballet by Balanchine or a stage production by Bob Wilson. Whatever the medium of its manifestation (and we will discuss a few others), a conceptual work clearly consists in the "gesture" of proposing something to the artworld; but this gesture in no wise requires that we consider all its perceptual details. As Binkley said (see above) of *L.H.O.O.Q.,* and as can obviously be said of *Bottlerack* as well, the act of proposing these objects is still not the artistic object to be considered: a simple "description" tells us (from this point of view) as much about it as attentive contemplation does, and the physical details of its production are irrelevant to an understanding of it. Indeed, even the word "description" is inappropriate to designate the mode in which the object offers itself, adequately, to reception, for if a "simple description" can adduce an infinite number of details, all eminently necessary and never too precise when it comes to giving an accurate idea of a painting by Vermeer—or Pollock, it is certainly superfluous for understanding a ready-made. Whether the bottlerack has fifty or sixty prongs, or what the exact color of the metal it is made of happens to be is certainly not relevant to its artistic significance. Indeed, what a ready-made or Oldenburg's happening calls for is not a (detailed) description, but rather a *definition,* because what counts in works of this kind is neither the proposed object as such, nor the act of proposing it as such, but the *idea* behind this act.[16] Just as the durable object, if there is one, refers to the act, so the act refers to its underlying idea, or, as is more commonly said today, its 'concept'—which, like any concept, calls not for "description," but definition.

I have just said "like any concept," but this should not be permitted to obscure the fact that the terms "idea" and "concept" are being

---

15. A hole the size of a grave that was dug in the presence of the public and immediately filled up again, in Central Park, behind the Metropolitan Museum, in 1967.
16. "To know the art is to know the idea; and to know an idea is not necessarily to experience a particular sensation, or even to have some particular experience." Binkley, "'Piece': Contra Aesthetics," p. 266.

used in a rather special sense here, one difficult to define, although these terms are quite common, and, doubtless, more familiar to everyone than is their logical or philosophical meaning. I know of no better way to specify that meaning than to recall what they are taken to mean in everyday, *practical* usage, when we say, for example, "That's a good idea,"[17] or when an industrialist or merchant talks about a "new concept" in discussing the principle underlying the function or advertising of a product.[18] This comparison with the economic sphere will doubtless help us better distinguish Duchamp's work from its physical supports, since the ready-made is usually an industrial object. The bottlerack, as a household convenience, has its concept, *Bottlerack,* as an artistic act, has another; the ready-made qua work consists in the second, which has very little to do with the first: it consists not in the act, but in the idea of exhibiting a bottlerack.

Our attention has thus shifted from an object to an act that is not physical, but rather cultural, and from this act to its concept. This brings us face to face with the notion of conceptual art, or, rather (I will come back to this point), of *conceptual works,* among which I have high-handedly ranged Duchamp's ready-mades, which antedate the birth of this notion by more than half a century—or, more precisely, the birth of this concept, because it is one, and a rather ingenious one at that. But I am not alone in thinking that the ready-mades were, *avant la lettre,* the earliest examples of conceptual art[19]—which means, for me, works whose object of immanence is a concept, in the sense defined above, and whose manifestation may be either a definition ("to exhibit a bottlerack") or a realization (the exhibiting of a bottlerack).

17. "Conceptual art is only any good when the concept is." Sol Le Witt, "Paragraphs on Conceptual Art," *Artforum* (June 1967), p. 83. [I have translated Genette's French translation.]

18. Heard from the mouth of a florist: "Mother's Day (or perhaps Valentine's Day) is a brilliant concept."

19. This is, for example, Joseph Kosuth's view as well, "Art after Philosophy, I and II," (1969), in Gregory Battock, ed., *Idea Art: A Critical Anthology* (New York: Dutton, 1973), p. 80: "All art (after Duchamp) is conceptual (by nature)." I do not know if Duchamp applied this label to himself (my general impression is that he very prudently avoided all labels), but we know that he applied it to Warhol as early as 1964: "If you take a can of Campbell's soup and duplicate it fifty times, the reason is that the retinal image doesn't interest you. What interests you is the concept of putting fifty cans of Campbell's on a canvas" (*New York Herald Tribune,* 17 May 1964). [I have translated Genette's French translation.]

I will return to the implications of this definition (that of a conceptual work), but I must first cite, without going into the details of what is an important chapter in the history of modern art,[20] a few examples of works more or less officially (that is, self-defined as) conceptual—if only to illustrate the diversity of their media of manifestation.

It is well known that Oldenburg's *Invisible Sculpture*, already mentioned, was termed "conceptual" by an official of the city of New York.[21] In June 1969, Robert Barry sent a contribution to an exhibition in Seattle, reduced to (the object of) this message: "Everything I know but am not thinking of at the moment, 1:36 P.M., June 15, 1969, New York." In December of the same year, the same artist organized an "exhibition" at the Amsterdam Art and Project Gallery which consisted in this sign, posted on the door of the gallery: "For the exhibition the gallery will be closed."[22] In 1972, Chris Burden arranged to have himself tied up in a bag and dropped (I do not know for how long) on a California freeway; this work bore the somber title *Deadman*, though the sinister promise was fortunately not kept.

It is thus by retroactive analogy that I describe Duchamp's ready-mades as conceptual, but also, for example, Andy Warhol's *Brillo Boxes* (1964), which are pseudo-ready-mades, because they are faithful handmade imitations. The same applies to a few interminable, deliberately monotonous (putting it mildly) films by Warhol, such as *Sleep* (1963), which shows us a sleeping man for six hours, or another, whose title I do not know, which shows us the Statue of Liberty for twenty-four; Rauschenberg's *Erased De Kooning Drawing* (1953);[23] the oversized imitations of comic strips by Lichtenstein, with their typographic screen

20. See especially Irving Sandler, *The New York School: The Painters and Sculptors of the Fifties* (New York: Harper and Row, 1978) and *American Art of the 1960s*.

21. "This is a conceptual work of art and is as much valid [sic] as something you can actually see. Everything is art if it is chosen by the artist to be art." Monroe C. Beardsley, "The Aesthetic Point of View" (1970), in John W. Bender and H. Gene Blocker, eds., *Contemporary Philosophy of Art: Readings in Analytic Aesthetics* (Englewood Cliffs, N.J.: Prentice-Hall, 1993), p. 386, citing the consulting architect Sam Green.

22. See Ursula Meyer, *Conceptual Art* (New York: E. P. Dutton, 1972), p. 41. I say "consisted in" for the sake of brevity, but the status of this "work" is subtler, and the sign posted to the door is only one of its instruments, as the bottlerack is nothing more than an instrument of the work *Bottlerack*.

23. At least if this work is reduced to the concept designated by its title; but, since the result was not an absolutely blank sheet of paper, nothing prevents us, pace Binkley ("'Piece':

scrupulously restored, or his sarcastic *Brushstrokes* (1965-1966), which utilizes the same technique, a mechanistic mockery of expressionist action painting*; Jasper Johns's flags, targets, numbers and letters; Christo's packagings of public buildings, along with the various manifestations of Land Art*; the countless "sculptures" of the 1960s which consist in rolls of wire-netting, piles of rubble, rags or ropes, coins scattered on the ground, and so on.

All these examples more or less belong to, or present themselves in the guise of, what are called the plastic or visual arts. However, as I have said, *Invisible Sculpture* consists more in an event than a persistent object, despite its title (which is, moreover, ambiguous); this is, fortunately, even more clearly the case with Burden's exhibition. Certain musical or literary works seem to me to be no less typically conceptual: John Cage's silent recital, for instance,[24] or a number of Oulipian[25] productions we cannot correctly or fully appreciate if we do not grasp the principle informing them. The lipogram provides a perfect illustration: George Perec's novel *The Void* (1969), which contains no "e"s, is the best known achievement in the genre. But if we agree to describe lipograms, $S+7$s, and so forth, as conceptual, how can we refuse to apply the term to the results of Raymond Roussel's famous "procedure"—and how can we then avoid going back, in similar fashion, from Cage to Satie? It can thus be seen that the conceptual is a regime (this term is provisional) capable of pervading all the arts and all modes of presentation: not only material objects and physical events, but also ideal objects like the *text* of *The Void*. It may perhaps seem that I am unduly enlarging the field of action of a very narrowly restricted type of art, one whose vogue was, like all vogues, very brief. But, before justifying (and in order to justify) doing so, I intend to enlarge it even more.

---

Contra Aesthetics," p. 265), from "looking for aesthetically interesting smudges on the paper," as if it were a sort of particularly pale Twombly.

24. *4' 33", Tacet, Any Instrument or Combination of Instruments* (1952). The work is silent as far as the performance of the instrumentalist is concerned; for the time span indicated in the title, he produces no sound whatsoever. The happening, however, which is never the same from occurrence to occurrence, and may be recorded, consists of the growing reactions of the public, and other background noise.

25. [See Chap. 7, n. 4.]

## Conceptual Reduction

What in fact motivates this extension, or, rather, my feeling that the notion of conceptual art is applicable (more or less) to a large number of works typical of the Dada, Pop, and neo-Dada movements, and, as will appear, a few others besides, is the fact that, in works of this type, the object or event produced (or selected) is produced or selected, not for its aesthetic qualities in the prevailing sense, to be sure, but, on the contrary, because of the critical, paradoxical, provocative, polemical, sarcastic, or simply humorous character that attaches to the act of proposing as an artwork an object or event whose properties are ordinarily felt to be nonartistic or antiartistic: mass-produced industrial objects, or objects that are vulgar, kitsch, boring, repetitive, amorphous, scandalous, empty, or imperceptible, or whose perceptual properties matter less than the process they result from. From this vantage point, works as classic as Ravel's *Bolero* (in which the theme is repeated eighteen times, with constant variations and a gradual increase in the size of the orchestra), or, conversely, Haydn's *Farewell* Symphony (in which, one by one, the performers steal away from behind their music stands), can just as legitimately be described as conceptual. But it can also be said that all avant-garde works have, from the turn of the century on, been received in the conceptual mode by a public whose norms or habits they have consistently surprised, since, for this public, the fact of and the reason for the scandal provoked by them has taken precedence over detailed examination of the perceptual properties of the works that provoked the scandal. Thus *Luncheon on the Grass* was reduced to a naked woman sitting between two clothed men, *Olympia* to her shamelessness, Impressionism to its separate brushstrokes, Wagner to his leitmotifs. As for the artistic achievements represented by unrhymed poetry, atonal music, abstract painting, action painting*, or minimalism (among many others), the general public initially saw in them nothing more than formal or thematic "gimmicks," whose novelty was so striking as to make everything else insignificant, or even imperceptible.

But the shifts in aesthetic paradigms that characterize the evolution of modern art have not been the sole factor militating in favor of conceptual reception. I have already mentioned the venerable *Farewell*

Symphony, which we reduce to being the illustration or exploitation of a gimmick if we focus too exclusively on its most conspicuous feature. The *Dissonant* Quartet, the *Unfinished* Symphony, the *Raindrop* Prelude, Debussy's *La Mer,* and a large number of other musical works thus suffer (if that is the word), almost inevitably, from the too evocative or too demonstrative nature of their titles. A painting like Brueghel's *The Fall of Icarus*[26] lends itself rather well to a contrastive experiment that is conclusive in this regard. Show the picture to a spectator who does not know it without telling him the title: he will attend to the whole of the landscape and seascape, the central figure of the plowman, the morning light, etc. In short, he will look at the picture without, perhaps, so much as noticing, to the right of the ship at anchor, the tiny detail comprised by the leg—still protruding above the surface of the water—that belongs to the otherwise invisible, plunging Icarus. Tell another spectator the title at the outset; his whole perception of the painting will inevitably organize itself around the question, "Where is Icarus?", then around the famous leg of the presumed hero of the scene, and, finally, around the procedure that consists in evoking this legendary event by way of a minimalist synecdoche bordering on a guessing game ("find the pilot").[27] I can imagine the response of someone steeped in eighteenth-century painting, whose upbringing had instilled in him a taste for historical scenes, mythological landscapes, court portraiture, and nothing else, upon being suddenly confronted with a humble still life by Chardin—for us, the very type of the most substantially pictorial painting. His reaction would most probably have been to burst into laughter, like the public confronted with Monet's landscapes in 1872—unless he simply vented his astonishment at the fact that, as Pascal more or less puts it, an artist could have had the vain design of drawing our attention "to an image of things whose originals we do not at all admire!" Such a reaction, in which attention is focused exclusively on an idea ("Chardin means to provoke us with a painting that represents an ordinary set of kitchen utensils!"), would constitute a typically conceptual reception of a work which certainly does not deliberately solicit one.

26. See Danto, *The Transfiguration of the Commonplace,* pp. 116–119.
27. The same kind of search is provoked, if less chance of success, by the (identical) title that Georges Salles spontaneously gave, in a speech inaugurating it, to the large, rather cryptic painting composed by Picasso for the foyer of the Unesco House in Paris.

As this example shows, a conceptual reception can be lacking in pertinence; surely we must say that conceptual receptions are always *more or less* pertinent, the "more" being applicable to, for example, Duchamp's *Bottlerack,* and the "less" to Chardin's (I know very well that Chardin never painted a bottlerack, but I also know that he could have; he has, in any case, painted bottles), about which Proust, responding de facto to Pascal, wrote simply that "Chardin found it beautiful to paint because he thought it beautiful to the eye."[28] Between the "more" and the "less," we have, for example, *The Fall of Icarus* or *Olympia,* which are surely not devoid of humorous or provocative intent, though that does not annul the pictorial properties of these paintings.[29] But what holds for conceptual receptions also holds for perceptual ones: if it is surely not very relevant to consider a zip by Barnett Newman, a monochrome by Reinhardt, an L by Morris (or, more generally, the productions of minimalist painting and sculpture), a dripping* by Pollock, or a compression by César[30] as simple conceptual provocations, it would be no more legitimate to admire the "brilliant technique" of *Brillo Boxes,* the "elegant contours" of *Fountain,* or the "powerful choreography" of Oldenburg's gravediggers.

Most inconveniently, this question of legitimacy goes beyond the bounds of the subject at hand, for it very insistently throws up the question of authorial intention. If it is illegitimate to treat *Fountain* as a Brancusi, the reason is that, knowing Duchamp did not intend us to, we

28. Marcel Proust, *Contre Sainte-Beuve* (Paris: Pléiade, Gallimard, 1971), p. 373 [tr. *On Art and Literature, 1896–1919,* trans. Sylvia Townsend Warner (New York: Meridian, 1958), p. 325].
29. It seems to me that this is even more clearly the case with certain of Picasso's assemblages, like the celebrated *Bull's Head,* made of a bicycle seat and handlebars (1942, Picasso Museum, Paris): here one must pay equal attention to the ingenuity of the procedure, and the sculptural effect of the whole. That, at any rate, was what the artist wished (see Pierre Cabanne, *Le siècle de Picasso* (1975) (Paris: Folio-Essais, Gallimard, 1992), vol. 3, p. 116 [tr. *Pablo Picasso: His Life and Times* (New York: Morrow, 1977), p. 339], for he drew a functional distinction between this work and the ready-mades it may remind us of. Two bronzes later taken from *Bull's Head* accentuate this difference.
30. In a certain way, these two series are antithetical. Minimalist works lend themselves to conceptual interpretation (as early as the early 1950s, Thomas Hess interpreted Newman in this fashion: see Sandler, *The New York School,* p. 13) because of their attenuation of perceptual detail; but a dripping or compression lends itself to the same sort of interpretation by virtue of the obviously random *proliferation* of detail. In a sense, nothing is more concrete and perceptual, but, at the same time, nothing is more nondescript—whence the temptation to reduce these objects to the process that gave rise to them, the dripping or compression.

consider his intention an intrinsic part of his act, as if it were inscribed in the object that perpetuates it; if it is not legitimate to take *[recevoir]* *One (Number 31)* as a good gag, the reason is that, knowing Pollock had nothing of the comedian about him, we find in the arabesques of his flowing paint a record of his passionate seriousness. But, after all, ignorance of or indifference to the artist's purposes has its prerogatives, and, to repeat, everyone is free to admire a urinal or smile at a tangle of drippings. I will put off my consideration of this vexed subject, essentially a matter, I think, of the complex relations between the artistic and the aesthetic, in order to return to the question of the regime of immanence of conceptual works. Since the conceptual function of a work is always partially *attentional*—since, that is, it always depends on the type of attention the work is given by its audience—this question should now be formulated in the following new terms: what is the regime of immanence of a work (whatever the work in question) for *the person who* (legitimately or not) receives it *as* conceptual?

From the foregoing, it follows, in my view, that the conceptual state depends on and proceeds from a mental operation (conscious or not) which consists in reducing the object or event in whose guise the work is presented to the act of presenting this object or event as a work; and, further, in reducing this act itself to its "concept," an object which is plainly ideal, and capable of prescribing other objects or events we would consider, from this standpoint, as equivalent or identical: the concept "exhibit a bottlerack," which I have extracted, by *reduction,* from the perception of a bottlerack exhibited in an art gallery, can manifest itself indefinitely in each further occurrence of this act, if there are any—just as the text of a literary or musical work can manifest itself indefinitely in all its correct occurrences or copies. But the ideality of the concept, both in this artistic sense and in the logical sense, is not identical to that of an allographic work such as a literary text, musical composition, or recipe, and the reduction that gives rise to it is not identical to allographic reduction, which leads us from the copy of a book or the performance of a sonata to the ideality of their object of immanence.

That these two operations are not identical becomes obvious when both are in evidence and bear on the same object. Take a copy of *The Void:* a first—allographic—reduction enables me, if I know how to read, to distinguish the "contingent" properties of the copy (individual properties, such as having a stain on page 25, or generic properties, such as containing 306 printed pages) from the "constitutive" properties of the text, or properties of immanence: for instance, that of containing so many words, of telling such-and-such a story, etc. I thus go from the book to the text, and, obviously, I can leave it at that. But, while making this first reduction, which is an inherent feature of any reading, I may also suddenly become aware, at some point (if I haven't already been told about it), of a peculiarity of this text (which also happens to be a peculiarity of this copy): the letter "e" never occurs in it. From there, I can (but am not obliged to) embark on a second operation, which I will call *conceptual reduction;* it consists in reducing the text to this negative particularity, that is, to the fact of being a "lipogram in 'e.'" (Indeed, the concept to which I reduce *The Void* can—by virtue of a reduction which is even more drastic, because it eliminates one feature of the definition—be the more generic concept "lipogram" tout court. It seems to me, however, that that reduction would be too drastic to be pertinent, because a lipogram in, for example, "y," does not hold the same interest as one which requires its author to overcome the difficulty of leaving out "e"s, the French language being what it is.) I make the same double reduction, of course, if I go from a performance or score of *Bolero* to its musical text, and from this text to its instrumental concept, etc. Obviously, in the case of works that appear to be autographic, like *Bottlerack,* only the conceptual reduction (if any) is carried out; it leads me directly from the physical object to the concept informing its exhibition as art.

But pointing out that the conceptual and allographic reductions are not identical obviously does not suffice to define the difference between these two operations. I will attempt to do so now (let me note straightaway, however, that what is involved is, as I see it, a difference of degree), by examining it through the prism of the difference between their results.

The effect of allographic reduction, as we saw above, is to constitute a singular ideality, or ideal individual, such as a literary or musical text. Such an object, though ideal, nevertheless answers to the logical definition of an individual, ultimate in its kind and thus not susceptible, as Lalande says, "of any further determination." This applies, of course, to the text of *The Void,* an ideal individual, or, ideality aside, to Duchamp's bottlerack, a singular (albeit multiple) physical individual. But the *concept* (lipogram in "e" or ready-made) to which I reduce, more or less legitimately, this ideal text or physical object, does not, for its part, have anything of the individual about it. Indeed, it is, like any concept in the ordinary sense of the word, typically generic: the lipogram and ready-made are, after all, genres, if ever genre there was. Every singular manifestation of a conceptual "gesture" is an individual, but the concept to which it can be reduced is generic and abstract, and capable, depending on the degree of abstraction involved, of describing a set of individual manifestations, specified and diversified to varying degrees, in accordance with a tree-structure of this kind:

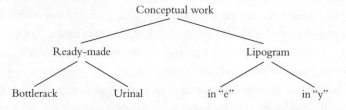

The proviso concerning "degree of abstraction" pretty much explains, I hope, why I have presented the difference between the two reductions as a difference of degree: I am not sure that the difference between individual and species admits of degrees, but I am sure that there are degrees in the logical hierarchy of classes: the genre "lipogram" is further from the individual *The Void* than is the species "lipogram in 'e.'" It will doubtless have been understood that any judgment which consists in reducing a work to its genre[31] is merely one conceptual reduction among others. But *reducing* a work to its genre is a much more powerful (more reductive) operation that *assigning* it to its genre. To say *"The Charterhouse of Parma* is a novel" is simply to assign it to its genre. The reduction would consist in assuming one had said everything there was to say about *The Charterhouse of Parma* once one had said it was a novel. If we refuse to make this reduction, the reason is that we believe, reasonably enough, that *The Charterhouse of Parma* is *not* a conceptual work.

31. [The French word *genre* means, among other things, both genus and (literary) genre.]

Thus the regime of immanence of conceptual works *qua conceptual works* may be defined, in relative, gradualistic fashion, as a *hyper-allographic regime,* in the sense, essentially, that their object of immanence (the concept) is not only ideal, like a poem or sonata, but also generic and abstract. But I have added the specification *"qua conceptual works,"* which means, among other things, *whenever* and *to the extent that* they are received as such. Depending on the case, this mode of reception can be legitimate and pertinent (this, as I see it, is in essence the mode of reception of ready-mades and officially conceptual works: it is a matter of indifference to me whether Arsène Lupin replaces the bottlerack in the museum with another, identical or not, purchased or stolen from the BHV[32]); it can also be aberrant (Chardin's *The Copper Fountain* regarded as a proto-Dadaist provocation), or manifestly insufficient and thus situated midway between the two others: that *The Void* is a lipogram does not prevent it from being *this* lipogram, that is, a singular text; manifestly, the right way to read it (to my mind) lies somewhere between the naive reading by a reader who fails to notice the absence of "e"s, and total reduction of the work to the concept "lipogram in 'e.'" This appropriate reading would consist in making a detailed examination of "the way it is constructed," in an attempt to discern the detours and verbal maneuvers that enabled the author to avoid the famous letter altogether.[33] If someone told me that a Harlequin novel had—an eminently conceptual gesture—been secretly written, in compliance with the norms and style required of all works in this series, by Maurice Blanchot, this would not free me of the obligation to go take a closer look myself; quite the contrary, in fact. And if he failed to tell me *which* Harlequin it was . . .

The variable pertinence of conceptual reception entails three consequences of very unequal importance; I want to round off my consideration of this subject by indicating what they are. The first is that we can never declare in advance and in absolute terms, as Binkley does, that

32. See Chap. 1, n 14 and 51.
33. They say that, as he was writing this novel, Perec, after long practice, ended up spontaneously "thinking" in *e*-less French; the flexibility of the human mind, enhanced by Oulipian gymnastics, makes a feat of this sort almost believable. The implication is surely that the work of circumvention and substitution, guided by a duly memorized and assimilated principle, is (nonetheless) carried out somewhere below the threshold of consciousness.

the "description" of a conceptual work is a more adequate manifesta-tion of it than its realization. This is because conceptual reduction is an operation each of us has to perform for himself, for each work and in his own manner; from this standpoint, it is, all in all, unfortunate that those visiting the Arensberg Collection of the Philadelphia Art Museum know in advance what to expect. What holds for a good (and, a fortiori, a bad) gag holds for a conceptual gesture as well: it loses something when it is, as they say, "given away." It loses even more as a result of institu-tionalization or regimentalization in "movements," groups, and other workrooms jealous of their labels and dues payments. A conceptual ges-ture is by definition (more or less) reducible to its concept, but it is not up to it to say why, to what extent, or how. Duchamp was well aware of this, but not everyone can be a Duchamp.

Second consequence: since one is always (more or less) at liberty to receive a work in either a "perceptual" mode, that is, by considering the proposed object for its own sake and attending to its individual prop-erties,[34] or in a conceptual mode, that is, by making one's way from the object back to the act, and from the act to the concept, or, again, ac-cording to some combination of these two attitudes of reception, it fol-lows that the conceptual state is not a stable *regime* which excludes its contrary and is backed up by a constitutive tradition, as the allographic state of music, for example, has been since the (gradual) invention of notation. A work can function in the allographic regime only if if be-longs to an artistic practice which has, globally, become allographic thanks to consensus and cultural convention: there can be no allograph-ic work without an allographic art.[35] In contrast, the conceptual state applies (or fails to) case by case, work by work, as determined by the fluc-

---

34. This category also accommodates ideal objects, insofar as they are "perceived" by the mind via their physical manifestations in their "ultimate" individuality. From a strictly logical stand-point, the real antonym of *conceptual* is *individual* rather than *perceptual,* for the properties of a concept are also perceived (by the mind). I will nevertheless sometimes use *perceptual* when what I have in mind is the "perception" of any object, even ideal, as an individual—which excludes nothing apart from concepts.

35. This does not mean, be it recalled, that an "art"—in the much broader sense in which Hegel, among others, divides the "system" of the arts into five canonical arts (architec-ture, sculpture, painting, music, and poetry)—belongs in its entirety to one of the two re-gimes; by "allographic art (or practice)," I here mean, for example, not the whole field of music, but that (already considerable) part of it which today functions in the allographic regime; the institution of music as a whole makes possible the allographic functioning of each of the works belonging to it.

tuating relation between the intention of the artist and the attention of the public, or, rather, of the individual receiving to the work. Thus there is no conceptual *art;* there are only conceptual *works,* which, furthermore, are more or less conceptual, depending on their mode of reception. And this conceptual character also plainly affects the perceptual state, since the two modes of reception are, with respect to one another, in a relation like that of communicating vessels, in which the quantity of liquid remains, of course, constant: the reception accorded a work is, in fact, always simultaneously perceptual and conceptual; we legitimately call "conceptual" those works which various individual and/or cultural motives incline us to treat in this fashion rather than the other.

The final consequence, which goes well beyond the scope of this volume, and which I here mention only provisionally, relates to the aesthetic function of conceptual works—of, in sum, their concept. If we take the Kantian definition of the judgment of taste as our standard of reference, such a function is highly paradoxical, since, as is well known, judgments of taste exclude all determinate concepts. And if we look to the Goodmanian criteria to define the aesthetic object as a locus of infinite (active) contemplation, thanks to the inexhaustible character of its symbolic functioning, it becomes hard to see how an object of thought as peremptorily defined as is the concept of a ready-made could inspire such contemplation. The provisional answer, it seems to me, is that, even if the definition of a conceptual gesture, like "exhibiting a bottlerack," is simple and exhaustive, the *meaning,* and hence the function of this gesture, is left, for its part, undefined, open, and suspended, like that of any other (natural or artistic) aesthetic object. We do not know exactly what Duchamp or Barry *meant to say* in exhibiting a bottlerack or inviting the public to a closed exhibition, no more, doubtless, than they do; we do not know any more precisely, all recorded declarations of intention aside, what these works actually *tell* us.[36] Thus conceptual works are also, after their fashion, inexhaustible in their functioning. They are concepts whose *effects* are not conceptual, and which accordingly can, on the figurative level, as we say [*au second degré*], please or displease in their turn, without a concept, and (secondarily), without end.

36. "Dada and Neo-Dada have prepared us to treat any object whatsoever as a work of art. But what this means, precisely, is far from clear" (Thierry de Duve, *Résonances du ready-made* [Nîmes: Jacqueline Chambon, 1989]). Of course, what Mona Lisa's smile or "The Death of Lovers" "means, precisely" is no closer to being clear.

# CHAPTER 10

# Will This Kill That?

THE DISTINCTION BETWEEN REGIMES, THOUGH BASED MORE ON cultural traditions and social conventions than on considerations of essence, clearly remains, despite the existence of intermediate regimes like those of multiple autographic works or iterable performances, the fundamental precondition for artistic immanence. This historical dichotomy is irreducible, in the sense that, wherever the allographic regime operates, it cannot forgo the ideal object its operation is based on: any iteration, any conversion of a realization into a (de)notation, or, reciprocally, any reading or dictation, presupposes, explicitly or implicitly, a detour by way of this ideal type, for which the autographic regime as such offers no equivalent. To attempt, in radically empiricist fashion, to reduce the regime of immanence of a literary or musical work to a collection of physical objects or events with no relation to a type is radically to exclude the possibility of defining, or even *conceiving,* the relation of equivalence between these various objects or events, to refuse to recognize them as copies or occurrences of the *same* text, and therefore, at the limit, to condemn oneself to treating each copy or occurrence as a distinct work, in a universe à la Funes[1], where

1. [The reference is to Borges's story "Funes el memorioso."]

the irreducible singularity of each grain of sand precludes appealing to a mental construct as spectral as "grain of sand." Once again, the onto-logical extrapolation of Ockham's razor makes for very costly savings. Though one should not multiply idealities unnecessarily, it is hardly very reasonable to make do with fewer than are needed.

The other (the only) possible way the two regimes might be uni-fied—one which is, this time, not theoretical, but real—would be for the historical process of gradual transition from the autogaphic to the allographic to reach completion. According to Nelson Goodman, we remember, all the arts must have been autographic at the outset;[2] some subsequently "emancipated" themselves by adopting a more or less no-tational system—"some," or, better, nearly all, since the only art whose emancipation *Languages of Art* contests is painting (though, presumably, certain forms of sculpture face the same sort of insuperable obstacle). I will not review Goodman's argument in detail; its very categorical conclusion ("the answer . . . is no") is that no system of notation can be applied to this art, which therefore can never become allographic.[3]

But it was not long before Goodman toned his argument down a bit. I must first recall that a number of modern painters, like Mondrian, Vasarely, or Warhol,[4] and doubtless others as well (whose minimalist style may have made for a certain affinity among them, since it lent itself bet-ter than others to faithful reproduction), had no objection to the multi-plication of their works. Let us also bear in mind that observers like Benjamin or Malraux made themselves (to varying degrees) the her-alds of "technical reproducibility" and the Imaginary Museum, which were to free future generations of the need to become familiar with originals; Prieto no longer accords such originals, which he associates with "collectionism," anything more than commercial and/or fetishistic value. But the text that may have inspired Goodman's semi-retraction, although it was published well before *Languages of Art,* is this comment

2. On the limits of this hypothesis as far as the verbal aspect of literature is concerned, see Jean-Marie Schaeffer, "Nelson Goodman en poéticien: Trois esquisses," *Cahiers du Musée national de l'art moderne,* no. 41 (Fall 1992): 85–97.

3. Nelson Goodman, *Languages of Art: An Approach to a Theory of Symbols* (Indianapolis: Bobbs-Merrill, 1968), p. 198.

4. Dora Vallier, *L'art abstrait* (1967) (Paris: Livre de Poche, 1980), p. 180 [tr. *Abstract Art,* trans. Jonathan Griffin (New York: Orion, 1970), pp. 182–183]; Richard Wollheim, *Art and Its Objects* (1968) (Cambridge: Cambridge University Press, 1980), p. 172.

of Strawson's: "It is only because of the empirical deficiencies of reproductive techniques that we identify [particular paintings and works
of sculpture] with the works of art. Were it not for these deficiencies, the
original of a painting would have only the interest which belongs to the
original manuscript of a poem. Different people could look at exactly
the same painting in different places at the same time."[5] In a response to
Joseph Margolis, delivered at a conference held at the beginning of the
1970s, Goodman reconsiders his position on this subject in terms that
manifestly, albeit implicitly, echo Strawson's:

> Professor Margolis argues that painting is not irrevocably auto-
> graphic, that what we now regard as reproductions might come
> to be as acceptable as the original picture. I have explained some
> strong reasons why this is unlikely to happen; but I have not main-
> tained that painting is inalterably autographic. For an art to be-
> come allographic depends upon the establishment of a practice of
> classifying instances into works in a manner independent of his-
> tory of production. If and when reproductions of a picture come
> to be accepted as no less original instances than the initial paint-
> ing, so that the latter has only the sort of special interest or value
> that attaches to the manuscript or first edition of a literary work,
> then indeed the art could become allographic. But it cannot be-
> come so by fiat; a practice or tradition must first be established,
> later to be codified by means of a notation.[6]

This response is curious, because, for one thing, Goodman covers
his retreat by denying, rather impudently, that he had ever gone so far
as to claim that painting could not develop into an allographic art. For
another, he very clearly states the sociocultural conditions such a development would call for; but he begins by accepting the terms proposed
by Margolis, Strawson, and many others, who do not exactly affirm the
existence of an authentic transition (by way of usage, tradition, reduction, notation) to the allographic regime, but simply point to future
progress in the techniques of reproduction. It is, indeed, the possibility
that these techniques might be perfected which is invoked by the artists

5. P. F. Strawson, *Individuals: An Essay in Descriptive Metaphysics* (London: Methuen, 1959),
p. 231, note. Cf. P. F. Strawson, "Aesthetic Appraisal and Works of Art," in *Freedom and Resentment and Other Essays* (London: Methuen, 1974), p. 184.
6. Nelson Goodman, *Problems and Projects* (Indianapolis: Bobbs-Merrill, 1972), pp. 135–136.

and theoreticians I mentioned a moment ago, along with countless others for whom a "perfect" reproduction makes an experience of the original superfluous. But to say "reproduction" (perfect or not) is by no
means to say notation, reduction to a type, and the whole mental
process, individual or collective, presupposed by the allographic regime;
"reproduction" only implies a well-made imprint. That a faithful imprint can be "closer" to the original than a new realization which complies with a correct notation does not in any way alter this difference of
principle, which we have already noted. That consensus and convention
are also required before a good reproduction can be accepted as valid
(in its fashion) does not change anything either, since the consensus in
question is patently not of the same nature as allographic consensus.[7]
What doubtless explains the ease with which Goodman shifts from one
mode to the other is the fact that, in both cases, the validity of the copy
is established "without reference to its history of production"; but I am
not sure that a photographic print (or a recording or a cast) can be validated in these terms. What makes a photo a photo is not faithfulness to
a "model" of the sort that could be ratified by convention, so that we
might accept as "valid as a photo of Pierre" a photo of his look-alike
Jacques; it is, rather, the fact that the photo really is a photonic imprint
taken from this model.[8] A reproduction can, then, no more be validated
without reference to its mode of production than a proof of an engraving can be validated by something other than the fact of having been
pulled from the original plate. Reproductions and allographic instances
doubtless have in common the fact that both require a convention in
order to function, but *it is not the same convention*. In short, the possible
("improbable") improvement of reproductions to the point of absolute
perfection would not make painting an allographic art, but, at the most,
an autographic art with multiple products.[9]

7. On the difference between technical reproducibility and amenability to notation, see
Nicholas Wolterstorff, *Works and Worlds of Art* (Oxford: Clarendon, 1980), pp. 72–73.
8. See Jean-Marie Schaeffer, *L' Image précaire* (Paris: Seuil, 1987).
9. What more nearly evokes (albeit in very rudimentary fashion) the operation of an allographic regime in painting is the kind of drawing made for children to color in, where the
colors to be used are identified by numbers. Warhol's *Do It Yourselfs* sought to turn this procedure of painting-by-numbers* to account. One also hears that Vasarely boasted of being
able to paint by telephone; but what does one *not* hear about Vasarely? We would have to
determine whether he actually did, and what the results were.

Theoretically, the former development will not necessarily preclude the latter, but it is highly probable that it will, in fact, do so by making it superfluous; whenever we have a relatively satisfactory technique of reproduction at our disposal, we do not go to all the trouble of creating a notational system that is hard to establish, and, by definition, always reductive. Photographic reproductions, however imperfect they may still be, have already gradually taken over many of the functions of copies (we will encounter these functions again); similarly, everyone is aware of the negative repercussions the record industry has had on the musical activity of amateurs. Digital recordings are on the point of replacing scores, especially in the case of certain kinds of contemporary music, more difficult (or even impossible) to score, or whose methods short-circuit notation. "Eventually," says Pierre Henry, "we will no longer have concerts, but only digital recordings. We will be able to go back over such recordings, mixing them differently to create successive versions, just as a score of Beethoven's is performed differently in different periods. For electronic music, the record *is* the score; it represents the exact configuration of what we want the work to be at a given moment . . . ."[10] Thus music may eventually "regress" from the allographic to the multiple autographic regime, for we obviously should not take the composer's "the record *is*" literally: that the record is replacing the score (even if it improves on it) does not mean that the record *is* a score; something *is* not what it supplants. Painting, for its part, could "progress" towards the same state, while literature could rejoin it by virtue of a strictly digitalized neo-orality. But let us not make unwarranted use of risky and (partially) depressing prophecies. We often know, or think we do, that "this will kill that"; but we are never entirely certain where this and that are.

10. Interviewed by Anne Rey, *Le Monde,* 18 October 1990.

# PART II

# The Modes of Transcendence

*T*HE OTHER MODE OF EXISTENCE OF WORKS, WHICH I HAVE christened *transcendence,* encompasses all the extremely diverse and by no means mutually exclusive ways a work can obscure or else surpass the relation it maintains with the material or ideal object it basically "consists in"—all the cases in which "play" of one sort or another springs up between the work and its object of immanence. In this sense, transcendence is a secondary and derivative mode, a complementary, and, on occasion, compensatory supplement to immanence. If it is possible to conceive of an immanence without transcendence (as, until now, most[1] theoreticians of art have implicitly done), it is impossible to conceive of transcendence without immanence, since transcendence is something that happens to immanence, not the other way around; transcendence transcends immanence, but the relation is plainly not reciprocal. But this, as it

---

1. But not all, because reflections on the "reproducibility" of autographic works (Benjamin, Malraux, and others, recently joined, as we shall see, by Goodman himself) bear on a typical case of transcendence.

were, logically secondary status does not imply that some works are empirically exempt from transcendence: if all works do not exhibit transcendence in all its forms, no work, as we will see, completely eludes it. I have conceded that it is possible to *conceive,* not that one could actually *encounter,* a work without transcendence.

The various cases of transcendence, as I just said, are quite diverse, but it seems to me that one can group them, without excessive strain, in three modes. The first is that of transcendence by *plurality of immanence.* Here a work immanates, not in one object (or a group of more or less closely related objects, such as Rodin's *Burghers of Calais* or Vivaldi's *Four Seasons),* but in several nonidentical, concurrent objects; the symbolic formula for this mode might be "n objects of immanence for 1 work." The second mode is that of transcendence by *partiality$^2$ of immanence;* it occurs whenever a work is manifested in a fragmentary or indirect manner. The formula for this mode would run, roughly, "1/n object of immanence for 1 work." The third arises from operal *plurality of effect:* a single object of immanence, in this case, determines or serves as support for several works, in the sense that, for example, one and the same picture or even text does not exercise the same function, or, as Goodman says,[3] the same operal "action" in different situations or contexts, if only because it does not find (or *provoke*) the same "reception" in each. Here the formula would be "n works for 1 object of immanence." What follows will, I hope, explain and qualify these outrageously summary formulas.

2. In the sense, obviously, of "being a part of." I need, by extending the sense of *partialité,* to coin this neologism [in French, the word means only "partiality" in the sense of "non-neutrality"] in order to avoid the unduly negative connotations attached to terms like *lacuna* or *incompleteness;* partial immanences, as we will see, do not always involve lacunae.
3. Nelson Goodman, "L'art en action," *Cahiers du Musée national de l'art moderne,* no. 41 (Fall 1992): 7–14.

CHAPTER 11

# Plural Immanences

THIS MODE OF TRANSCENDENCE AFFECTS THE TWO REGIMES OF immanence in different ways (and to varying degrees); and it finds occasions to operate in both regimes, some of them limited to one or another "art." The feature common to all these forms is that the work immanates in several nonidentical objects, or, more exactly (since, strictly speaking, no two objects in this world are absolutely identical), in two objects *not deemed to be* identical and interchangeable, in the sense in which we generally assume that two casts of a cast sculpture *are*. This proviso, let us recall, underlies the distinction between *multiple* and *plural* objects. A cast sculpture or a print is (generally speaking) a multiple work (a work with multiple immanence); the works we are now about to consider are works with plural immanence. This distinction, which is of course more cultural than "ontological," is also more gradual than categorical, since, as we have seen, prints pulled from the same plate are often so different that specialists do not at all regard them as equivalent. If they are, nevertheless, considered to be "multiple" and not plural, the reason is doubtless that their differences generally stem from defects in the production process (deterioration of the plate or, in the case of sculpture, the model) rather than conscious design; these differences are, in a word, accidental and unintended. But cases of deliberate differentiation

are not completely excluded, so that the transition between the two situations, which we will encounter again later, is a fairly continuous one.

To my mind, the works that are incontestably plural in this sense[1]
are those whose plurality is not a technical byproduct, but, rather, results
wholly from authorial intention, as when an artist, after producing a
painting, text, or musical composition, decides to produce a new version of it, different from the first in one degree or another, yet sufficiently similar to (and derivative of) it for cultural convention to treat
it as *another version* of the same work rather than *another work*.

The motives for such a decision can vary considerably from one art
to the next, and so can its effects. One reason for this diversity lies in the
difference between the two regimes of immanence. A painter can produce what is commonly called a *replica* in order to compensate, in some
sort, for the autographic nature of his art, which prevents him from fur-
nishing a number of people with as many instances of the same picture;
writers and composers are clearly not confronted with the same impossibility, since the same text can be printed (or reproduced) in enough
copies (often, more than enough) to meet public demand. A plural allographic work is such, then, for reasons that generally have nothing to
do with those making for autographic pluralities, which result from one
(or more) processes that are no less specific.

## Replicas

In the autographic regime, plurality of immanence is determined by the
widespread existence of what are customarily called[2] works with *replicas,* or *versions.* The most relevant definition of "replica" is the one found
in Littré:[3] "a copy of a statue or painting executed by the author him-

1. That is, in the sense of works with plural *immanence. Operal* plurality is characteristic of
the third mode of transcendence. I can see no way of avoiding this terminological confusion, which is not, in any case, particularly troublesome.
2. To be honest, usage is rather confused and fluctuating here: works of this type are sometimes also described as "duplicates" or "doubles," while the word replica is often used to
refer to simple copies made by someone other than the original artist, especially when one
is speaking of Classical sculpture.
3. [Maximilien Littré (1801–1881) compiled a still authoritative French dictionary. According to *The American Heritage Dictionary of the English Language,* ed. William Morris (Boston:
Houghton Mifflin, 1976), "replica in its strictest sense is reserved for a copy by the origi-

self." In sculpture, the practice of (duplicate) casting, like that of indirect carving performed with the help of pointing machines, tends to make the notion of replica hazy by blurring the borderline between unique and multiple works; as far as I know, instances of sculptors producing copies of their own work are quite rare.[4] The art most conducive to the production of replicas is, accordingly, painting, where it goes without saying that a copy, even by the original artist, cannot conform absolutely to its model, so that *replica* inevitably means a perceptibly different *version*. I say "inevitably" and "even by the original artist" in deference to the assumption that the intention here is maximum fidelity, though that is in fact not the usual motive for the production of replicas, as we will see. But I should first give a few examples of this practice, which goes back, I believe, to the fifteenth century; for obvious reasons, its beginnings were probably (though I know of no historical study of the subject) contemporaneous with the revival[5] of easel paintings, which were intended for patrons or private customers, and could well give rise to new orders for the "same" picture. The earliest example I am aware of is Leonardo's *Virgin of the Rocks,* the first version of which (Louvre) dates from 1483, and the second (National Gallery, London) from 1506, though the latter may have been painted by Ambrogio di Predis "under the master's supervision." The van Buuren Collection in New York includes a slightly smaller version of *The Fall of Icarus* by Brueghel (Royal Museum, Brussels), though the attribution of these two paintings, roughly datable between 1555 and 1569, is a subject of dispute. Of El Greco's *Christ Driving the Money-Changers from the Temple* (between 1595 and 1605, Frick Collection), there exist not only three copies, but also a very faithful replica (between 1600 and 1610, National Gallery, London), which counts as authentic. A somewhat smaller replica of *The Fortune-Teller* by Caravaggio (c. 1596, Pinacoteca Capitolina) may be found in the Louvre;[6] the poses and colors are slightly different from those of the original (which,

---

nal artist. But it is widely accepted for any close reproduction, and it is acceptable to [some] in the still less literal sense of 'close reproduction in miniature.' "]

4. Though it is said that Bernini redid his bust of Cardinal Borghese (Borghese Gallery, Rome) because of a crack that appeared with the last blow of the chisel.

5. Revival, because this type of painting, essentially unknown in the Middle Ages, was not unknown to the ancient Greeks, who practiced painting on wooden panels from the fourth century B.C. onwards.

6. It is believed that there was a third version, which is now lost.

however, is in poor condition). Of Watteau's *The Embarkation for Cythera's Island* (1717, Louvre), there exists a replica painted for Julienne (Charlottenburg Castle, Berlin); not only did the painter copy his own work, but the replica was also produced in part, according to Eidelberg, using oil counterproofs, and thus by way of imprint.

> [The Louvre and Berlin paintings] are of the same size and, since the restoration of the Paris painting, of comparable tonality. . . . [But] the Berlin painting is more crowded (twenty-four persons, instead of eighteen). On the right, Watteau added a couple of lovers accompanied by three putti; in the background, a young man pours roses into a girl's apron. . . In addition, he replaced the bust of Venus with a full-length sculpture of the goddess. . . . But above all, the mountains in the background and on the left have disappeared, replaced by a large azure and pink sky.[7]

Chardin made replicas so frequently that we should almost cite the whole catalogue of his works. I will mention only the most famous example, *Saying Grace* (Salon of 1740, Louvre). We know of four replicas of this picture; they represent different kinds of authenticity and different kinds of variants. The one in the Louvre,[8] the one in Gosford House, which counts as a copy retouched by the author, and the one in the Hermitage (the only signed painting in the series) all very closely resemble the original; the essential difference resides in the nature of the objects on the floor. The authenticity of the replica in Rotterdam (which doubtless dates from 1760) is contested. A major addition, a fourth figure carrying a platter, to the left, differentiates it from the others; such an addition, which makes the painting nearly twice as wide and results in a horizontal arrangement, obviously takes us beyond the realm of mere replicas.[9] *The Rehearsal of the Ballet on Stage* by Degas (c. 1874) exists in two versions. Though they are of the same size,[10] one

7. Margaret Morgan Grasselli and Pierre Rosenberg, *Watteau, 1684–1721* (Washington, D.C.: National Gallery of Art, 1984), p. 408.
8. It may now be seen on the third floor of the Cour carré [Square Court], not far from the original.
9. *Soap Bubbles* (c. 1733) is a special case, because the three extant paintings (Metropolitan Museum, National Gallery in Washington, Los Angeles County Museum of Art) differ appreciably; they appear to be three replicas of an original that is now lost. See the essay by Philip Conisbee published by the LACMA in connection with the comparative exhibition of 1990–91.

is in essential oils and the other in pastels, making for an appreciable difference in tone: that of the second is warmer. The best-known version of Renoir's *Moulin de la Galette* (1876, Orsay Museum) could be described as a replica, since it very probably derives from another version, sold for a memorable sum at Sotheby's in New York; the latter painting, which is smaller, has a blurrier line, and is therefore sometimes described as "more Impressionist." It was doubtless painted in situ, later serving as model, in the studio, for its (larger) older sister.[11] The *Moulin* went under the hammer in May 1990; the same month, Van Gogh's *Portrait of Dr. Paul Gachet* was sold at another mind-boggling auction, held, this time, at Christie's. The painting auctioned off was, again, the original; but the relationship between it and its replica (Orsay) is better known than in the case of the Renoir. The first portrait was painted on 4 June 1890, and kept by the painter until his death; the second is a copy with variations (the yellow books have disappeared, the flowers on the table are no longer in a vase, the tones are brighter and the background is plainer), painted on 7 June by Van Gogh himself, at the sitter's request.

The artistic revolutions of the twentieth century have not curtailed the practice of making replicas to the extent one might think, as is shown by two examples, one due to Picasso, the other to Rauschenberg. The two versions of Picassos's *Three Musicians* (one in the MoMA in New York, the other in the Philadelphia Art Museum) both date from the summer of 1921; the order in which they were painted is not known, obviously making it impossible to tell which is the original and which the replica. Tradition sometimes describes the two realizations as "simultaneous," an adjective which, if taken literally, would suggest that the artist used both hands at the same time, one for each painting. A virtuoso like Picasso would surely have been up to a performance of that sort, but "simultaneous" should doubtless be construed to mean that the two pictures were painted "in alternation"; both interpretations rule out the possibility that Picasso copied his own work, and thus the status of replica

10. Both are painted over a pen-and-ink drawing on paper mounted on canvas, and both are in the Metropolitan.

11. Some prefer to regard the first version as a preliminary sketch, but, if it is one, it is a very elaborate sketch indeed; moreover, there is a version in the Museum of Copenhagen with a better claim to the title. These distinctions are, plainly, relative in the extreme, and the status they define often owes a great deal to commercial considerations: if it had been described as a sketch, the *Moulin* sold by Sotheby's would probably not have fetched $78,100,000.

in the strict sense. Moreover, the differences between the two pictures are appreciable, since two of the three figures have been switched around, while the dog on hand in New York is missing in Philadelphia. Here, then, we find ourselves at the limits of the field covered by the word "replica"; but we plunge back into it with the two versions of *Factum* by Rauschenberg, two assemblages of photos, printed pages, and splotches of paint laid on in the expressionist manner. I can do no better than to quote Irving Sandler's commentary on these works:

> His work constituted a challenge to the moral stance of the Abstract Expressionists, to their insistence that in order to be worthwhile a picture had to be found in the struggle of painting. They deemed without value a picture that was not a unique event evolving from anxious existential action but was a matter of aesthetic performance. To undermine this notion, Rauschenberg in 1957 made a gestural combine-painting titled *Factum I* and then executed a near-duplicate of it. This raised the upsetting question of whether the "found" picture was any more valuable than its "made" near-copy, and how could one tell. Critics were quick to grasp the issue; one wrote that when one discovers that *Factum I* has a twin, "with its patient, scrupulous duplication of every dribble and tatter, one is forced to admit that the same combination of impulses and discipline that produces more conventional pictures is also operating here." In time, the subtle differences in the two versions became more pronounced to viewers, and indeed of greater interest than the similarities, complicating the issues raised.[12]

The critical function of this iconoclastic replica, converging with that of Lichtenstein's fake brushstrokes*, may seem to be entirely at odds with traditional practice, and one might suppose that Rauschenberg was profiting from the occasion to subvert it too. But it seems to me that such a performance, however special its materials and techniques might make it, brings out, through exaggeration, a feature common to the whole of that practice: namely, the change in status that accompanies the transition from original to replica. In figurative painting, the original "directly" represents a real (Gachet) or imaginary (the Blessed Vir-

12. Irving Sandler, *The New York School: The Painters and Sculptors of the Fifties* (New York: Harper and Row, 1978), pp. 180–181. The two paintings are in private collections in Milan and Chicago, respectively.

gin) object. The replica, by virtue of the fact that the artist has copied his own work, represents the same object, but indirectly (transitively). It also represents (in a different sense) the original, because it *takes its place*—having, in the vast majority of cases, been ordered and painted with precisely that end in mind—while adding the artistic (and commercial) premium that comes with authenticity. In nonfigurative painting, especially action painting*, the original does not represent anything; it presents the trace of a pictorial act, such as brushwork*, dripping*, etc. A faithful replica, if a Pollock or a Kline had ever hazarded so risky an undertaking, would not have effected a more radical change in status than did Chardin's or Van Gogh's replicas. In both cases, the original is "about" something (the object depicted, an expressive act), and the replica is, for someone aware of its genesis, inevitably "about" the original. It is, therefore, second-degree painting [*peinture au second degré*].

The most common motive for the production of replicas is, as I have said—and as is obvious—commercial demand, a demand certain artists are manifestly more inclined to satisfy than others. Chardin's accommodating attitude is often explained as the consequence of a lack of imagination that led him to repeat rather than renew himself, but we must not neglect the fact that all such "repetition" brings its share of renewal with it, even when its traces are barely perceptible; I will come back to this. The case of the bust of Cardinal Borghese reveals another motive, which is obviously less common, and also specific to sculpture: accidents in the final stages. A third motive might be a patron's refusal to purchase a replica because he is dissatisfied with some detail; such disputes are, however, more likely to be resolved by corrections which the picture in its final state will show no signs of, unless subjected to very close scrutiny. It is well known that the first version of Caravaggio's *St. Matthew and the Angel* (1602), deemed too realistic, was refused, to be replaced by the one that can be seen today in the Church of San Luigi dei Francesi; the original, which the artist kept in his possession, was destroyed in the Kaiser-Friedrich Museum in Berlin during a 1945 air raid. However, the differences in the arrangement and expressions of the figures (which we know about, of course, from reproductions) rule out any notion that this is merely a copy by the original artist: the second picture represents a genuinely new work on the same theme. The history of painting and sculpture teems with examples of this sort. I will come back to this distinction in a moment; it is not only, nor even essentially, a quantitative one.

Indeed, if a replica is defined as a copy by the original artist, it is self-evident that no replica can be absolutely true to its model, as I have already said, even in cases (which would appear to be rather rare) where the artist does his best to make as faithful a copy as he can. As a matter of fact, an artist who "repeats" himself tends (contrary to the ordinary[13] copyist, who strives for conformity) to be drawn toward variation, whether or not his new client has requested it—as we can see by leafing through, say, Chardin's catalogue.

Such variation may be formal or thematic. The simplest formal variant stems from a change in format,[14] made by diminishing or enlarging the field of a painting—we have seen an example or two in Chardin—or by changing its scale, as with the two *Moulin de la Galette,* and, even more conspicuously, the two *Poseuses* by Seurat.[15] The latter kind of modification seems a bit less frequent, perhaps as a result of the utilization of various tracing procedures, such as those I mentioned in connection with *The Embarkation for Cythera's Island.* Another possible formal variant is stylistic, like the difference in touch between the two *Moulin de la Galette* or the two *Gachet.* Thematic or iconographic variants may consist—to be very schematic—in additions (the skimmer on the floor in the Hermitage *Saying Grace,* the left section of the Rotterdam version), omissions (the lost original of *Soap Bubbles,* which we know from a print, included a sort of bas-relief on the entablature in the foreground, missing from the three extant versions), inversions (Harlequin and Polichinelle in *The Three Musicians),* or substitutions: the two versions of Chardin's *Still Life with a Cat and Fish* also include, in one case, a mortar (Rothschild Collection), and, in the other (Kansas City Museum), three pastry molds and a piece of fruit. An in-depth study of

13. This adjective is restrictive; later we will come across cases of free copies, generally the work of artists of greater stature.
14. Replicas that have exactly the same dimensions as the original are extremely rare. I believe it is safe to say that varying the dimensions of a replica is standard practice with "honest" copies, so as to avoid fakes; this holds for copies by the original artist as well.
15. The original is at the Barnes Foundation, the "little version" in the National Gallery in London. There exists a reduced version of Ingres's *Bather of Valpinçon* (1808), known as *The Small Bather,* or *The Interior of the Harem* (1828), whose background displays considerable variation. Both paintings are in the Louvre.

these procedures of variation, even if it dealt only with Chardin, would fill an entire volume.

I have attributed the status of (unique) work with plural immanence to works with replicas, but this is certainly not self-evident, and calls for explanation. As this explanation also applies to allographic works (and, it seems to me, can be couched in the same terms in both cases), I will not offer it until we have examined them as well. But, before quitting the autographic regime, we should try to describe a little more precisely the difference between replicas and two similar phenomena, of which one is absolutely, and the other relatively, characteristic of this regime: multiple works (or works with multiple proofs) on the one hand, and what I will call works with *remakes* on the other.

The essential difference between the multiple works of printmaking or cast sculpture and the plural works we are interested in here clearly flows from a difference in method: an imprint is supposed to guarantee the identity of its products in mechanical fashion, whereas an artist who copies his own work is not supposed to guarantee the identity of his products in mechanical fashion, but even has license to produce partial (thematic) or global variants (involving format or style)—something which, indeed, tends to be encouraged. Yet the reliability of the various procedures for taking imprints is entirely relative: if, in photography, the prints produced in a single run are indeed indiscernible, the number of acceptable casts of a cast sculpture is limited, at a minimum, by wear and tear on the model and other hazards of the casting process, during which the "quality" of the casts steadily declines. In printmaking, the differences are even more noticeable, generally leaping to the eye, inasmuch as wear on the plate, the abrasion of the burrs and grooves, has a marked effect on the prints. As Jean-Jacques Rousseau says somewhere, "every copy of a print has its peculiar defects, which serve as its personality." Furthermore, nothing prevents the artist from stepping in to alter a print (or the plate itself) in order to accentuate its "personality" in the course of a run: this was, as we know, standard practice for Rembrandt, whose "method [consisted in] putting in slight changes or small additions so that his prints could be sold as new."[16] Such retouching clearly constitutes an

---

16. Svetlana Alpers, citing Arnold Houbraken, *Rembrandt's Enterprise: The Studio and the Market* (Chicago: University of Chicago Press, 1988), p. 100.

intermediate case, which lies somewhere between the proof and the replica with variants. But, all these nuances or deviations notwithstanding,
cultural convention accords a common identity to all proofs of "multiple" works. It effectively annuls their differences by treating these as
purely technical, setting each proof in an (optional) relation of artistic
equivalence with all the others: *The Thinker* immanates in this particular cast or (*vel*) in another, the assumption being that, when you have
seen one, you have seen them all. Works with replicas, in contrast, stand
in an (additive) relation of complementarity: *Saying Grace* immanates
in a certain painting *and* in these others, so that looking at one of them
does not free you of the obligation to look at the others; you will not
have exhaustive knowledge of this work (if that is a meaningful notion)
until you are familiar with every version of it.[17] This distinction is
undoubtedly reinforced by the fact that the task of taking multiple proofs
can be (and usually is) entrusted to simple craftsmen, while it is a defining condition of a replica, in the sense under consideration here, that it
be realized (at least in part) by the original artist. The most striking indi-
cation that the world of art accepts this distinction is the fact that it readily organizes comparative exhibitions that bring together different
versions of the same paintings, but far less frequently puts on exhibitions
which include several prints from the same plate, and, doubtless, never
holds shows involving different casts of the same statue or prints of the
same photograph.

It is, again, the fact that replicas are produced by the original artist
which distinguishes the relation between works and their replicas from
that between works and their remakes.[18] To *remake** is to make again, or
to make over, starting out afresh with the same thematic or formal motif,
but without copying an already existing work.[19] This is the relation that

17. To be sure, such partial knowledge, which we will return to in connection with the second mode of transcendence, is not negligible, and can give rise to a more intense, more
authentic aesthetic relation than a rapid comparative survey. Completeness is no more necessary a condition for the aesthetic sense, which takes what it wants where it wants, than
"perfection" is.

18. [Genette proposes *reprise* as a translation of "remake," noting, however, that the French
term is less exact, that an alternate, *réfection,* which literally means "remaking," has the wrong
connotations (it means repairs, as in street repairs), and that "remake," in English, is always
a movie (in contemporary hit-parade French, it can also be a song).]

19. Of course, the sharpness of the distinction between these two procedures does not preclude mixed or uncertain cases. I must confess that I cannot say what relationship obtains

unifies, for example, Michelangelo's four *Pietà,* or Cézanne's countless paintings of *Mont Sainte-Victoire*—or else, to take two works related by remake [*en reprise*] that are as close as possible to one another, the two *Mont Sainte-Victoire Seen from les Lauves.*[20] The contrast between this pair of very similar paintings and, let us say, the pair formed by the *Pietà* in St. Peter's (1500) and the one in Santa Maria del Fiore (1550),[21] which everything in the style and arrangement of the figures conspires to distinguish, shows how variable the distance between works related by remake can be: all the two pairs have in common is that each pair taken separately has the same subject matter. But, having spoken of "related" works, I need to make this genealogical metaphor more precise (for the *Saying Graces* are also related pictures) by spelling out that the two very different *Pietà,* or the two very similar *Sainte-Victoire,* are sister-works (daughters of the same father); in contrast, two *Saying Graces* are not only brothers, but one is also the son of the other, since the second proceeds, by way of the artist, from the first, while the artist produces the second by way of the first.

Works related by remake not only resemble one another to widely varying degrees, but can also arise from very different intentions, depending on whether the artist contents himself with returning to a favorite motif[22] (even if he does so as obsessively as Cézanne) without seeking to create any sort of opposition between the resulting works, or else sets out to organize them in what is generally called a "series," based on a principle of deliberate variation, as Monet did with his *Haystacks* (fifteen paintings exhibited together in May 1891) and *Rouen Cathedrals* (twenty paintings exhibited in May 1892 and arranged in a chronological pattern beginning at dawn and ending at dusk). The practice of producing remakes with variations has, as is well known, become widespread in contemporary art—especially (or, indeed, above all) in nonfigurative art, where structural analogies have come to replace

---

between Goya's two *Mayas* (1800 and 1801–1803, Prado), in which the pose, expression, and décor are so similar.

20. Venturi 798, 1902–1904, Philadelphia, and Venturi 1529, 1904–1906, Basel.

21. [The *Pietà with St. Nicodemus,* currently housed in a museum a short distance from the Florence cathedral.]

22. Favored by the artist, but also by patrons and the public: one need only recall the untold *Annunciations* or *Madonna and Childs* that an artist of the Middle Ages or the Renaissance must have had to turn out in the course of his career, enthusiastically or not.

the sameness of subject matter of an earlier age: consider De Kooning's *Women,* Jasper Johns's flags, targets, and cards, Newman's zips, Rothko's fuzzy rectangles, Motherwell's repetitive *Elegies,* Albers's concentric squares, Reinhardt's black monochromes, etc.

I will not devote as much time to this vast question as it deserves, not only for lack of competence, but, above all, because it lies outside our subject. Like works with multiple immanence, but for a diametrically opposed reason, works related by remake fail to meet the definition for cases of plural immanence. Works with multiple immanence fail to do so because the multiple is (or is considered to be) too similar to determine a plurality that would compel us to regard it as a single work taking the form of several objects. As to works related by remake, cultural convention prefers to treat them as fully autonomous,[23] since the original artist has not copied his own work. In the latter case, of course, we no longer have a work with plural immanence, but simply several distinct works; their thematic or formal kinship calls their autonomy into question no more than does, say, the thematic similarity between two novels by Balzac, or the stylistic similarity between two symphonies by Mozart. ("No more than" does not, however, mean *not at all;* I will come back to this point.)

To say "cultural convention prefers" is to acknowledge the relatively arbitrary nature of these distinctions, even if, to repeat, the existence of copies made by the original artists provides a fairly solid grounding for the category "work with replicas." Like all methodological decisions, this one will not command unanimous assent, resting as it does on essentially pragmatic considerations (does this way of describing things have more advantages or disadvantages than another?): after all, the fact that a painter has copied his own work does not logically imply that two pictures must be regarded as constituting a single work. But why should the fact that a work is produced by imprint imply, any more compellingly, that the two prints or casts constitute two instances of what the artworld unanimously considers to be, this time, the *same* sculpture or the *same* engraving? Operal identity is not a given: it is

---

23. Or perhaps, on occasion, prefers to treat each series as a unique work with several parts, as with the Arena Chapel frescoes or the Brancacci Chapel, even if their unifying principle, narrative in the latter case and variational in the former, is not the same. I will return to this thorny question of the relation of the parts to the whole.

constructed on the basis of subtle and eminently variable criteria, which are determined by usage. We will encounter this question again after we have considered pluralities of immanence in the allographic regime.

## Adaptations

Plural works of this type, be it recalled, cannot arise, like replicas in painting, from the need to provide several admirers of a work with more or less identical copies of it, since the distinguishing feature of the allographic regime is to allow unlimited reproduction of the instances of manifestation of an ideal, unique object of immanence; should the original artist copy his own work, he would simpy produce one more such instance.[24] In literature, music, choreography, or the other allographic arts, then, there is no practice strictly parallel to that of making replicas. But versions of certain kinds, especially in literature and music, have at least one feature in common with them: these versions stand on an equal footing with the original text or score, and thus distribute the work's immanence over two or more objects. This is the situation created by what are generally known as "adaptations," whether they are destined for a particular public, as when Michel Tournier brought out a children's version of *Friday; or, The Other Island* under the title *Friday and Robinson: Life on Esperanza Island,* or have a particular practical purpose, like the "stage versions" of plays by Claudel that were once considered unplayable in their original form: *The Tidings Brought to Mary, Break of Noon,* or *The Satin Slipper.*[25] Everyone is familiar with Claudel's stage versions, because they have been published and belong, as such, to his œuvre; but it is a well-known fact that performances of already published plays often involve minor adaptations which, in certain cases, no edition preserves any trace of. In music, the most typical example of adaptation is that of ballet scores

24. This even if such a copy can, as an autographic object, have a particular aesthetic and/or commercial value: it is said that certain surrealist poets, in the poverty of their younger years, lived in part off the sale of manuscripts which, though they were, to be sure, autographs, were yet fairly multiple.
25. I do not put in this category stage adaptations of prose fiction, such as were very often produced in the nineteenth century, even if they are the work of the original author; the reason is that usage treats them, not unreasonably, as distinct works. See Gérard Genette, *Palimpsestes* (Paris: Seuil, 1982).

which have been subsequently rearranged as "suites for orchestra": for example, *Daphnis and Chloe* (1909-1912), *The Firebird* (1910-1919), *Petrushka* (1911-1914), *The Soldier's Tale* (pantomime 1918, suite 1920), and many other early twentieth-century works that today form part of the repertory or a composer's catalogue in these two (at least[26]) competing forms (the second of which is generally a reduction of the first).

In addition to these modes of adaptation common, mutatis mutandis, to all allographic practices (stage productions or choreographies must, for example, be adapted to new spatial and technical conditions when they move from one theater to another), there are others which are characteristic of certain arts. I will mention three: one, *translation,* is peculiar to literature, the two others, *transcription* and *transposition,* to music.

If the adaptations just evoked can be considered exceptional or peripheral, translation of literary works is, in principle, a universal phenomenon. Even if many works are never translated, each is at least a candidate for translation into as many languages as possible; some, indeed, have been translated several times into the same language. To be sure, the operal identity of a text and its translation is not granted by everyone, beginning with a considerable number of writers. Goodman, faithful to his principle that a (literary) work is absolutely identical with its text, categorically rejects this identification: for him, a translation cannot but be a new work, since, by definition, it takes the form of a new text.[27]

But this straightforward and, for a nominalist, philosophically convenient position hardly conforms with common usage, which allows us to say, indifferently, "I've read a French translation of *War and Peace,*" "I've read *War and Peace* in French," or simply, in the same situation, "I've read *War and Peace.*" It will doubtless be objected that these expressions are merely metonymical, like *"War and Peace* is in the living room," but it does not seem to me that we are dealing with the same kind of metonymy in both cases: the figural displacement [*glissement figural*] is more noticeable (and, as it happens, more "ontological") between the

26. "At least," because the plurality of immanence of some of these works (like the literary works mentioned earlier) proceeds from another factor as well, to be examined later.
27. Nelson Goodman, *Languages of Art: An Approach to a Theory of Symbols* (Indianapolis: Bobbs-Merrill, 1968), p. 209.

text and its copy than between the text and its translation. The special
case of translations made by the author himself (Nabokov, from Russian to English in the case of, at least, *King, Queen, Knave, The Gift,* and
*Despair,* and, it is said, from English to Russian in the case of *Lolita;*
Beckett, from English to French in the case of *Murphy* and *Watt,* and in
the opposite direction for most of his subsequent works) tends to justify this view: it is quite artificial to consider the French and English versions of *Molloy* as two distinct *works,* rather than as two *texts* (and thus
two objects of immanence) of the same work. The criterion for the latter judgment is plainly not faithfulness to the original, which we rarely
verify, and which is by no means guaranteed by the fact that the translator and author are identical (indeed, it is the other way around: an
author is naturally at greater liberty than a translator to make changes
in his own text, just as a painter has greater freedom in copying his own
painting than a copyist does). Rather, the criterion is clearly the authorial source as such. When we must decide whether several objects of
immanence—texts, paintings, scores, etc.—belong to the same work,
the fact that they have been produced by the same author counts for a
great deal, even if it is not, of course, a sufficient condition (that *Père
Goriot* and *Eugénie Grandet* are by the same author does not suffice to
make them the same work), or even, properly speaking, an entirely necessary condition, as will appear.

However, if we deem an authorial translation (or a translation revised by the author and hence "authorized," like, beginning in 1985, the
French translations of Kundera) to be another text of the same work, it
becomes quite difficult not to extend this recognition to translations by
others [*allographe*], which obviously display widely varying degrees of
fidelity to the original, but on a scale that owes nothing to the fact that
they have been made by someone other than the author. The reason,
which nobody resists in practice, is that, if a *text* is surely defined by
literal identity (sameness of spelling),\* a literary *work* is defined, from
one text to the next, by semantic identity (sameness of meaning\*, as one
might put it), which the passage from one language to another is supposed to preserve—not totally, to be sure, but sufficiently well and accurately enough for the reader to have a legitimate sense of operal identity.
As is well known, the limit on total fidelity stems from the impossibility
of simultaneously respecting what Goodman calls the semantic values

of denotation and exemplification; as is also well known, this uncertain relation weighs more heavily upon translations of "poetic" texts, where the accent lies, more than it does elsewhere, on what Jakobson termed the "message," which in fact means the linguistic medium. How far translinguistic operal identity can be extended is thus variable, and the public handles this situation with a flexibility that, here again, owes more to common usage than to a priori principles. In any event, when we declare that a translation is unfaithful, we are rarely unable to say what it is unfaithful *to:* a translation of *The Imitation of Christ* would have to be most unfaithful indeed in order to do service as a translation of *Journey to the End of the Night.*

Since musical works as such have nothing to do with the plurality of languages, the phenomenon of versions unified by a semantic identity transcending linguistic differences is unknown in music. Musical works are, however, subject to two factors capable of operating an overall transformation on the whole of a text; this transformation is governed by a principle just as simple as that governing translinguistic conversion. The multiplicity of aural parameters might even authorize two more such principles: thus it would be possible to distinguish faster and slower, or louder and softer versions of the same "score." But such variations are generaly left to the performer's discretion; they function as options of performance, and hence of manifestation.[28] The two factors of overall transformation actually exploited are, as is well known, a change in pitch (and therefore, as a rule, in key), or *transposition,* and a change in timbre (a change in instrument), or *transcription,* which, moreover, often entails transposition. Here the criterion for operal identity is not, as in the previous case, semantic, but rather structural. A transposed and/or transcribed composition retains a structure defined by the maintenance of identical rhythmic values and melodic relationships determined by intervals that are deemed equivalent (the structure C, half-note—D, quarter-note—C, half-note is structurally assimilated to the structure F, half-note—G, quarter-note—F, half-note). Like the se-

---

28. Differences in tempo and intensity can function as principles of composition, but they have the status of internal variations: a phrase played forte repeated piano, or at another tempo or even with a different rhythm. Of course, differences in key and instrumentation can play the same role, and often do: this was the "basis of the language" of classical development.

mantic criterion in the case of literary works, the structural criterion owes its pertinence more to usage than to natural fact, and nothing prevents us from rejecting it and defining the identity of a musical work in terms of its pitch or timbre. Goodman does so with timbre (and, I suppose, key): "A more substantive consideration might be found in the relation of a work to its siblings for other instruments. As we have seen, specification of instrument is an integral part of any true score in standard musical notation; and a piano work and the violin version of it, for example, count strictly as different works."[29]

It is not, we know, entirely accurate to say that "specification of instrument is an integral part of any true score in standard musical notation," unless we maintain, at the risk of departing from common usage and so giving up the possibility of accounting for it, that the score of *The Well-Tempered Clavier* and countless other baroque works are not "true" scores, or that their notation is not yet "standard." For usage declines to treat as two "strictly" different works not only a version of *The Well-Tempered Clavier* for piano and another for clavichord, but also the original version of Beethoven's Concerto in D for violin and a transcription of it for piano. But I will come back to this theoretical question, which every instance of plural immanence poses, at the end of this chapter.

Aside from cases of internal variation, in which transposition and transcription do not yield new versions, but play a role in development, these two kinds of transformation are generally made either to meet the needs of a performance, or simply for the performers' convenience. A melody composed for tenor can be lowered a few notes to bring it within the range of baritones or mezzo-sopranos (as in the case of the *Winterreise,* composed by Schubert for a voice of his own tessitura, but which we today tend to associate with the deeper voice of a baritone; a mezzo-soprano like Christa Ludwig sang it readily); we choose a single tessitura for the melodies in the cycle *Nuits d'été,* which Berlioz apparently intended for several male and female voices; the role of

29. Goodman, *Languages of Art,* p. 206. [Genette remarks about his French translation of this passage:] *Transcription* is my translation of the English "siblings," while *comptent strictement* is a literal translation of "count strictly": I interpret this phrase to mean "count in the strict sense" rather than "count absolutely." The sentences which follow in Goodman seem to leave room for certain personal predilections: a transcription for violin of a piano work that preserved a C-sharp would be, says Goodman, a more acceptable version (of the same work) than a transcription which converted it to D-flat.

Rosina in the *Barber of Seville,* originally for mezzo-contralto, was long given to sopranos, while that of Nero in *The Coronation of Poppea,* composed for castrato, is, on stage,[30] often sung an octave lower by a tenor (and thus, as it happens, without a change in key); and so on. The list of these modifications in tessitura is endless. In the instrumental domain, they generally come about as the result of transcriptions from one instrument to another, although it is well known that Schubert's Impromptu, Opus 90, N° 3, composed in G-flat in 1827, was published in 1855, and for several decades thereafter, in G, a more accessible key for amateurs.

One knows about interinstrumental transcriptions above all because of the special case of "reductions" of orchestral or vocal works for piano. This was a specialty in which Liszt earned a name for himself, to the profit—or at the expense—of Beethoven (the nine symphonies), Schubert (the lieder), Wagner, and many others. Throughout the nineteenth century, reduction fulfilled, for the music-loving public, the same function of distinguished popularization that records perform today.[31] Transcriptions in the other direction, in which works for piano are scored for orchestra, are also well known: among those made by the original composer, we may cite Liszt's *St. Francis of Assisi Preaching to the Birds,* or *Mother Goose* and *Alborada del gracioso* by Ravel; an example of transcription by someone other than the composer is provided by Musorgsky's *Pictures at an Exhibition,* expanded by, again, Ravel.[32] These orchestrations obviously aim to exploit the potential of a work with a view to broadening its audience (let us not forget that, for many composers, the piano version of a work is a stage in its genesis). But instrumental transcription can take the most varied forms. I have already mentioned the piano version of Beethoven's *Violin Concerto,* but it is well known that Bach (very freely) transcribed, for clavichord or organ, several concertos by Vivaldi, as well as his own Partita

30. And sometimes on records as well—for example, in the performance conducted in 1981 by Nikolaus Harnoncourt, in which Eric Tappy plays Nero. However, in most recordings of the opera, preference goes to the original tessitura, and the part is given to a soprano (Elisabeth Söderström, conducted in 1972 by, again, Harnoncourt).

31. But Stravinsky himself reduced three movements of *Petrushka* for piano, and the whole of *Petrushka* and the *Rite of Spring* for four hands.

32. There exists a recording by Horowitz of the original version; it is so strange that many regard it as a (free) reduction of Ravel's orchestration.

for Solo Violin in E for organ; the Chaconne of Bach's Partita N° 2 in D-minor for Solo Violin was transcribed for piano by Busoni, and by Schumann for . . . violin and piano. Haydn's *The Seven Last Words of Our Savior on the Cross,* composed in 1785 for string orchestra, brass, and ketttledrums (the program called for an introduction, seven sonatas, and an earthquake), was reduced for string quartet around 1790, then expanded around 1801, doubtless by Michael Haydn, into a cantata for voice, choir, and orchestra. *Transfigured Night,* composed by Schön-berg in 1899 for two violins, two violas, and two cellos, was arranged for string orchestra in 1917; and the list continues.[33]

Literature and music offer the most typical cases of works with competing or supplementary versions, but, as goes without saying, the phenomenon can occur throughout the allographic domain. There are innumerable recipes with variants (not counting, of course, optional ways of making them that are left unspecified), and if architecture ex-ploited the possibilities of multiplication opened up by its allographic regime, there would be plans with variations, prescribing buildings that, while differing slightly, would resemble one another closely enough to have the same operal identity. There doubtless exist plans of this sort that I do not know of.

## Revisions

All the pluralities of immanence mentioned so far (including, inciden-tally, those of autographic works with replicas) were intended as sup-plements or *alternatives:* in the minds of their creators, the "stage version" of *The Satin Slipper* or the two "orchestral suite" versions of *Daphnis and Chloé* were by no means intended to suppress and replace the full or original versions of these works. Indeed, some of these adaptations, im-posed by practical necessity, were doubtless nothing more than com-promises or stopgaps; this certainly holds for most translations as well as for most reductions for piano. The "new versions" we now turn to owe

33. Let me recall that some of these transcriptions (but the name is quite inappropriate in this case) entail no transposition or modification in the number of players, and so require no changes in the written version: the same score can prescribe a part for violin or flute, piano or clavichord.

their existence, in theory, to an entirely different impulse, whose aim is to correct or improve. Their function would plainly be *substitutive,* if practical obstacles did not get in the way: an author who has come to be dissatisfied with a finished, and even published, work, produces some time afterwards (the lapse of time involved varies considerably) a version which more closely conforms to his new intentions or capacities, or, occasionally, public taste.[34] Only the fact that he is not in a position to destroy the extant copies of the work in its original state affords posterity an opportunity to study and compare what will from then on be, de facto, two or more versions, and, perhaps, to reflect upon the aptness of the modification or the legitimacy of its own preferences.

The successive editions of a work, when there *are* successive editions in an author's lifetime, almost always contain minor rectifications, usually involving silent corrections of slips or typographical errors (it is well known that, until the beginning of the nineteenth century, first editions generally teemed with mistakes, because galleys were not proofread; the second, and, at last, emended edition of a work was, as a rule, the first correct one). Thus, the second, 1858 edition of *Madame Bovary,* first published in 1857 in two volumes by Michel Lévy, contains more than sixty corrections. The impressions of 1862, 1866, and 1868 were left unaltered, but a newly set one-volume edition had appeared in the meantime with 208 additional corrections, and, in 1869, a revised reprinting of this edition brought 127 more. In 1873, Flaubert transferred the novel to a new publisher, Charpentier, whose "definitive" edition included yet another 168 corrections.[35] This text, the last to be revised by the author, is the one adopted by all serious modern editors, for whom previous texts have been rendered obsolete by the final revision and now count as corrupt, even if copies of these earlier editions continue to be traded on the old and rare book market, often at prices justified by their value for bibliophiles. From the standpoint of the author's final intentions, it is fortunate that these purchases are not too often made with reading in mind.

34. For obvious reasons, this motive is particularly powerful in cinema. A recent example of such adjustment is provided by Giuseppe Tornatore's *Cinema Paradiso* (1989), whose somewhat heavy-handed original version was spurned by Italian audiences; the director thereupon produced a drastically cut version, which enjoyed huge (and deserved) success.
35. See the edition by C. Gothot-Mersch (Garnier, 1971), pp. 362–363. An edition of the novel was also brought out by Lemerre (1874); it was apparently based on the original edition and not corrected by Flaubert.

Editorial policy is much the same, of course, with regard to hand-written corrections made by the author in a copy of the last edition published during his lifetime, and adopted only after his death. This holds for the emendations (essentially additions) made by Montaigne in a copy of the 1588 ("Bordeaux") edition of the *Essays,* or those made by Balzac in a copy of the Furne edition (1842), designated in his will as "the final manuscript of *The Human Comedy.*"[36] But the fact that such corrections were not actually published in the author's lifetime some-times raises doubts as to the definitive, and therefore binding, nature of these "final intentions," which never reached the fateful "passed for press" stage: the corrections of *The Red and the Black* found in what is known as the Bucci copy, or those of the *Charterhouse* (inspired, in part, by Balzac's criticisms) in the Chaper copy, generally rank as passing whims, and are relegated to the status of variants by modern editors.

In all these cases, the slight nature of the differences and the virtu-ally unanimous consensus as to the choice of text have forestalled the emergence of significantly different, competing versions intended for public consumption, even if examination of the "variants" given by scholarly editions sometimes sows a few healthy doubts about the osten-sible uniqueness and stability of the text. But it occasionally happens that emendations go beyond the merely local, taking the form of a stylistic and/or thematic revision of the whole, and so giving rise to what can only be called a new version. Earlier, when discussing what establishing a text involves, I cited the examples of *The Cid* and *The Life of Rancé,* of which there are, today, two versions in circulation, one original and the other "definitive." This has also been the fate of Senancour's *Ober-man(n),* of which there are three versions (1804, 1833, 1840); the first and last are in competition today.[37] In all three instances, the revised edition

36. This corrected copy has been published in a facsimile edition by Bibliophiles de l'orig-inal, edited by Jean A. Ducourneau, 1965–1976.
37. The 1804 version was adopted by André Monglond (Arthaud, 1947), and taken up again by Georges Borgeaud, among others (UGE, 1965); the 1840 edition was chosen for the edi-tion prepared by Jean-Maurice Monnoyer (Gallimard, Folio, 1984). The name "Oberman" acquired a second *n* in 1833; the resulting change in the title provides a handy way of iden-tifying the versions, if we discount, as most do, the one in the middle. (Senancour's inten-tion to censor himself in this version is supposed to have been checked by Sainte-Beuve, who wrote the preface to it.)

is characterized by greater stylistic,[38] and even, in Senancour's case, thematic[39] moderation (the anticlerical passages have been toned down). *Justine,* a case of a rarer sort, evolves in the opposite direction (*The Misadventures of Virtue,* 1787; *Justine or the Misfortunes of Virtue,* 1791; *The New Justine,* 1797); moreover, the third version is marked by a change in narrative voice (shift to the third person). But examples are legion, and bear witness to adjustments of all kinds. In *Manon Lescaut* (1731-1753), the transformation is both thematic and stylistic. The various revised versions of Claudel's plays[40] have been revised (independently of the "stage versions") in very different senses of the word, which one would be hard pressed to sum up in a single formulation. *Nadja* (1927-1962) was the object, according to the author himself, of "minor attentions," which "testify to a certain concern to say things better" (or what he imagines to be better); these "attentions" were accompanied by the elimination of an episode and the addition of a few photo illustrations.[41] The original text of *Passengers of Destiny,* published in censored form in 1943, was fully restored in 1947, then modified, like *The Communists,* for the edition of the *Œuvres romanesques croisées* (1966). *Man's Hope* (1937) was revised in 1944, *The Talker* (1946) in 1963. *Friday; or, The Other Island* (1967) saw, in 1972, the addition of two new episodes, drawn from the children's version. I would be unhappy with myself if I did not round off this entirely arbitrary selection with *Thomas the Obscure* (1941), whose 1950 second edition, published, like the first, by Gallimard, is embellished with a foreword of highly characteristic ambiguity: "There is, for every work, an infinity of possible variants. The present edition adds nothing to the pages entitled Thomas the Obscure begun in 1932, deliv-

---

38. Be it recalled that, in Corneille's case, the 1660 edition contains major revisions not only of *The Cid,* but, to varying degrees, of all the early plays.

39. This also holds for La Rochefoucauld's *Maxims,* from their first (1665) to their fifth and final edition during the author's lifetime (1678). The editor, Jacques Truchet (Garnier, 1967), presents both editions in parallel format, with this explanation: "We thought it crucial to reproduce the first edition of the *Maxims* in its entirety; it is perhaps more vigorous than the definitive edition itself."

40. *Tête-d'or,* 1889–1894; *The City,* 1893–1901; *La jeune fille violaine* [a version of *The Tidings Brought to Mary*], 1894–1898; *The Exchange,* 1894–1951; *Break of Noon,* 1905–1958; *Proteus,* 1913–1926, to cite only the major instances. These dates are the dates of composition, not publication.

41. The Pléiade edition of the Complete Works opts for the late version, which it places, curiously enough, among the texts of the 1920s, without listing the variants from the original.

ered to the publisher in May of 1940 and published in 1941; but as it subtracts a good deal from them, it may be said to be another, and even an entirely new version, but identical at the same time, if one is right in making no distinction between the figure and that which is, or believes itself to be, its center, whenever the complete figure itself expresses no more than the search for an imagined center." Translation (which will hold no surprises for anyone who has followed me this far): a work can have several texts.

Serious scholarly editions (be it said without pleonasm), present and to come, give (or will give) all the successive versions of a text. In so doing, they create an effect of multiplicity that is doubtless hard to justify in the face of authorial disavowals, yet manifestly justified after the fact (with increasing frequency) by the inalienable rights of a curious public. This is one manifestation among others of the predominance of the reception of works over their production, or the privilege of posterity—of which we will soon encounter a still more unmistakable illustration.

Versions disavowed by their author can, then, with the active cooperation of sharp-eyed specialists, be "dredged back up" by the public. The same holds for works that their author disavows without granting them the benefit of a new version (I am going beyond the scope of our subject for a moment): consider, among other instances, *Inquisiciones* (1925), which Borges very quickly repudiated, to the point, supposedly, of feverishly hunting down and destroying all the remaining copies, and (so he said) of authorizing a first edition of his *Complete Works* in 1953 (Émécé) to the sole end of making the exclusion of this book memorably official. An unpublished work can also be disavowed, but in that case, of course, the author can proceed to make the salutary auto-dafé himself (the same applies to autographic works that have not yet been sold). He does not always do so (consider the first edition of the *Sentimental Education*), or is not always in a position to do so, in which case he can entrust the task to his executor, who, naturally, does just as he pleases: think of Max Brod. It is said (but, like all famous last words, the story is a fabrication) that Proust, on his deathbed, tersely ordered Céleste Albaret to "erase everything," which testifies to impressive confidence in the destructive capacity of the eraser (among other things). What Céleste did is well known; it amounted to the same thing.

Needless to say, music (in written form) offers analogies. Some of the best-known examples (at least to me) are in Stravinsky (*The Firebird,* 1910, revised in 1945; *Petrushka,* 1911, revised in 1947; the *Pulcinella suite,* 1922, revised in 1947). Each of the two versions of these works, which have unintendedly come into competition with one another, has its defenders; in all three cases, the competing versions have been performed and recorded equally often.[42] Further examples are provided by Boulez, whose "works are, with rare exceptions, either unfinished ('evolving,' on the principle underlying the work in progress*), or else revised or due to be revised":[43] this is true of *The Sun of the Waters,* twice "rectified"[44] after its publication in 1948, and *The Bridal Face,* composed in 1946 for two voices, two ondes martenot, and percussion, orchestrated in 1952, and revised again in 1990 for a (definitive?) version which the critic I have taken this information from amiably describes as "music of the 1950s adapted to the taste of the end of the century"—which in no way determines in advance the taste which the next version, if there is to be one, will be adapted to.[45]

The situation of opera is, generally speaking, more confused, for reasons having to do with the complexity of this type of art and its dependence on all sorts of factors; the result is that revision of the kind we are considering has, in opera, a status midway between correction and adaptation. We know that Mozart would sometimes modify his operas according to the availability of certain singers, striking or replacing arias

42. The situation of Bruckner's Eighth Symphony is similar: performers and publishers continue to do battle over the three versions released during composer's lifetime (1887, 1892, 1895). The 1935 Hass edition is mysteriously (as far as I am concerned) described as "synthetic."

43. Gérard Condé, "Remaniements," *Le Monde,* 2 August 1990.

44. The term is Boulez's. On the reasons for and the modalities of this "rectification," see Pierre Boulez, *Par volonté et par hasard* (Paris: Seuil, 1975), pp. 58–59.

45. The relation betwen the *Book for Quartet* (1948–1949), which, incidentally, remains unfinished, and the 1968 *Book for Strings* is more complicated, and, perhaps, temporary, since the second version so far expands (in terms of both the number of performers and the development) only the first two movements (1a and 1b) of the first version. It is not very clear if this transformation is meant to be corrective and substitutive, as in Stravinsky's case, or supplementary and alternative (as with Haydn's *Seven Last Words*); as far as performance and publication are concerned, it is the latter, at least de facto. Boulez himself (*Par volonté,* pp. 61–62) assimilates this case to that of the various *Mont Sainte-Victoires,* a very rough comparison, at least in terms of my categories, since, with Boulez, the second version plainly results from work on the first, which is not usually the case with Cézanne.

to meet the wishes of his dear prima donnas; this is by no means an exceptional case. The reception the public accords a work, pressure from the censors, and diverse considerations of decorum carry at least equal weight: the avatars of *Fidelio* during Beethoven's lifetime (from 1805 to 1814), of *Tannhäuser* (original version, 1845, Parisian version, 1861), *Simone Boccanegra* (1857-1881), *Don Carlo(s)* (original version in French in five acts, 1867; Italian translation, 1868; Italian version in four acts, 1884) deserve an entire chapter. The avatars of *Boris Godunov* would seem almost simple if we considered only the autograph versions that appeared in Musorgsky's lifetime (first version, rejected, 1869; second version, performed in 1872, proscribed in 1874); but the posthumous fortunes or misfortunes of this work—due to the successive interventions of Rimsky-Korsakov (1896, and again in 1906), Shostakovich (1959), the illustrious musicologist Joseph Stalin, who ordered a return, for a time, to the (second) Rimsky-Korsakov version, and a few other people as well, including nearly all the opera directors, conductors, and managers involved—have been such that, from successive choices through arbitrary suppressions to inspired mixing, one never encounters two productions based on the same score.[46]

This last example takes us beyond the question of revisions regarded as legitimate because they have been made by the author (an artist always has the right, and, doubtless, the obligation, to revise his work for as long as it does not satisfy him, or whenever it no longer satisfies him). The reason invoked to justify revision by someone other than the author is, of course, the desire to improve works deemed imperfect or clumsy, especially, in music, works considered to be clumsily orchestrated. This was the main motivation for Rimsky-Korakov's revisions of *Boris Godunov*, and also of *Khovanshchina*,[47] which, incidentally, Musorgsky had not finished orchestrating. Thus the desire to make improvements stems from a subjective (even if collective) judgment that can always be rescinded in the name of a change in taste: this was the justification for the restorations later undertaken by Shostakovich in the two cases just mentioned,

46. At last word, the "second original version [*sic*], complete and definitive (1874), an edition established [in 1928?] by Pavel Lamm on the basis of the composer's autograph manuscripts" and performed in 1992 by the Paris Opera after a production by the Teatro Communale in Bologna, counts as the most reliable version.

47. Produced in 1886, after Musorgsky's death. The original version—orchestrated, however, by Shostakovich—was published in 1960.

at a time when it was thought preferable to return to (or, at least, come closer to) the original version. The history ("the tradition") of musical performance, especially of orchestral music, is made up of this incessant movement of revision and de-revision: the debate about baroque instruments and the size of baroque orchestras is only one aspect or chapter among many. Every music lover knows that Schumann's orchestration of his own symphonies was so opaque and lifeless that they would have had small chance of surviving if they had not been touched up by Gustav Mahler, acting in his capacity as conductor; it is likewise a matter of record that various instrumental solutions, impossible in Beethoven's day, have enabled us to improve even his orchestrations.[48] Here too, however, aesthetic judgments vary; the modern principle of "respect for the text" sometimes leads us to go back to the original, or inspires other, possibly more respectful forms of "dusting off" the original scores. From the "purist" point of view, which—for different reasons—finds expression in the Goodmanian theory of notation, it is clear that performances which comply with posthumous revisions of this sort are simply not ("correct")[49] performances of the works in question; partially for that reason, Goodman's theory has been rather poorly received in the musical world, as is well known. It seems to me, however, that the debate is not well founded, or that it is only a quarrel over words: it would be enough for both parties to reach agreement about the meaning of "correct," and grant that a performance can be incorrect in the Goodmanian sense and yet better serve the work—as, for example, a correct performance of a successfully revised version can. Nothing prevents us from identifying a given performance (or score) with a label like "Schumann, *Rhenish Symphony,* Mahler revision," or even, if one feels it is necessary, "Schumann-Mahler," the way one says "Bach-Busoni."

48. See the chapter entitled "Le respect du texte: Faut-il retoucher les symphonies classiques?" in René Leibowitz, *Le compositeur et son double* (Paris: Gallimard, 1971).

49. I put "correct" in parentheses because, for Goodman, a performance of a given work that is not absolutely correct is simply not a performance of that work; "correct" is therefore simply a glaring pleonasm. Musicians (composers included), who know what the score is in this domain, correctly deduce that, on this definition, there are never *any* performances in this world. Once again, however, the quarrel is merely one of words, and Goodman is not the last (nor the first) to admit that an "incorrect" performance, in the Goodmanian sense, can "be better than a correct performance" (*Languages of Art,* p. 119–120). "Correct" is not exactly an aesthetic predicate.

I myself do not feel it is necessary, and I do not think that Mahler did either; for such an attribution gives a bit too much credit to the reviser.

A work its author considers finished at a given moment does not always see publication. Moreover, there exists a practice midway between publishing something and abandoning it to the "gnawing criticism of the mice," namely, "prepublication" in a journal (for example, *Madame Bovary* in the *Revue de Paris,* 1856-1857), in periodic "installments" (*David Copperfield,* 1849-1850), or as a newspaper serial; this last was, in the nineteenth century, a widespread form of publication practiced by many novelists, from Balzac to Zola, who did not, for all that, lapse into the genre of the "serialized novel."[50] Such prepublications, which often involve only selections or else are partially censored, give an author the opportunity to stand back and judge his work from a certain distance, weigh up the reaction to it, and, possibly, revise it for publication in book form. The resulting "variants" sometimes attest to significant reworking; this is true of certain poems by Mallarmé ("Futile Petition," "Summer Sadness," "The Beautiful Suicide Victoriously Fled"), both versions of which appear in the Pléiade edition.[51] Goethe took advantage of the staggered publication of his *Works* to bring the successive versions of his *Faust* before the public:[52] *Faust, a Fragment* in the seventh volume, in 1790; *Faust, a Tragedy* in the eighth volume (of a new edition of his collected works), in 1808; a draft of *Faust, Part II* in *Dichtung und Wahrheit,* in 1816; the Helen episode in 1827, in the fourth volume of a third collected edition; and other fragments in the twelfth volume, in 1828. The definitive version was to appear posthumously in 1832, in Volume 41. The publication, also staggered, of *Remembrance of Things Past* (even if it did not reach back far enough to encompass the *Ur-Remembrances* entitled *Jean Santeuil,* abandoned in 1899, and *On Art and Literature,* abandoned in 1908 and published for the most part posthumously)[53] gave rise to a phenomenon of a different sort. The *Swann's Way* published in 1913 was never to undergo

50. Lise Queffélec, *Le roman-feuilleton français au XIXe siècle* (Paris: PUF, 1989).
51. Other "first versions," just as provisionally definitive, went unpublished: for example, the first versions of "The Clown Chastised," "The Afternoon of a Faun," and "Sonnet in X."
52. With the exception of the 1775 *Urfaust,* which went unpublished until 1887.
53. Other works have the same ambiguous status (of a preliminary draft deliberately abandoned by the author in favor of a new version, but ultimately elevated to the status of a "work" by posterity, on the initiative of sensible editors). Among them are Joyce's *Stephen*

revision; however, the rest of the novel, which Proust then regarded as nearly complete, but which could not be printed until 1918 due to adverse circumstances, was, as is well known, augmented and revised. I do not think it would be entirely impossible to reconstitute the 1913 version of *Remembrance of Things Past* by excising these additions, to the extent that they can be identified; but I am by no means a die-hard advocate of the idea that this dubious operation should be pursued.[54]

The three versions of *The Temptation of St. Anthony* owe nothing to the process of prepublication, since the first two (with the exception of a few extracts from the second, published in *L'Artiste* in 1856) did not make their way into print until after Flaubert's death. These versions are thus matter for a genetic study, that is, a study focusing on the evolving states of a work prior to its publication—or, rather, they would be, were it not for the fact that their author considered first one and then the other to be definitive. The first, completed in 1849 and censored, as is well-known, by Louis Bouilhet and Maxime Du Camp, was reluctantly abandoned, then taken in hand for a revision that consisted essentially in cuts (from 591 to 193 pages); this yielded the second version, finished by 1856. Flaubert was dissuaded from publishing it by, again, external circumstances (the *Madame Bovary* trial). A third attempt to recast the text was undertaken in May 1869, after the publication of *The Sentimental Education;* in June 1872, it culminated in a third version (published in April 1874), which was, this time, different from the others in a positive sense—to put it in the received terms, to save time, the text was less dramatic in form and more philosophical in spirit. Thus it is probable that if Flaubert's friends had not dissuaded him from publishing the first version, he would not have set out to produce the second, and that if the second had been published on time, he would never have written the third. Probable, but not, after all, certain: *The Temptation* might also have met *Oberman(n)'s* fate. Today, at all events, we have at our disposal three markedly different versions whose operal

---

*Hero,* a fragment of a draft of the 1914 *Portrait of the Artist;* abandoned in 1907, it was posthumously published in 1944.

54. On the present state of the problems that editing *Remembrance of Things Past* poses—they seem to be growing more complex, rather than moving toward resolution—see the dossier "Proust, éditions et lectures," *Littérature* 88 (Dec. 1992).

unity no one, to my knowledge, contests (which is not the case with the two *Sentimental Educations*), and whose genealogy is such that no one can regard the first two versions as mere drafts of the third.[55] Thus we here find ourselves on the point of crossing the threshhold of the highly problematic, even suspect, category I will call genetic states.

## Genetic States

In theory, this category is by no means peculiar to allographic works, since every work has its genesis—even the most inspired, rapidly executed sketch is the result of a process, however brief. What makes it more difficult to observe the stages in the genesis of an autographic work is the fact that, in many instances, each stage effaces (drawing), covers (painting), or even destroys (carving) the previous one. But to cover, at least, is not quite to annihilate, especially in light of contemporary methods of investigation. The genesis of a pictorial work is therefore not completely inaccessible to observation after the fact; indeed, for several decades now, the cinema has in certain cases rendered it perfectly observable as it unfolds—witness Hans Namuth's and Paul Falkenberg's *Jackson Pollock* (1951), or Henri-Georges Clouzot's *The Picasso Mystery* (1956), among many other films. Even making full allowance for the influence of the observer on the observed, the latter movie, at least, enables us to compare, second by second, the successive states of a single work by looking at freeze-frames, and thus makes it possible to study, evaluate, and, possibly, deplore the compulsive process of transformation that leads from one state to another. I doubt that we have many equally instructive documents on the genesis of literary works at our disposal, but, theoretically, nothing prevents us from producing them.[56]

55. There exist, moreover, drafts of the first and third versions (the second being nothing more than a copy of the first, with certain passages struck). The three "definitive" versions may be found in vols. 8 and 9 of the "Club de l'honnête homme" edition of the *Œuvres complètes* (and elsewhere as well).

56. I mean that there is nothing to prevent a writer at work from allowing someone to film him for several hours, from erasure to erasure. Today we can produce a sort of artificial, approximative reconstitution of this sort of process (though not at actual speed) by simulating it on the computer screen after dating and transcribing handwritten corrections.

These very special conditions aside, the genesis of a pictorial work involves two modes of elaboration, commonly referred to as sketches [*esquisses*] and drafts [*ébauches*].[57] A sketch, let us recall, is a preliminary state (which may itself be preceded by drawings or partial studies) that is drawn on its own support and is physically independent; it later serves as a model (signal) for the final execution of a painting, and, in some cases, allows a client or patron to form a judgment of it.

Unless it is deliberately or accidentally destroyed, a sketch thus bears witness to the genesis of a painting, and may be compared (and sometimes preferred) to the final work; its physical and artistic status is identical to that of a rough draft [*brouillon*] in literature or music. *Ébauche* is the name given to a state of incompletion, whether temporary (work in progress)* or definitive, of something which was in principle destined to become the final work. An abandoned *ébauche* can very well constitute an artistic (or, at any rate, aesthetic) object in itself, but it bears witness to nothing but itself: it has the status, which it in some sense shares with that of the manuscripts of, say, *The Life of Henry Brulard* or *The Trial,* of an unfinished work. Nevertheless, an underdrawing [*ébauche*] detected under the final painting by means of X-rays does indeed bear witness to a state (a stage) that can be compared to the final state, like a preliminary sketch or a rough draft. Its relative inferiority is simply due to the fact that our access to it is precarious, but its documentary value, at least for specialists, is not diminished thereby, and is often crucial. I have not, however, forgotten that our present subject is not the documenta-ry value of sketches or the underdrawings brought to light by one or another technical device,[58] but, rather, their more or less legitimate contribution to the plurality of immanence of the works they pave the way for. This question of principle is posed in the same terms, physical and technical differences notwithstanding, in the case of allographic genetic states.

In literature, these states consist in what geneticists usually call "pre-texts," that is, the states of a text prior to the "final" text attested by a

57. [*Esquisse* is a more comprehensive term than "sketch"; thus oil sketches are also called *esquisses. Ébauche* is often translated "first draft," but can also be used to refer to what are called underdrawings in English.]

58. Including cinematic devices: the stages revealed by *The Picasso Mystery* are, typically, underdrawings.

first edition, or, if there is no first edition, the last handwritten or typed copy reviewed by the author (whether produced by the author or someone else): notes, plans, scenarios, "first drafts" [*ébauches*] in Zola's sense (scenarios written out in full), various rough drafts, and "fair copies" of intermediate states of a manuscript. These preliminary states have, materially speaking, the same status as an autographic *sketch* [*esquisse*] whenever the author, out of "physical abhorrence of the struck passage" (Le Clézio), prefers to correct his work by producing a new copy (of his own work), leaving the previous one as is.[59] They have the status of a draft [*ébauche*] whenever, in particular, he corrects his work by erasing words or passages where they stand, on the same page, which, in such cases, generally provides evidence of its evolution to the trained eye (or optical instruments) of the specialist.[60] Most writers utilize both procedures, like Flaubert or Proust: every state of one of their pages bears traces of several changes. Of course, dossiers on pre-texts are only available in the case of authors who keep their rough drafts for the record or the edification of posterity; this is a very recent practice that does not go back much further than the beginning of the nineteenth century.[61] Hugo, Flaubert, Zola, Proust, and Valéry are thus, for the moment, the major (French) suppliers of "modern manuscripts" (though Hugo's are not exactly rough drafts[62]). The Balzacian pre-text consists above all in corrected galleys (as many as fourteen sets in the case of *César Birotteau*);

59. This is apparently also the case with Giraudoux and Christa Wolf: see Almuth Grésillon, *Les manuscrits modernes: Éléments de critique génétique* (Paris: PUF, 1994). When an author, in his "abhorrence of the struck passage," goes to the extreme of destroying the previous version, nothing remains, obviously, of this vanished "sketch" except, sometimes, indirect testimony; but the "sketch" as such has nevertheless existed.

60. If I am not mistaken, Kafka proceeded, as often as he could, in particularly maniacal fashion; he tortured the "wrong" word until it had been transformed (correction by "writing over" a word) into the "right" one—as we all occasionally do at the level of a single letter. Emblematically: the *ich* of *The Castle* transformed into *er* or *K.* See Gresillon, *Les manuscrits.*

61. Earlier autograph manuscripts which have been preserved or rediscovered, like that of *Rameau's Nephew* or Saint-Simon's *Mémoirs,* are final versions, as is the manuscript of the *Decameron,* the only important literary autograph (with drawings and corrections) that has come down to us from the Middle Ages (see Paul Zumthor, *La lettre et la voix* [Paris: Seuil, 1987], pp. 141 and 166). Rough drafts in the true sense are, here, drafts of unfinished works, like the manuscript of Pascal's *Pensées,* which is, again, unique—though we know that, in the case of the *Pensées,* this has by no means precluded a formidable posthumous plurality, due to variations in the order of presentation. I will come back to this point.

62. See Jean Gaudon, "De la poésie au poème: Remarques sur les manuscrits poétiques de Victor Hugo," *Genesis* 2 (1992): 81–100.

Stendhal, classic in this regard, left only manuscripts of his unfinished works, which are, it is true, numerous and crucially important *(Lucien Leuwen, Henry Brulard, Lamiel)*. But it seems that contemporary writers—for reasons I will come back to—have followed the lead of Louis Aragon, who bequeathed all his manuscripts to the CNRS[63] for study; this promises to create a considerable number of further opportunities for comparison,[64] until the—most probably[65] negative—effects of writing with word processing programs begin to make themselves felt.

For genetic specialists, from whom our knowledge of these states necessarily derives, their publication is little more than a by-product of the basic task, which is to decode, transcribe, date, and reconstruct (as far as possible) the genetic process, and then, possibly, to interpret it in critical and theoretical terms. Moreover, in presenting this by-product, the specialists are often torn between rigorously "establishing" texts and publishing them in readable, or even attractive and easily accessible form. Evidently, it is these somewhat artificial productions—like the famous "new version" of *Madame Bovary* proposed quite some time ago by Jean Pommier and Gabrielle Leleu,[66] or the many "sketches" in the new Pléiade edition of *Remembrance of Things Past*—which interest us here, since they alone offer the public (often illusory) access to something like an "unpublished first version."

In their most authentic forms, these "versions" are generally partial or fragmentary: it is quite rare for a genetic dossier to produce a complete, continuous text like that of the first *Temptation,* which, as we have seen, is not exactly a "pre-text," but a "definitive" text called into question, and put back on the drawing board, after it was "finished." The *Mémoires de ma vie* in three books, written by Chateaubriand between 1812 and 1822, provides an example of an authentic, continuous initial version, but it corrresponds to only the first twelve books (down to 1800) of the future *Mémoires d'outre-tombe*[67] (whose evolution to 1847

63. [Centre national de la recherche scientifique, a state-funded research institute.]
64. To say nothing of the practice, famously illustrated by Francis Ponge, of publishing dossiers on the genesis of a work during the author's lifetime: see *La Fabrique du pré* (Skira, 1971), or *Comment une figue de paroles et pourquoi* (Flammarion, 1977).
65. But not necessarily: an author can keep each successive state of a work on disk, no matter how often and how heavily it has been revised.
66. Corti, 1949; out of print, and, to date, not reprinted.
67. The two texts are available for comparison in the first volume of the edition prepared by Jean-Claude Berchet (Classiques Garnier, Bordas, 1989).

is, moreover, quite complex, and has given rise to several very different versions since 1850). These disinterred states usually reveal, above
all, changes in form, whether stylistic or structural: cuts, additions, and
changes in the order of episodes. More rarely, they testify to decisive
thematic revisions, the most spectacular I know of being the last-minute
substitution, made at Bulwer Lytton's suggestion, of a happy end* for
the original sad ending of *Great Expectations* (in which Pip is not reunited with Estella).[68] The most massive divergence has come about
as the result, not of a multiplicity of authorial versions in the proper
sense, but of an unfinished state and uncertainty as to the order in
which to put the fragments left by an author at his death. I have in
mind, of course, Pascal's *Pensées:* since 1662, editors have been hesitat-
ing between adopting the "objective" order in which the "packets" of
these fragments were found, the conjectural order of the *Apology for the
Christian Religion* of which they were very probably intended to be a
"precursor", and a "logical" order based on a purely thematic classification by subject, this last arrangement being by definition arbitrary, and
varying with the editor doing the classifying. I will not venture into this
labyrinth, whose last twist and turn we have yet to see, as everybody
knows; certain is that, even if the "material" remains exactly the same
from one edition to the next,[69] differences in the way it is arranged give
rise to as many different *texts,* in the etymological sense of the word.
The inevitable quotation: "Let no one say that I have said nothing new;
the arrangement of the subject is new .... Words differently arrranged
have a different meaning, and meanings differently arranged have different effects."[70] The same observation holds, on a different scale, for
vaster ensembles like *The Human Comedy* or Hugo's complete works.[71]

68. 1860; the original ending was adopted in 1937, for a limited edition, by George Bernard
Shaw, who introduced it, perversely enough, as the *"real* happy end."
69. This does not preclude many conflicting readings of the manuscript. Some are famous,
like the "armed troops [*troupes*]" of the king, long distorted into "armed fat red faces [*trognes*]":
at least those who are sure that "troops" is the correct reading take "fat red faces" to be a distortion. The question is, of course, beyond my competence.
70. Ms. 431, 225 [tr. *Pensées,* in *The Provincial Letters, Pensées, Scientific Treatises,* trans. W. F. Trot-
ter (Chicago: Encyclopedia Britannica, 1952), p. 175].
71. In Hugo's case, the Jean Massin edition (Club français du Livre, 1967) has adopted, whenever possible, the chronological order of composition, breaking up collections of poetry published in Hugo's lifetime. As to *The Human Comedy,* the most respectful arrangement of which
is the one made by le Furne and later emended, there exists at least one chronological edition (Roland Chollet, Rencontres, 1958–1962), and another which follows the historical order
of the subject-matter (Albert Béguin–Jean-A. Ducourneau, Formes et Reflets, 1950–1953).

The problematic nature of these effects of plurality, induced by unearthing and exploiting genetic states, does not only have to do with the arbitrary choices or the compromises between readability and authenticity inherent in their mode of presentation—the modern taste[72] for the fragmentary and the unfinished, disorder and variation, which guarantees the success of these publications, might well bring the public to put up with ever more faithful forms of presentation, or even to take a somewhat perverse pleasure in their inevitably rebarbative nature. The more serious objection to the effects of plurality so created turns on the fact that such "versions," whether continuous or fragmentary, neat or unkempt, were, for their authors, nothing more than preliminary states which had not yet been invested with a truly operal function, and accordingly did not constitute true objects of immanence in their eyes. To treat them as versions is therefore clearly a betrayal or high-handed violation of the author's intention, which defines the status of the work.

But this founding or legitimizing intention is not always certain. When an artist leaves a manuscript, painting, or sculpture behind, whether at his death or in order to turn to another work, he does not attach a certificate to it attesting that it is finished or unfinished, so that posterity will not be left in doubt as to its intentional status: thus it is not entirely certain how Picasso regarded, from this standpoint, *Les Demoiselles d'Avignon.*[73] Similarly, the artist's intention is not always definitive: the example of works that are revised, sometimes very heavily, after being published or exhibited, makes this obvious. The artist's "final intention" is never anything more than the most recent to date, and we have seen that even scholarly editions often do not consider themselves bound by it. Hence it is not surprising that the public, whose reception of works is bound by fewer scruples, has tended to throw off the shackles of so fallible a criterion.

72. Modern in a rather broad sense, for, if it is pronounced in our day, it goes back at least as far as German Romanticism.

73. All that can be said with certainty about this subject is that, after a long, turbulent period of gestation, the picture was shown in the fall of 1907 to friends who expressed rather negative judgments of it, with the exception of Uhde and Kahnweiler. Picasso thereupon put it aside and did not touch it again, either because he considered it already finished, or because he deemed it unworthy of being finished—until 1923, when Jacques Doucet bought it on André Breton's advice.

The sometimes naive promotion, in the France of the 1970s, of the notion of *text* at the expense of that of *work* was both a sign of and factor in this emancipation. The "formalist" gutting of authorial intention, taken to the extreme of the symbolic murder of the author,[74] and the "structuralist" valorization of the autonomy of the text both militate in favor of treating genetic materials as full-fledged literary objects, in the name of the irrefutable, obvious fact that a pre-text is also a text. The somewhat mythical "closure of the text" thus paradoxically ends up authorizing the concept of the "open work,"[75] whose genetic mutability is one aspect among others. This concept once again places the work—as understood here—beyond (or above) the plurality of texts of all kinds and of widely varying status which the work gathers up and federates under the aegis of a wider, and, in this sense, transcendent unity.

We could devise other terms to describe this paradigm shift, which, to repeat, goes back, by subterranean paths, to Romanticism and its cult of the fragment: aesthetic judgment is free to fasten upon any object whatsoever, whether natural or man-made: for example, an amorphous rough outline, a chaotic draft, a fragment of a sentence, a mutilated or rough-hewn block of marble,[76] a chance assemblage, an "exquisite corpse," automatic writing, or an Oulipian[77] production. But a "simple" aesthetic object, whenever it is also a human artifact, always suggests the presence of an aesthetic intention—rightly or wrongly, and generally in such a way as to make it impossible to decide (who can say whether the "beauty" we find in an anvil or harness is fortuitous or deliberate?). That suggestion, legitimate or not, can invest it with an

---

74. Roland Barthes, "La mort de l'auteur" (1968), in *Le bruissement de la langue* (Paris: Seuil, 1984), 61–68 [tr. "The Death of the Author," in *The Rustle of Language,* trans. Richard Howard (New York: Hill and Wang, 1986, pp. 49–55)] and "De l'œuvre au texte" (1971), in *Le bruissement de la langue* (Paris: Seuil, 1984), pp. 69–78 [tr. "From Work to Text," in *The Rustle of Language,* trans. Richard Howard (New York: Hill and Wang, 1986, pp. 56–64)]. The first and most famous attack on the relevance of authorial intention is that of Monroe C. Beardsley and William K. Wimsatt, "The Intentional Fallacy," *Sewanee Review* 54 (1946): 468–487, also in *The Verbal Icon* (Lexington: University of Kentucky Press, 1954), chapter 1.

75. Umberto Eco, *The Open Work* (1962), trans. Anna Cancogni (N.p.: Hutchinson Radius, 1989).

76. A familiar filiation, at once obvious and paradoxical, links a surviving fragment like *The Belvedere Torso* with the skilful *non finito* of a Michelangelo, and, bridging four centuries, a Rodin.

77. [See Chap. 7, n. 4.]

artistic function, thus making it the object (or one of the objects) of immanence of a work.

## Mutability

Oral "literature" (recited or sung), transmitted by bards, minstrels, and other popular storytellers, is marked by another kind of multiplicity, which stems from the share of improvisation[78] each performer brings to it. In this mode of transmission, as Menendez Pidal has said of the *chanson de geste,* every work "lives on variants" and revisions.[79] The scribal tradition exemplified by the manuscripts published in the Middle Ages extends this constitutive variability to writing, not only in consequence of the inevitable "errors" of transcription, multiplied by the precarious conditions of collective dictation in the scriptorium, but also because these manuscripts, in the case of the most "oral" vernacular genres (*chansons de geste,* beast epics, fables, and drama—novels are not entirely excluded from this category[80]), are often mere adjuncts (and, for us, witnesses) to the oral tradition, like the famous "minstrels' manuscripts," of which the illustrious Oxford manuscript of *The Song of Roland* may well be an example. The minstrel's license to improvise is thus bequeathed to the scribe, who "inflects" in his manner a text that is a bit his and a bit someone else's. Thus a work like *The Song of Roland* has come down to us in the form of at least seven texts, widely differing in date (from the beginning of the twelfth to the fourteenth century), dialect ("French," Anglo-Norman, Venitian), versification (from assonance to rhyme), and thematic inflection (from the epic to the novelistic); the critical methods of classical philology have failed in their attempts to assign a reductive genealogy to all these forms. Along with other "neo-traditionalists,"[81] Paul Zumthor has been an enthusiastic,

---

78. When this "share" expands to take up the whole of a performance, we once again find ourselves in the autographic regime; the work then consists, theoretically, in this unique, unparalleled performance. Clearly, however, such a situation is purely hypothetical, since pure improvisation is a purely imaginary notion.

79. Ramon Menéndez Pidal, *La chanson de Roland et la tradition épique des Francs,* trans. I. M. Cluzel (Paris: Picard, 1960).

80. Zumthor, *La lettre et la voix.*

81. See, among other works, Bernard Cerquiglini, *Éloge de la variante: Histoire critique de la philologie* (Paris: Seuil, 1989), which concludes that computer inscriptions, "an always tran-

eloquent commentator on this "mutability of the text" (I would be more inclined to say "of the work," which undergoes mutation from one text to the next); I can do no better than quote the following passage by him to characterize it:

> The term *work* cannot, therefore, be understood in its modern sense. It refers, however, to something that undoubtedly had real existence, as a complex but easily recognizable entity, made up of the sum of material witnesses to current versions. These were the synthesis of signs used by successive "authors" (singers, reciters, scribes) and of the text's own existence in the letter. The form—meaning nexus thus generated is thereby constantly called in question. The work is fundamentally unstable. Properly speaking it has no end; it merely accepts to come to an end, at a given point, for whatever reasons. The work exists outside and hierarchically above its textual manifestations, as schematized in the accompanying diagram.

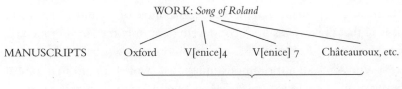

WORK: *Song of Roland*

MANUSCRIPTS    Oxford    V[enice]4    V[enice] 7    Châteauroux, etc.

TEXTS: the *Songs of Roland*

> It will be understood that I do not mean by this to indicate the archetype of a chronological stemma. We are dealing with something existing on a different plane. Thus conceived the work is dynamic by definition. It grows, changes, and decays. The multiplicity and diversity of texts that bear witness to it are like special effects within the system.[82]

---

sitory record," as read on the screen, "an ephemeral visualization" (p. 115), are the forms of publication best adapted to the constitutive variability of texts of this type. This neo- (in this case, very neo-) traditionalism provides unmistakable evidence of the same paradigm shift that the recent valorization of pre-texts bears witness to.

82. Paul Zumthor, *Essai de poétique médiévale* (Paris: Seuil, 1972), p. 73 [tr. *Toward a Medieval Poetics,* trans. Philip Bennett (Minneapolis: University of Minnesota Press, 1992), pp. 47–48]. Obviously, what Zumthor here calls "manifestation" is what I call "immanence"; but it so happens that, in the scribal regime, every manuscript is simultaneously an object of immanence (one of the "texts") and of manifestation (its unique instance). Just as obviously, what Zumthor calls "multiplicity and diversity" is what I have christened "plurality."

As will have been noticed, this exemplary case is also an extreme one, since plurality of immanence is here combined with a plurality of authors, validated, as it were, by the abiding anonymity of works of this type—or our uncertainty as to their attribution, which is epitomized by the controversy over whether Homer actually existed. Unlike the cases evoked earlier, the operal unity of *The Song of Roland,* for example, is not even founded on the authorial identity unifying the three *Oberman(n)s* or the three *Temptations,* but simply on a "community" of themes and a sense of the continuity of a tradition which assures us that each reciter and/or scribe himself felt that he was following (with a certain license) in the footsteps of a predecessor, whose work he was carrying on. These criteria are obviously shaky, and their legitimacy entirely a matter of custom. There is, after all, a community of themes from Sophocles to Corneille and from Corneille to Cocteau in that other kind of tradition constituted by hypertextual series; yet we hardly consider gathering up all these *Oedipuses* in the unity of a single, pluritextual work. The (supposed) continuity of an oral tradition, or a scribal tradition still close to the oral, is, perhaps, a more reliable guarantee of the unity of a work; it is all that prevents us from considering not only the "medieval epic," but *The Song of Roland* itself as nothing more than a *genre* in which each text represents an autonomous individual (work). Yet, from a logical point of view, there is a good deal to be said for treating such works as genres. I will come back to this point in a moment.

## Performances

As we saw above, works of performance consist in events that are, strictly speaking, unique and noniterable. But, since performances, even if they are largely improvised, like jazz variations, are nearly always performances of execution, the continuity of the work performed or the theme which undergoes variation encourages us to compare successive realizations, which we treat as so many versions of the same pluri-occurential work, called "Gérard Philipe's Rodrigo," "Maria Callas's Violetta," or "Charlie Parker's *Lover Man.*" The fact that duration of persistence is not a feature of this type of work, at once autographic and ephemeral, makes observations of this kind somewhat conjectural ("his timbre has grown darker," "he's playing it more briskly than yesterday," etc.), except when they are based on the kind of indirect testimony that has been provided, from the beginning of the twentieth century, by the "reproductions" constituted by recordings, films, or audiovisual materials. These make it possible for anyone to appreciate the differences between two interpretations of the *Winterreise* by Fischer-Dieskau, two renditions of the *Ninth Symphony* by Karajan, or two successive takes of *Koko,* from a single session, by the "Charlie Parker Reboppers."[83] For those less alert to this kind of "mutability," certain comparative radio or television programs, like the late lamented Sunday show *Tribune des critiques de disques* [Record Critics' Forum], might make instructive listening. Here again, there is no need to point out that the success of certain "integral" jazz recordings (all the takes of a single session), which are increasingly common, and, all in all, increasingly serious, and which were soon christened the *"Pléiades* of jazz," bear witness to the paradigm shift we have already repeatedly mentioned. (It will have been gathered that I am not only describing this shift, but am also helping make it.) In this sense as in many others, modern (and postmodern) aesthetic sensibilities have shown themselves to be typically pluralistic. By way of contrast—a bit sophistical, perhaps—let me recall that Greek tragedies, in the fifth and fourth century, were performed *only once.*

## Between Work and Genre

In diverse forms diversely legitimized by authorial intention, all these instances of plural immanence confront us with works whose identity transcends the diversity of the material or ideal objects they immanate in. This mode of transcendence is not relevant to *all* works, because there exist works, whether autographic, like the *View of Delft,* or allographic, like *The Princess of Clèves,*[84] whose object of immanence is unique— though that does not, as we will see, put them beyond the reach of other

---

83. New York, 26 November 1945, Savoy Records, 5853–1 and 5853–2.

84. The uniqueness of immanence of allographic works is less absolute than that of autographic works, for one would be hard put to find a text that has no variants whatsoever. For better or for worse, *The Princess of Clèves,* to the best of my knowledge, illustrates this poorly represented category.

factors of transcendence. But this mode is not at all rare, and the works which fall entirely outside its purview do so only because of the nonexistence or disappearance, intentional or not, of their preliminary states.

Such a description, be it recalled, by no means commands the consent of all theoreticians of art—if it did, there would have been no need to advance it. As we have seen, Nelson Goodman, in particular, refuses to treat transcriptions (and hence, doubtless, transpositions as well) as versions of the same musical work, or translations as versions of the same literary work; he affirms that the identity between work and text is absolute. As regards music, his position is only apparently nuanced by the fact that he does not directly identify a work with its score, but with the compliance-class of its performances, for this is only to make the same identification indirectly. For Goodman, optional differences among several correct performances (for example, differences in tempo or expression) do not affect the identity of the work. They do not for me either, of course; this point is not at issue. The disagreement turns on whether we should accept or reject the idea that a musical work can encompass several distinct (ideal) scores, or a literary work several distinct texts.[85]

I certainly do not underestimate the advantages of this strictly nominalist or empiricist position, which eliminates the concept of transcendence, doubtless nebulous for some, and the entity, which the same people apparently have no use for, represented by a work distinct, however slightly, from the (unique or multiple) material objects that manifest it. Despite the neatness of the principle it rests on, however, this position seems to me to be logically uncertain and untenable in practice.

Uncertain, because it must break down into three options it has no means of choosing among. The first consists in affirming that Chardin produced only one *Saying Grace,* the first, that Flaubert produced only one *Temptation of Saint Anthony,* the first, etc., and that the other versions are merely copies or transcriptions of this one; neither the fact that they are the artist's own work nor the existence of all manner of variants modifies their minor (nonoperal) status. The second alternative consists in arguing, conversely, that the first *Saying Grace* (or the first two, etc.) and the first *Temptation* (or the first two, etc.) are merely sketches preliminary to the final state, which alone deserves to be called a work. The

---

85. I do not think Goodman says anything about the case of autographic replicas, but, to be consistent, he would have to be equally negative on this point.

third alternative is to say that Chardin or Flaubert produced several works that bear the same name, yet are distinct, as Cézanne's various *Mont Sainte-Victoire*s or Flaubert's two *Sentimental Education*s really are.[86] Over and above this uncertainty, this position seems to me to be in contradiction with the fact that Goodman admits the multiple nature of works of printmaking or cast sculpture. Here too, the nominalist position should be that each print or cast is a distinct work, or else that the model or plate is the only authentic work, and its proofs/casts merely reproductions derived by imprint. As we know, Goodman never even entertains the possibility of describing matters this way; I suppose he is prevented from doing so by his (justified) respect for ordinary usage, which treats the casts/prints as the "ultimate products," and therefore the true works, while regarding the models or plates as transitory stages in the process of production leading up to them.

It seems to me, however, that the very same ordinary usage also requires us to acknowledge the plurality of immanence of works with versions, whose "history of production," moreover (except in the case of works belonging to an oral or manuscript tradition and possessing collective plurality), benefits more from the authorial guarantee than does that of works multiplied by imprint through the—possibly suspect—labors of a craftsman. In my view, it is this departure from the common usage of the world of art which makes the nominalist position untenable. Cultural consensus quite clearly treats *Saying Grace, The Temptation of Saint Anthony, Petrushka,* and (today) even *The Song of Roland,* not as groups of works bearing the same title or as chronological series of states only one of which (which one?) is the work, but rather as distinct works with several versions: we have only to consult our card catalogues, monographs, or collections of complete works to convince ourselves of the fact. And a theory of works that does not account for the customary assumptions of the world of art is, to the extent that it does not, invalid. To be sure, the notion of a work with plural immanence is a mental construct, a bizarre entity one would like to be able to do without, on the principle of Ockham's razor. But ordinary usage is also a fact, and it lays down certain requirements quite as much as other facts do.

86. Though in very different ways, for the *Sainte-Victoire*s have the same "motif," which we can hardly say (or can say only very loosely) about the two *Education*s.

Respecting ordinary usage does not, however, free us of the oblig-ation to inquire into its criteria, or, simply, its motives. In the present case, it seems to me that the criteria of operal identity—that is, the mo-tives which induce prevailing usage to regroup a certain number of nonidentical objects and call them "the same work"[87]—are of several different kinds, none sufficient by itself. Among other such motives, we might mention thematic identity of the sort that unites, respectively, the various *Saying Graces*, the three *Temptations of Saint Anthony*, or *War and Peace* in Russian and French, but is absent from the two *Sentimental Edu-cations*;[88] identity of mode, whose absence makes us loath to attribute operal unity to the novel *Gervaise* and the play, or to the novel *Man's Hope* and the film (the slight difference in their titles indicates the dif-ference in medium clearly enough[89]); in music, identity of melodic, rhythmic, or harmonic structure, of the sort that persists after tran-scription or transposition; genetic identity, which makes the two ver-sions of *The Cid* one work (same author), but not *The Cid* by Corneille and *Mocedades del Cid* by Guillen de Castro (different authors), or which, again, unites two *Saying Graces* (copies by the original artist) but not two *Mont Sainte-Victoires* (beginning afresh with the same motif); or, finally, in the absence of these motives and under the conditions specified ear-lier, the continuity of the oral-scribal tradition that is assumed to make the various *Songs of Roland* a single work, but not the *Oedipus* by Voltaire and that by Corneille.

I have doubtless left out some of the relevant criteria, but little mat-ter (here): plainly, none of these criteria has anything of the absolute

87. Autographic replicas are not identical either with respect to their specific identity, since they exhibit perceptible differences, or their numerical identity, since every painting or sculp-ture is a distinct physical object. Allographic versions, which are ideal objects, do not, let me recall, have a numerical identity—or else, but this comes down to the same thing, their numerical identity is exhaustively defined by their specific identity (sameness of spelling)*, which is different for each of them.

88. This exclusion plainly implies that "thematic identity" is to be understood in a strong sense; stronger, at any rate, than the (vague) thematic kinship one can of course find in the two *Sen-timental Educations*, but also, just as easily (or with just as much strain), between those two works and *Madame Bovary*, or, by moving along a chain of associations, between any X and Y. A long critical study would be required to justify distinctions of this sort, established in common usage "by approximation"—which does not mean by chance.

89. [In French, *L'espoir* and *Espoir*.]

about it, and even less (so to speak) of the absolutely legitimate.[90] They are eminently gradualistic and elastic. (Where does thematic identity end? If the third *Temptation* is "less dramatic" than the other two, does it still belong to the same mode? Where does the line between the last version and the first hypertext lie, between the Venice *Roland* and Boiardo's *Orlando*[91] *innamorato?*). They are also highly susceptible to modification and evolution: we have seen to what extent changes in aesthetic paradigm have influenced the public's *operal tolerance,* by which I mean the capacity of one generation to treat as a version of a work what the preceding generation would perhaps have regarded as a mere genetic document, or even simply tossed into the waste basket. Conversely, however, a circumstance like the decline in the number of amateur concerts, and our familiarity with professional performances, more accessible thanks to records and the radio, have made us less tolerant of certain transpositions or transcriptions carried out for convenience' sake (Schubert's *Impromptu* transposed into G, the overture to *Tannhäuser* transcribed for piano for four hands), just as progress in photographic reproduction has made us more critical of hand-drawn copies.

If this borderline is fuzzy and unstable, the reason is doubtless that we have already crossed another, firmer and sharper, in passing from works with unique immanence (the *Mona Lisa, The Princess of Clèves,* the *Jupiter* Symphony) or multiple immanence *(Melancholia, The Thinker)* to works with plural immanence. The second borderline, of a logical kind, is the one that lies between an individual and a *class*—or, as one usually says in talking about art, a "genre." A work with unique immanence, as we have seen, is exhaustively and exclusively identified with a physical or ideal individual. A multiple (autographic) work is in fact a unique work whose multiplication by imprint in limited quantities is accepted as legitimate by the world of art. An allographic work, be it recalled, is multiple only on the level of its manifestations, not its immanence. In contrast, a work with plural immanence is identifed with a group or series of perceptibly distinct individuals, which, taken together,

90. But "inquiring into" these criteria does not oblige us to justify them: common usage is its own legitimation, simply by virtue of being common usage. We can only try to reconstruct the motives behind it.

91. [The French title is *Roland amoureux.*]

obviously make up a class. The identity of such a work is therefore that of a class, and constitutes what can be called—in contradistinction to the numerical identity of a physical individual and the specific identity of an ideal individual—*generic identity*. And, somewhat as[92] the numerical identity of a physical object transcends, as we will see, the plurality of its successive specific identities, so the generic identity of a class transcends the plurality of the specific identities of its members. A work like the *Mona Lisa* or the *Jupiter* Symphony, considered identical to a unique object of immanence, is an individual. *Saying Grace* or *The Song of Roland*, inasmuch as it is identical to a group of objects of immanence (paintings or texts), is a class; each of its objects of immanence is a member, or—to admit a term we refused to apply to instances of manifestation—an *exemplum* of this class. An instance or copy, as we have seen, is not an "exemplum" of its type, because only a class can be exemplified, and because a type is not a class; in contrast, an object of immanence of a plural work is clearly an exemplum—though it would certainly be preferable to call it a *member*—of the class (of objects of immanence) which constitutes this work. A copy (token*) of *The Charterhouse of Parma* is not "a *Charterhouse of Parma*" except in the figurative sense, by ellipsis or metonymy; but a *text* (type) of *The Song of Roland*, like the text of the Oxford manuscript (not the manuscript itself), is "a *Song of Roland*" in the literal sense: it is a member of the class of texts that constitutes *The Song of Roland*, a plural work which consists in the whole set of its texts, *their differences included*. (One would never say, except unthinkingly, that *The Charterhouse of Parma* consists in the whole set of its copies, their differences included.) The *Saying Grace* in the Hermitage is literally a *Saying Grace*, the two in the Louvre are literally two others. Neither *The Song of Roland* nor *Saying Grace* can, then, be described as individuals, or logically ultimate entities, as the *Mona Lisa* or *The Charterhouse of Parma* can; and what is not an individual can only be a class. In a previous chapter, I emended the term megatype, proposed by Stevenson, to *archetype*; this term obviously only applies to works (allographic by definition) whose diverse objects of immanence are types. Let us be more precise: *The Song of Roland* or *The Temptation of Saint Anthony*, works with several texts, are (inevitably) *archetexts*.

92. This "somewhat as" is very approximate, for these two cases do not involve the same form of transcendence.

The use (here legitimate) of this term, which I once applied, rather infelicitously,[93] to arche-operal categories, such as literary "genres" in the prevailing sense, indicates that the (onto)logical mode of existence of plural works is analogous to that of genres. Genres, in literature as in all the other arts, are classes of works (among other such classes)[94] which conveniently group works, some of which in turn group objects of immanence. The difference between these two kinds of groupings is that the criteria for operal groups are stricter (albeit fluctuating) than are those for generic groups. But, all in all, a work with plural immanence is a subgenre (a species) in a logical hierarchy that stretches, for example, from an individual (the Oxford text of *The Song of Roland*), through a species *(The Sons of Roland),* an historical genre (the *chanson de geste*), a "theoretical" (Todorov) or "analogical" (Schaeffer) genre (the epic), to still broader genres: poem, narrative, literary work, work of art, artifact, thing of this or of some other world. Quite obviously, in this hierarchy of concentric circles, the only logically defined limit is the one that runs between the individual and the first inclusive class. All the rest is a slippery slope, and the only landmarks are those established by usage.[95] In short, a work with plural immanence is, logically, a genre usage has decided to treat as a work, for one or another reason of which usage is sole judge. Nelson Goodman, whose ontology is apparently a kind of nominalism tempered by cheek, is happy to say[96] that he means to recognize only individuals, but that he reserves the right to take anything whatsoever (that is to say, necessarily, classes as well) as an individual.

93. This choice of words (Gérard Genette, *Introduction à l'architexte* (Paris: Seuil, 1979) [tr. *The Architext,* trans. Jane E. Lewin (Berkeley: Quantum Books, University of California Press, 1992)], obviously inspired by the valorization, common at the time I was writing, of the text over the work, was infelicitous, because what I in fact had in mind in making it were genres (among other things) considered as arche-works—I had not yet realized that certain works are already archetexts in the proper sense. But, as it happens, the term was not absolutely incorrect, since an arche-work is, a fortiori, an archetext.

94. Among other such classes: but the class of poems starting with A, or musical compositions with an A-sharp in the first measure, or paintings measuring 4' by 8', though just as pertinent as any other (everything is pertinent, the only question is to what) is not ordinarily considered a genre, because its defining criterion is not ordinarily to be found among the criteria which, however heterogeneous and traditional they may be, define genres.

95. The same cannot be said about the classifications of the naturalists, which are based on objective (biological) criteria.

96. See, for example, Nelson Goodman, *Of Mind and Other Matters* (Cambridge: Harvard University Press, 1984), p. 52.

In this sense, ordinary usage is very Goodmanian\*, since a work is, in this case, a class it treats as an individual.

This logical peculiarity may explain, in passing, a paradox pertaining to the "ontology" of works, which Goodman points out, rather elliptically, but on two or three occasions.[97] At issue is the existence of works which belong neither to the autographic nor to the allographic regime, because their "work identity" has not been established: for example (but Goodman mentions no other examples), musical works prescribed by a "non-notational" system that does not suffice to define their "transitive identity." Transitive identity is clearly the syntactic identity common to all correct copies of a text or score, an identity that a non-notational score is too imprecise to define. Involved here, then, are works which would belong to the allographic regime if they were prescribed with sufficient precision, but which, as things now stand, do not belong to it—yet which cannot be said to belong to the autographic regime either, since their identification does not depend on their "history of production," as does that of a painting or sculpture.

Jean-Marie Schaeffer[98] rightly draws a parallel between this case—which is, for the moment, clearly an exception—and that of literary works with plural immanence, like *The Song of Roland,* whose operal unity is thematic, and defined by a common "narrative framework." (I would be inclined to add "or a common dramatic framework," as in the case of the different versions of *Tête-d'or,* but it is doubtless enough to take "narrative" in the broad sense.) The case of musical works is analogous, mutatis mutandis: the operal unity of transposed works, for example, tends to be defined by a common *structural* framework, which standard notation is too precise to account for, because it necessarily specifies pitch; to indicate this common structure by way of a notation, it would, therefore, be necessary to have recourse to a looser system, which Goodman would describe as "non-notational." But the "insuf-

97. Nelson Goodman, *Problems and Projects* (Indianapolis: Bobbs-Merrill, 1972), p. 83, a paragraph included in the French translation of *Languages of Art,* p. 156, and illustrated in the latter, p. 227, by a diagram borrowed from John Cage. Another version of this paragraph is to be found in *Of Mind and Other Matters,* p. 139.
98. Jean-Marie Schaeffer, "Nelson Goodman en poéticien: Trois esquisses." *Cahiers du Musée national de l'art moderne,* no. 41 (Fall 1992).

ficience of identification" which he mentions also characterizes, in the autographic regime, pictorial works with replicas, whose identity is similarly defined by a common thematic and/or formal "framework."

It can be seen, then, that the apparently marginal status of musical works with "non-notational" scores merely constitutes a particular instance of what is in fact the pervasive category of works whose immanence is plural and whose identity cannot, as a result, be other than generic. Such works are, *in this sense,* neither autographic nor allographic, because only an individual can be autographic, when it is a thing or physical event, or allographic, when it is a "type," or ideal individual. The reason is that the distinction autographic/allographic discriminates, not between regimes of operality, but between regimes of immanence—except, of course, when a work, like the *View of Delft* or *The Princess of Clèves,* is exclusively and exhaustively identified with a single object of immanence. In all other cases, the identity of the work transcends that of its objects of immanence; it is generic, in the broad sense, that is, not only ideal, but abstract. It is easy to understand why a nominalist philosopher like Goodman regards such identity as spectral, and prefers to say that the identity of such a work has simply not been established, since, for him, identity is always individual. For him, then, such a work does not *exist*—which means, of course, that the status of work can be attributed only to each of its replicas, versions, or states: to each of its objects of immanence. If, on the other hand, and in conformity with (prevailing) usage, we regard such a group of objects as *one* work, it goes without saying that its identity is generic—and therefore *open:* if, tomorrow, someone discovered (there is nothing fantastic about this hypothesis) a "new" text of *The Song of Roland,* this discovery would not in any way modify the status of *The Song of Roland* as a class—except as far as the number of its members and the list of their properties was concerned. If, however, someone discovered a new (authentic) text of *The Princess of Clèves* (in which, say, the princess marries Monsieur de Nemours after the death of her husband), this new individual could not "be integrated" into the old one; to incorporate it, we would have to attribute a new (onto)logical status to *The Princess of Clèves*—it would no longer have the status of an individual work, but rather that of a generic, that is, plural work.

This type of transcendence, transcendence through plurality of immanence, is thus ultimately very easy to define—indeed, almost disappointingly so. Works with plural immanence are transcendent in the sense that they do not immanate where one might suppose they do, somewhat (and with good reason[99]) the way the "conceptual" work does not immanate in the object that manifests it. A work with plural immanence does not "consist" in each of its objects of immanence, but in their totality—a totality whose definition is established, or rather *modulated,* by ordinary usage alone.

99. A conceptual work (or one deemed conceptual) is indeed, as the name indicates, defined by a concept, and plural either in fact (Duchamp's ready-mades in several copies) or at least in theory: a work defined by "exhibiting a bottlerack" can undergo any number of realizations, not necessarily identical; changing the model in no way changes the "act." The sole limit lies in the functional ("aesthetic") tedium caused by repeating the procedure.

# CHAPTER 12

# Partial Manifestations

T HE SECOND MODE OF TRANSCENDENCE PROCEEDS FROM ESSENTIALLY
the opposite kind of relation: here the work goes beyond or exceeds its immanence. This mode is characteristic of all the situations in
which one, several, or even all the members of a work's audience are
confronted, knowingly or not, with an incomplete and, as it were, deficient manifestation of the work, some parts or aspects of which are momentarily or definitively inaccessible to them. This deficiency can take
one of two theoretically quite distinct forms: lacunary [*lacunaire*] manifestation (the *Venus of Milo* without her arms) or indirect manifestation (the *Mona Lisa* in a reproduction). Later I will spell out the sense
in which indirect manifestations are partial, though this is no great mystery; but we need to note at the outset that the term *manifestation* here
designates a moment situated, in some sort, between immanence and
reception. It is *distinct from reception:* clearly, every occurrence of the
reception of a work is partial, since no contemplation, reading, or audition lasts long enough or is sufficiently attentive to exhaust the work's
properties. This fact, which in many respects defines, or, as Goodman
says, is symptomatic of the aesthetic relation in general, cannot, for that
very reason, be the defining characteristic of a specific situation like the
one I am evoking here. In that situation, reception is partial, not because

of a subjective lack of attention, but rather because of the objective fact that absence or occultation has rendered one part or aspect of the object of immanence imperceptible. Manifestation is, again, *distinct from immanence* in the sense that the very notion of incomplete manifestation implies that the object of immanence includes, has included, or should have included aspects other than those it offers up to perception here and now:[1] the *Venus of Milo* once had two arms, which no one can see today; the *Unfinished* Symphony was to have three movements; *The Battle of San Romano,* only one of whose panels I can look at in the Louvre, has two others, which I have to go to London and Florence to see; the page missing from my copy of *The Charterhouse of Parma* is not missing from the (ideal) text of this work, nor, doubtless, from its other instances of manifestation; and so on. In all these cases, I am dealing with an incomplete manifestation of an object of immanence that may either itself be (or have become) incomplete (the *Venus*), or else may exceed this manifestation in one way or another *(San Romano, The Charterhouse),* and so merely be incomplete for me and others who, like me, have only limited [*lacunaire*] access to the object for the time being.

## Lacunary Manifestations

The (countless) instances of lacunary manifestation have various causes: the main ones seem to me to be plural immanence, partial loss or destruction, and dispersion. Works with plural immanence are, so to speak, all destined (if to varying degrees) to have dissociated and, therefore, incomplete manifestations in every occurrence: anyone who acquires a version of *Saying Grace,* reads a version of *Oberman(n),* or listens to a version of *Petrushka* is supposed to content himself, at least for the nonce, with a single object of immanence, or even to be unaware of the existence of the others, which, as we have seen, the artist would in certain

---

1. It is this situation that authorizes us to speak of a manifestation distinct from immanence, even in the case of autographic works in which, in principle and by definition, these two moments are one and the same. The notion of manifestation here seems to me to be similar to what Goodman terms *implementation* or *activation.* Nelson Goodman, *Of Mind and Other Matters* (Cambridge: Harvard University Press, 1984) and "L'art en action," *Cahiers du Musée national de l'art moderne,* no. 41 (Fall 1992): 7–14.

cases have liked to destroy. It is our modern taste for complete editions/ exhibitions with variants which leads us to regard these dissociated receptions as incomplete, and to organize comparative exhibitions of replicas or to publish editions that include all the versions of a work— with the result that every other form of manifestation bears the stamp of insufficience.

Works that are incomplete because they have been left unfinished are, obviously, incomplete only with regard to a broader or more ambitious operal project, the existence of which cannot always be attested. Nothing, except for the mark of authenticity represented by the artist's signature at the bottom of a painting or on a final corrected proof, guarantees that a work has been finished. Indeed, the notion of "finished work" is one Borges, after Valéry, chalked up to fatigue or superstition, and we have already come across a few cases of more or less belated disavowals of works once considered finished. A work that is momentarily "finished" can later be revised; conversely, a work its author regards as unfinished, like, perhaps, *The Demoiselles d'Avignon,* can be adopted as it stands by the world of art—which, by the same token, would consider any further modification sacrilege. The state of being finished is not an intrinsic, perceptible property, and, a contrario, one cannot always determine that a work is unfinished without referring to external evidence, be it only the testimony of the artist: we call Schubert's Eighth Symphony "unfinished" because we know the composer had projected a third movement, but we do not use the same word to describe Beethoven's nineteenth, twentieth, twenty-fourth, twenty-seventh, or thirty-second piano sonatas, which seem to get along quite well without a third movement.[2] When they are present, internal indications that a work is unfinished are, thus, eminently relative, depending as they do on generic norms certain works are supposed to satisfy, and also on whether the feature serving as one's point of reference is of a standard, variable, or counterstandard type.[3] A grammatically incomplete sentence (like "Yesterday, I met") doubtless signals (unless it is a case of reticence, or of aposiopesis, a trope generally identified by ellipsis

2. In the case of the thirty-second (Opus 111), Beethoven awakened a doubt of sorts by responding, cavalierly, to anyone who asked him why there was no third movement, "I didn't have the time!"

3. See Kendall Walton, "Categories of Art," *Philosophical Review* 79 (1970): 334–367.

points—*"Quos ego . . . "*) an unfinished state in a classical or standard regime, but may be a deliberately chosen closing tag in an "avant-garde" regime, which allows or encourages this sort of violation of the rules.[4] In classical music, a score that is not resolved on a perfect chord of the tonic can be considered unfinished, little jokes à la Haydn aside; in jazz, open phrases (ending, for example, on the leading tone) have been all but obligatory for half a century now, whereas ending on the tonic ranks as rather corny*. A poem that displays all the features of a sonnet except for the fourteenth line is undoubtedly an unfinished sonnet— barring a clearly signaled "counter standard" decision on the author's part. The disorderly and, as it were, crumbling fabric of *Lucien Leuwen* (the first two parts have been written out in nearly finished form, a third is made up of sundry rough drafts, there is an outline of the dénouement) offers abundant testimony to the fact that this work is unfinished, as does the disorderly state of *Lamiel,* but the outright inter-ruption of *The Life of Henry Brulard* is more enigmatic: the last sentence ("Tender feelings are spoilt by being set down in detail"[5]) constitutes a more than acceptable closing tag, and only external documents show that Stendhal had the intention, later abandoned, of carrying this auto-biographical narrative further. As to *The Charterhouse,* which was pub-lished during its author's lifetime, we must, of course, consider it a finished work,[6] but we also know, or think we do, that the conclusion was "precipitated" by the fact that the publisher was in a hurry; this doubtless accounts for its elliptical nature.

Works that are (or have become) incomplete as a result of mutila-tion or dispersion raise another fundamental question, and a very tick-

4. For reasons having to do with its theme, Richard Matheson's novella "Disappearing Act" (*The Magazine of Fantasy and Science Fiction,* March 1953, p. 38) closes on an aposiopesis of this sort. When the novella was first published in French, in the magazine *Fiction* (1956), a compositor who was more zealous than informed took it upon himself to complete the last sentence, which was, and should remain, "I am drinking a cup of cof."

5. [Trans. Jean Stewart and B. C. J. G. Knight (Chicago: University of Chicago Press, 1958), p. 347.]

6. The fact that it was published during the writer's lifetime is, here, a sign of this, but can-not be erected into an absolute criterion: a goodly number of eighteenth-century works appeared in partial installments that anticipated a conclusion which did not always come: consider, among others, *The Life of Marianne,* abandoned in 1741 after the publication of Part 11. Ten years elapsed before the publication of Part 11 of *Don Quixote,* largely provoked by (and so due to) Avellaneda's apocryphal version.

lish one: that of constituence[7], or the relation of the "parts" to the "whole." Possessing no more than a fragment of a hypothetical Greek vase represents neither the same degree, nor, doubtless, the same type of incompleteness as being left with only seven of Sophocles' one hundred twenty-three tragedies, or, again, as having read, of *The Human Comedy,* only *Père Goriot,* or, of *The Flowers of Evil,* only "Meditation." These situations of incompleteness are as diverse as the types of wholeness they impair;[8] we know, for example, that the mode of integration of *The Human Comedy* is not that of the *Rougon-Macquart,* which, in turn, is not that of *Remembrance of Things Past.* To mark off a few gradations on this infinite continuum, one can distinguish four major types, in what I hope is not merely an exercise in semantics.

A "part" may be considered a *fragment of an artistically indivisible individual,* one whose unity is conceived as an organic relation of cohesion: for instance, the arms of the *Venus of Milo* or the lines missing from Menander's *The Arbitration,* and, reciprocally, the extant parts of these works; or, again, the page torn out of my copy of *The Charterhouse* (and, reciprocally, the pages left in it). (After all, the five hundred thirty extant lines of *The Arbitration* are those left in the single extant *copy* of this comedy.) Cases of this sort are the only ones in which the effect of incompleteness is essentially inevitable—unless, of course, we valorize, ex post facto, this lacunary state, to which so many fragments owe some of their prestige, or adopt it as a new standard and produce deliberately "mutilated" works, like the classic or modern Roman busts whose lack of arms we no longer even notice, or the artificial ruins adorning our parks.

A part may also be regarded as an *element in a set* whose unity derives from an intentional relation bringing together autonomous elements: a movement in a sonata or symphony, a poem in a collection, a novel in a cycle, a panel in a polyptich. Here, as I have already said, the degree of integration varies widely, but it is entirely possible for the autonomous parts to serve as the objects of separate receptions; when custom does prescribe a relation of complementarity, it does not say which relation is

7. [*Appartenance.* This meaning of this word is that of the technical philosophical term 'appurtenance' in English; but the French word, unlike its English counterpart, does not carry a sense of being accessory or secondary, and is, moreover, current.]
8. See Boris de Schlœzer's distinction between "sets" and "systems," *Introduction à Jean-Sébastien Bach* (Paris: Gallimard, 1947), and also Richard Shusterman, "The Identity of the Work of Art," in *The Object of Literary Criticism* (Amsterdam: Rodopi, 1984), chap. 4.

involved. After an allegro movement in a symphony, we expect a slow movement, but know no more than that; when there is a closer thematic or structural relationship, like the one that obtains between the first and third movements of the Fifth Symphony (⌣⌣⌣—) or the five movements (the "idée fixe") of the *Fantastic* Symphony, this additional "cyclical" relation is neither predictable nor indispensable. Most dispersed autographic works[9] made up sets of this sort before their dispersion, like Murillo's *Cycle for the Franciscan Monastery* in Seville, his *Cycle for the Charity Hospital,* or, again, Chardin's "pendant" paintings.[10] Some of these sets, incidentally, do not display any discernable thematic unity. The Louvre has every right to be pleased at having recently reunited two long separated works by Fragonard—the pious *Adoration of the Wise Men* and the libertine *Bolt;* the art lover who ordered this pair of pendant paintings had a reasonably perverse sense of symmetry.[11] I said that "most" dispersed works once made up sets, but some dispersions work more harm than others, since they affect more closely related sets of works: one cannot but be pained (unless one is unaware of the situation) at not being able to see all three panels of *The Battle of San Romano* together.

A third type of integration, which is even looser, purely empirical, and not always intentional, conceives parts as *members of the same species* (or *family*): it is a "kinship" relation based on having the same source—works by the same author, or, in an even weaker connection, works from the same period or by artists in the same group. The one hundred sixteen or so lost tragedies of Sophocles are missing from a set of this kind (the missing tragedies in Aeschylus' trilogies belonged to more closely integrated sets[12]); there can be no doubt that we would judge this writer very differently if we did not have so "anthological" a knowledge of his

9. An allographic work cannot, obviously, be dispersed, even if its text has only come down to us in several complementary manuscripts which have various types of lacunae and are scattered over several collections.

10. Of *The Attributes of the Arts, Music, and the Sciences,* the third painting is in fact "lost," but, if it were to come to light in a private collection, the group would be considered dispersed (the first two pictures are in the Louvre).

11. Although Daniel Arasse, *Le détail* (Paris: Flammarion, 1992), p. 252, argues, in an ingenious interpretation, for the unity of the two works.

12. *The Suppliants* and *Prometheus Bound* are each the opening plays, *Seven Against Thebes* the last play in trilogies. Sophocles seems never to have produced a trilogy: *Antigone, Oedipus Rex,* and *Oedipus at Colonus* never made up such a set, any more than did Euripides' *Andromaque, Hecuba,* and *The Trojan Women.*

work (in the true sense of the word, because the tragedies that have come down to us owe their survival to choices made rather late in the day, for, possibly, pedagogical purposes). But it is equally true that knowing only one or two of Balzac's novels, to the exclusion of the rest of *The Human Comedy,* or only *The Human Comedy,* to the exclusion of all other nineteenth-century prose fiction, and so on, constitute further cases of lacunary, and, accordingly, deformed reception. An art lover whose knowledge of Impressionist paintings was restricted to works by Monet, or who knew, of Cubist paintings, only Picasso's, would at a minimum risk, say, attributing to an individual things that in fact derived from a collective enterprise and history—which was, indeed, meant to be collective in the case of both Impressionism and Cubism.

The last type of integration is not even empirical, in the true sense, but simply attentional and/or intentional: it is a matter of conceiving a work as a *member of a class*—in particular, a class of the more or less profoundly institutionalized kind the world of art (of all the arts) calls genres. Here, the existence of widely varying kinds and degrees of constituence[13] surely does not give rise to any sense of incompleteness: the sets known as genres possess an essentially conceptual unity, and, the fetishism of the collector aside, nobody who reads a sonnet or looks at a still life suffers because he cannot immediately convoke all the other sonnets or still lifes in Creation. On the other hand, knowing and recognizing the generic properties of works constitutes a (more or less) integral part of their reception. Generic differences can be as pertinent as differences between the arts, of which they are, plainly, secondary specifications, and it is not always easy (or worthwhile) to determine whether we have shifted from one genre or one art to another: if we do not respond to a painting the way we respond to a book, or to a book the way we respond to a piece of music, neither do we look at a *Madonna and Child* the way we look at a landscape, or listen to jazz the way we listen to classical music, while poetry and prose are often treated, not without reason, as two distinct "arts" rather than two literary "genres." Awareness of genre (whatever the contents or intensity of that awareness) may be considered irrelevant at the purely aesthetic level (a painting, poem, or sonata can produce the "same" sort of pleasure, which

13. See Jean-Marie Schaeffer, *Qu'est-ce qu'un genre littéraire?* (Paris: Seuil, 1989).

Kant, as is well known, defines in terms that transcend divisions between the arts, and even the sphere of the arts in general), but it is harder to do without them at the level of artistic appreciation in the true sense of the word. Aesthetically, contemplation of the *Knidian Aphrodite,* without her arms and head, may be sufficient unto itself. Artistically, it is not a matter of indifference to know whether the statue is an original or a copy, that it is mutilated, dates from the fifth and not the third century, is by Praxiteles and not Phidias, represents Aphrodite and not Artemis—and first of all, perhaps, to know that it is a statue, and what a statue is.

These rather commonplace considerations, and the distinction between the aesthetic and the artistic which they imply, are of a typically functional kind; for the moment, I cannot pursue these matters any further. Let me simply point out that, just as all receptions of a work are always "incomplete" in view of the inexhaustible nature of its aesthetic features, so, in a certain sense, every manifestation is always deficient in view of the inexhaustible nature of its artistic constituence. Incompleteness is thus an inherent feature of any relation to a singular work of art; a work endlessly evokes, from one association to the next, and in the most diverse ways imaginable, the latent totality of the world of art—in the way a single note, as Valéry says somewhere, evokes the totality of the musical universe.[14] This endless evocation, this appeal that every work implicity addresses to all the others, amply deserves, I think, to be called *transcendence.*

## Indirect Manifestations

I mean by "indirect manifestation"[15] everything that can provide more or less precise knowledge of a work, whenever the work itself is definitively or temporarily absent. The absence of a destroyed work becomes definitive for all of us the moment it is destroyed: no one will ever see the *Athena Parthenos* or *Colossus of Rhodes* again. The absence of a lost work is not necessarily definitive: it is possible that someone will some-

14. Paul Valéry, "Poésie et pensée abstraite" (1939), in *Œuvres,* vol. 1 (Paris: Pléiade, Gallimard, 1957), p. 1327 [tr. "Poetry and Abstract Thought," in *Collected Works,* vol. 7, trans. Denise Folliot (New York: Pantheon, 1958), p. 67].

15. A notion accepted by Nelson Goodman, "L'art en action," *Cahiers du Musée national de l'art moderne,* no. 41 (Fall 1992): 7–14.

day find, at the bottom of a sand-choked well, the original of the *Kni-dian Aphrodite* or one of Sophocles' lost tragedies. However, I understand by temporary absence, above all, relative absence due to distance—for example, the absence, for me, in the place where and at the moment when I write this sentence, of the *View of Delft,* of which I nonetheless have, before my eyes, a "good" photographic reproduction in color: an indirect manifestation, doubtless more accurate (more complete) than a black and white photograph, and, doubtless, a fortiori more accurate than a verbal description. But my "doubtless" is in fact (as is often the case) rather dubitative, for these comparisons can run in the other direction: a good description can be more precise than a bad copy. At all events, I can put an end to this "absence" by making the trip to The Hague; this would permit me to replace the indirect manifestation with a direct manifestation *in praesentia,* which is obviously the manifestation par excellence. But "manifestation par excellence" does not necessarily mean (entail) *best possible reception:* attentive examination of a reproduction can very well tell me more about a picture than casting a rapid glance at it while being jostled by a milling crowd at an exhibition, or, simply, while inhibited by too strong an emotion, as in the case of Marcel watching Berma. After all, since translations (I will come back to this point) are also indirect manifestations, my reception of *War and Peace* is better when it is mediated by Boris de Schlœzer than when it is based on stupid contemplation of the original text—let us say for the time being, if only to dismiss the excessively purist notion that reading a translation has "nothing to do" with the artistic relation.

It can be seen that the field of indirect manifestations is virtually unlimited, since it encompasses even vague knowledge acquired by hearsay, like that of the high school student who, when asked if he had read *Madame Bovary,* answered, "Not personally," or else, "A friend of mine has seen the movie." We will not explore this field to that point, even if this scrap of knowledge is better (or worse), and is at all events something other, than nothing at all. But we would do well to draw a distinction between the two regimes at the outset, for the modes of indirect manifestation are not quite identical.

The autographic regime possesses essentially four such modes: copies made by hand (on a "signal"); reproductions made by imprint (including "recordings"); documents, if one stretches this term to cover

all representations that do not seek the greatest possible visual equivalence (prints after paintings, photographs of sculpture or architecture,
or verbal descriptions[16]); to which one must add, but doubtless as an
example of an unintentional, indirect manifestation derived from other
manifestations, the fact that replicas can function as indirect manifestations of one another: the Louvre *Saying Grace* can, accompanied by a
few verbal indications, give me a sense of what the one in the Hermitage looks like. All these manifestations, which make up the famous
Imaginary Museum, generally perform functions (we will consider
them later) the originals also perform. We would, however, do well to
bear in mind the large number of works, today lost, that we only know
in this indirect manner: Roman copies of Greek statues; paintings
"which have been lost but preserved in the form of prints," like Vouet's
*Entombment,* or photographed before their destruction, like Caravaggio's *Saint Matthew and the Angel,* already mentioned; verbal descriptions of the "Seven Wonders of the Ancient World." Certain of these
witnesses are simultaneouly indirect and lacunary, like the *Knidian
Aphrodite* in the Louvre, which is a mutilated copy.[17] What is today
called a "detail" in art books is generally a fragment that has been
picked out and then magnified (at least relative to the scale of all the
accompanying reproductions): it is thus at once partial and indirect, and
its dimensions have been modified. But the fact is that our relation to
ancient art (a few architectural works aside) comes essentially by way
of these indirect manifestations. However, certain contemporary art
forms (Land Art*, happenings*, temporary installations, the packaging
of buildings, bridges, etc.) are inherently made for receptions of this
sort, by way of posters, postcards, genetic documents, and so on.

By definition, there are neither reproductions nor copies in the
allographic regime (since these can only give rise to new instances), but
there do exist, as in the autographic regime, indirect manifestations by
way of documents (summaries and digests* of literary works, verbal
"analyses" of musical works) and versions; I will not reconsider the

16. The black and white photo may be regarded as an intermediate case, because it does not
attempt to provide chromatic equivalence.
17. My "simultaneously" is resultative: this copy must have been whole to begin with, and
later mutilated; today, however, we proceed in the opposite direction, taking casts of mutilated works.

function, fully intentional, of translations in literature and transcriptions in music. Millions of readers know millions of texts only "in translation," and, for one or two centuries, millions of music lovers knew certain musical works only as reduced for piano. A considerable number of ancient works, including the post-Homeric epics, have been transmitted to us only in the form of summaries, or, in certain cases, as a combination of fragments (lacunary manifestation) and summaries (indirect manifestation), like Livy's *History*.[18] If so few Latin translations of Greek texts have come down to us,[19] the obvious reason is that educated Romans read Greek; but the consequence—an important one— was near total ignorance of Greek literature in the Middle Ages. Let me also recall that *Rameau's Nephew*, the autograph manuscript of which had been lost, was, between 1805 and 1821, known to the public only in the form of a German translation made by Goethe from a (corrupt) copy held by the Hermitage, and, from 1821 and 1823, in the form of a translation made from German back into French.[20]

We should, perhaps, add to these four entirely canonical modes (copies, reproductions, documents, and versions) a fifth, which, obviously, did not have a similar purpose at first, but which can, under certain circumstances, perform a more or less similar function: I have in mind works of the kind I have called, by extension, "hypertextual" (actually, *hyperoperal*), that is, derived from earlier works by transformation or imitation.[21] One can imagine, and perhaps find, readers and art lovers perverse enough to know the *Aeneid* only through Scarron, the *Odyssey* only through Joyce, Sophocles only through Cocteau, Giraudoux, Sartre,

18. Of one hundred forty-two books, thirty-five have come down to us; most of the gaps have been filled in, so to speak, by second-century summaries which, even before the original was lost, served as schoolbooks. For a general discussion of the forms and functions of textual reductions, see Gérard Genette, *Palimpsestes* (Paris: Seuil, 1982), chaps. 46–52.
19. A Latin version of the *Timaeus,* which goes back to the fourth century, is often cited as an exception. See L. D. Reynolds and N. G. Wilson, *Scribes and Scholars: A Guide to the Transmission of Greek and Latin Literature* (1968), 3d ed. (Oxford: Clarendon, 1991), p. 119.
20. In 1823, Brière published the "Vandeul" copy; in 1884, Tourneux published another copy that had been bequeathed to posterity by Catherine II. Monval found and published the original manuscript only in 1891.
21. See Genette, *Palimpsestes;* Nelson Goodman and Catherine Elgin, "Variation on Variation," in *Reconceptions in Philosophy and Other Arts and Sciences* (London: Routledge, 1988), chap. 4, pp. 66–82.

or Anouilh, *Las Meninas, Luncheon on the Grass,* or *The Women of Algiers* only through Picasso, Pergolesi only through Stravinsky, Picasso himself only through Lichtenstein, Vermeer only through Van Meegeren, or even, *horribile dictu,* the *Mona Lisa* only through Duchamp—or again, moving from one art to another, the Rouen Cathedral only through Monet (like Marcel in Combray), and Hogarth only through Auden's and Stravinsky's *Rake's Progress.* We need to recall that, throughout the Middle Ages, the Homeric epics were known only by way of Latin narratives purportedly translated from Greek and attributed to "Dictys Cretensis" and "Dares of Phrygia," supposedly veterans of the Trojan War—narratives Father Le Moyne believed, as late as 1670, to have been the authentic sources for the *Iliad*. Let us not unduly mock these ignorant assumptions, whether merely imaginary, or else belonging to a bygone age: "variation" or parody often brings out features that would otherwise go unnoticed, while imitation, as we have known at least since Proust, is "criticism in the act," and hence a precious touchstone of a style, if nothing else. It might perhaps be preferable not to limit ourselves to reading Saint-Simon, Michelet, or Flaubert "in" Proust, but I have no doubt that we read them better in the light (or under the magnifying glass) of his pastiches.

We cannot qualify as an "indirect manifestation" the fact that certain (usually fragmentary) classical texts have come down to us in the form of quotations included in other, later texts—by Diogenes Laertius and Athenaeus of Naucratis, or even Plato, who cites untold bits and pieces of verse—since, by definition, an (accurate) quotation is simply one more occurrence of a text. In painting, on the other hand, "quotation" can only consist in including in a picture a partial or complete copy (or in today's pop* style, a reproduction) of an earlier one, of which the new work accordingly offers us an indirect manifestation. This practice of including "a painting in the painting" is ancient;[22] it can involve a work by the same artist (the *Grande Jatte* in Seurat's *Les Poseuses,* Matisse's *The Dance* in *Still Life with "The Dance"*), or by another, either identifiable (the still life by the master in Maurice Denis's *Homage to Cézanne*) or of less certain attribution. Again, the painting may be purely "imaginary,"

---

22. See André Chastel, "Le tableau dans le tableau" (1964), in *Fables, formes, figures,* vol. 2 (Paris: Flammarion, 1978), pp. 73–98; Pierre Georgel and Anne-Marie Lecoq, *La peinture dans la peinture* (Paris: Adam Biro, 1987).

that is, made up for the painter's immediate purposes, like the landscape, a self-parody en abyme, which occupies the place of honor in Courbet's *The Artist's Studio*. But, in this case, of course, it is not possible to speak of an indirect manifestation, except in a rather subtle and purely conventional sense: the painting en abyme is *supposed* to represent, transitively, another painting that it in fact constitutes in perfectly intransitive fashion.[23] Finally, a manifestation can be indirect in several senses, or at several levels, like the *Olympia* included in Manet's portrait of Zola, which clearly seems to be a painted representation of the photograph of a print made after the painting.[24] In every instance in which the painting in the painting is not merely imaginary, it goes without saying that this indirect manifestation could, if the original were destroyed, become a witness to the work: if the still life Venturi 341 were to burn up tomorrow, Maurice Denis's picture would continue to manifest it for us in its fashion, along with a certain number of other reproductions, of course.

I have not yet said in what sense indirect manifestations are partial manifestations, but I presume that the following explanation verges on the superfluous: copies, reproductions, replicas, descriptions, etc., share some but not all of the features of the work they are based on. Thus, even a faithful copy will not have the same underlying texture as the original; a photographic reproduction will not have the pictorial thickness, a black and white photo the colors of its model; a print will preserve only the linear contours of the model, a description will contain only verbal indications of the features it denotes, and so on. In short, if lacunary manifestations are quantitatively partial, we can say that indirect manifestations are qualitatively so. But, unlike lacunary manifestations, indirect manifestations replace the features they omit with features of their own. Thus, for the pictorial properties of a painting, a reproduction substitutes its photographic, and a description its linguistic, properties, while a translation substitutes its own linguistic properties for those of the original, and so forth.

23. But a painting can also figure, en abyme, in the same picture as its "model," which will thus be present in two forms, as living model and as image. This is the theme—a pioneering theme, in many respects—of the various renditions of *Saint Luke Painting the Virgin* (by, for example, Martin Van Heemskerck, circa 1532, Museum of Rennes).
24. See Gérard Genette, "Le regard d'Olympia," in *Mimesis et semiosis: Littérature et représentation. Miscellanées offertes à Henri Mitterand* (Paris: Nathan, 1993), pp. 475–484.

Lacunary manifestations are for the most part the result of accident, and, as such, lack an intentional function, even if their audience usually knows how to turn them to good use. In contrast, indirect manifestations are intentional, typically functional artifacts. One does not make a copy or translation without intending to use it to some end, or even several—though this is not always sufficient warrant against unforeseen or even deviant utilization: if a Rembrandt can serve as an ironing board, a copy of it can also have the same, or some other, function. It seems to me that the intentional and/or attentional functions of indirect manifestations can essentially be ranged in one of two categories, corresponding to different senses of the verb "to represent"—"denote" and "replace" [*suppléer*]—although this classification is by no means rigid, and permits considerable switching from one category to the other. Thus, the primary intentional function[25] of a copy is to replace the original work, while that of a reproduction, especially in art books, is rather to denote it. But nothing prevents us from using a copy to denote a work, if need be, or from framing a big reproduction and hanging it on the living-room wall. In the case of works that are themselves denotational, a reproduction can serve to designate, not the work itself, but, transitively, the object this work represents: in a travel agency, a photo of a Canaletto can function as an invitation to vacation in Venice; conversely, in the shop of someone who makes reproductions, it can, very intransitively, illustrate (exemplify) the quality of his work. The copy of Michelangelo's *David* that has replaced that statue in front of the Palazzo Vecchio could denote it in an outdoor course on the history of art. The copies en abyme just discussed are typically denotational; conversely, certain copies signed by great artists tend to undergo a change in status and become an integral part of the copyist's *œuvre,* where, like Picasso's "variations," they acquire something approaching the rank of an original work: for example, Manet's copy of *The Barque of Dante* by Delacroix,[26] which is usually considered with an eye to the copyist's style rather than his fidelity to the original. The primary function of a trans-

25. If we leave aside *student copies,* which have a pedagogical function. However, it is not always possible to tell, after the fact, which function a copy was originially meant to fulfill; and, here again, there is nothing to prevent people from using it as something other than what it was intended to be.

26. Museum of Lyons. The original [of the two copies] is in the Metropolitan.

lation is obviously to stand in for the original, although many (Chateaubriand's Milton, Nerval's *Faust,* Baudelaire's or Mallarmé's Poe, Claudel's *Oresteia,* Rilke's *Cimetière marin,* Valéry's *Eclogues*) have acquired a value of their own and are counted as part of the translator's *œuvre*. Today, Liszt's transcriptions are part of his work, like Ravel's orchestrations, Scarron's burlesques, Proust's pastiches, or Giraudoux's adaptations.

## The Imaginary Museum

The special case of the "technical reproducibility" of autographic works, particularly pictorial ones (for the technical reproducibility of works of sculpture is as old as sculpture itself), has come in for a great deal of comment, sometimes exaggerated, because some discern in this reproductibility, in order to celebrate or deplore it, the beginnings of a change of regime for painting. I will not again take up this debate, which I have already touched on, but it is a fact that "technical reproduction" has today become the instrument of what might more modestly be called a transition toward a *quasi-allographic* regime in painting. Its most positive cultural aspect is a phenomenon Valéry saluted in 1928 (including in it the recording of musical works and their diffusion by radio) as a "conquest of ubiquity"; its most negative aspect is what Walter Benjamin, even while adopting Valéry's enthusiastic views, feared would be the loss of the "aura" surrounding the here and now of unique works.[27] In contrast, Luis Prieto, as we have seen, carries his valorization of technical reproduction to the point of entirely excluding considerations of authenticity from the domain of the aesthetic relation: he calls a concern for authenticity "collectionism," stigmatizing it as a confusion of aesthetic and economic values, a new form of the fetishism of commodities. This position is surely exaggerated, for attachment to the unique object, and perhaps even the desire to possess it, are in many respects part of the aesthetic relation, which is not, for all that, a factor contributing to alienation: if

27. Paul Valéry, "La conquête de l'ubiquité" (1928), in *Œuvres,* vol. 2 (Paris: Pléiade, Gallimard, 1960), p. 1284 [tr. "The Conquest of Ubiquity," in *Collected Works,* vol. 13, trans. Ralph Mannheim (New York: Pantheon, 1964), p. 225]; Walter Benjamin, "The Work of Art in the Age of Mechanical Reproduction" (1935), in *Illuminations,* trans. Harry Zohn (New York: Schocken, 1969), pp. 217–251.

it's not your cup of tea, don't spoil it for others. It is, rather, "technical reproduction" itself which is simultaneously liberating and alienating, as Benjamin quite ably showed. But this ambivalence, quite banal, when all is said and done, also marked the transition of music and literature to the allographic regime, inasmuch as no notation can preserve the irreplaceable feeling of a particular performance.

The irresolvable debate over the advantages and disadvantages of indirect manifestation takes its most aggressive form in the accusation Georges Duthuit levels against Malraux,[28] whom he charges with being, at a minimum, the gravedigger of the true artistic relation by virtue of his exaltation of the Imaginary Museum,[29] whereas Benjamin had at least had the merit of deploring the disappearance of this relation. As a matter of fact, *The Voices of Silence* examines a much broader phenomenon, of which the museum without walls is only the most extreme manifestation. The museum tout court, a quite recent invention, after all, would be more representative of the phenomenon in question: that of the *metamorphosis* of works, which is as old as art itself, and which the modern age and its technology have only accelerated: "Metamorphosis is not an accident, it is the very life of the work of art."[30] We can distinguish three aspects of this phenomenon, which are also relevant to a discussion of transcendence, though in very different ways. The first consists in actual modification of autographic works as a result of the effects of time: objects of art are damaged, polychrome sculptures or buildings lose their color, paintings get dirty, works are restored or stolen. The second consists in the way the reception of works evolves and the meaning the pub-

28. Georges Duthuit, *Le musée inimaginable* (Paris: Corti, 1956). More generally, the virulent attacks launched against *The Voices of Silence* seem excessive to me: it is as if one had to rail against this book (which does not deserve so much honor or so much vituperation) to establish one's credentials as a serious critic of art. A more balanced consideration of the book may be found in Maurice Blanchot, "Le musée, l'art et le temps," in *L'amitié* (Paris: Gallimard, 1971), pp. 21–51.

29. The text Duthuit attacks is the one dating from 1947. This *Psychologie de l'art* in three parts was to become *Les voix du silence* in 1951 (Gallimard) [tr. *The Voices of Silence,* trans. Stuart Gilbert (Garden City, New York, 1953)]; the definitive edition, now out of print, was published in 1965 (yet another work with versions, then). I cite the "Idées-Arts" edition (André Malraux, *Le musée imaginaire* [Paris: Gallimard, 1965] [tr. *Museum without Walls,* trans. Stuart Gilbert and Francis Price (Garden City, N.Y.: Doubleday, 1967)]), which is also out of print.

30. Malraux, *Le musée imaginaire,* p. 224 [*Museum without Walls,* p. 224].

lic attaches to this. This evolution is both caused and symbolized by the Museum, agent of a "destruction of surroundings"[31] that tears works from their original contexts and functions; but, more generally, what is involved here are the attentional [*attentionnel*] modifications effected by History, by the manner in which each period, if only by way of its own productions, alters our relation to the works of the past: "every great art modifies those that preceded it . . . . Works of art are restored to life in our world of art, not in their own . . . . It is what is said *to us* by these sculptures and these paintings that matters, not what they have said."[32]

I will come back to these two sets of realities, which characterize what will be our last mode of transcendence. The third set has more specifically to do with the Imaginary Museum as such; it consists in certain consequences—derivative, and, sometimes, perverse effects—of photographic reproduction, especially photographs of works of sculpture and other objects in relief. These effects owe their existence, essentially, to two technical aspects of photographic practice: lighting,[33] which appears to alter relief ("the angle from which a work of sculpture is photographed, the manner in which it is framed and centered, and, above all, a *carefully studied* lighting—the lighting of some famous works is beginning to share a degree of attention that once was granted only to film stars—may strongly accentuate something that until then had only been suggested"[34]), and a change in scale that valorizes the "minor" arts by fictitiously endowing miniatures with the dimensions of major sculpture:

> The specific life which is given to a work by an enlargement of it attains its greatest strength in the dialogue permitted— indeed, demanded—by a comparison of photographs. The art of the Steppes was a highly specialized form, but if its bronze or gold plaques are shown beside a bas-relief, in the same format, they themselves become bas-reliefs, as do the seals of the ancient

31. Ibid., p. 220 [tr., p. 220].
32. Ibid., pp. 222, 234, 239 [tr., pp. 222–223, 234, 239. I have modified the translation of the last sentence].
33. Linked to photography and, in some sort, promoted by it, lighting effects have found autonomous application both in light shows on public buildings (it is well known how much this practice [widespread in France] owes to Malraux's efforts as Minister [of Culture]), and also in the lighting of objects in museums. The latter is an example of the effect the imaginary museum has had, in its turn, on the artistic direction of real museums [*muséographie*].
34. Malraux, *Le musée imaginaire*, p. 82 [tr., p. 82].

Orient, from Crete to the Indus. Thus, there has come into being a world of sculpture far different from that of the museum. More complex, because it ranges from curiosities to master-pieces, from figurines to colossi. . . . The enlargement of seals, of coins, of amulets, of figurines, creates truly *fictitious arts.*[35]

As a result of such effects, which can be celebrated or decried, but whose reality is undeniable, indirect manifestation is clearly on the way to emancipating itself and joining, in its turn, the ranks of "creative"—that is, transformational—practices.

Analogous or parallel effects are produced by the techniques used in reproducing the performing arts by means of recordings (Benjamin evoked, in terms characteristic of his period, the cinema, that art which, like photograpy, springs entirely from a "technique of reproduction"). It is well known that aural norms have been modified by various amplification techniques, which deserve most of the credit for the revival of ancient instruments that were long judged to be too soft, and for the resulting rediscovery of ancient and baroque music. These techniques are also responsible, doubtless, for new interpretive styles encouraged by studio conditions (Karajan's "intimate" Wagner, Schwartzkopf's or Fischer-Dieskau's sophisticated singing). Certain opera casts, impossible to bring together on a stage (Krips's *Don Giovanni,* Kleiber's *Marriage of Figaro,* Karajan's *Rosenkavalier,* or Sawallich's *Capriccio*), have given rise to a more demanding public while turning production policies, performers' careers, and the economics of the opera topsy-turvy. Artistic directors of record companies, like Walter Legge, have assumed decisive roles in the world of music; certain studio orchestras, like the Philharmonia, have dethroned concert orchestras; many jazz ensembles have flourished only long enough to record a few takes; and performers like Glenn Gould have abandoned the concert halls to devote themselves to recording. These technical procedures have, thanks to manipulations of all sorts (sound-editing, multiple tracks, mixing), made possible performances that are constructed measure by measure, note by note. Heifetz has thus been able to play Bach's Concerto for Two Violins by himself, Elisabeth Schuman to perform the two roles of Hansel and Gretel, Natalie Cole to sing *Unforgettable* in a duet with her father Nat twenty-seven years after his death,

35. Ibid., pp. 103, 111, 184 [tr., pp. 102–103, 110, 186].

and Bill Evans to carry on a four-handed dialogue with himself in his *Conversations with Myself*, like Noel Lee in a performance of Debussy's *Six Épigraphes Antiques*. Saint-Saëns's Third Symphony has been recorded by the Chicago Orchesta, conducted by Daniel Barenboïm in Chicago, with Gaston Litaize on the organ in Chartres; the *Rhapsody in Blue* has been recorded by an orchestra conducted in 1977 by Michael Tilson Thomas, with Gershwin himself at the piano, in a recording of the 1930s. More recently, *Tosca* was sung and filmed in situ: Zubin Mehta conducted the orchestra from the studio, while the singers appeared by way of video screens set up on the scene of the action in Rome. And I have already pointed out the change in regime of immanence undergone by music in its electronic forms, composed directly for magnetic tape and digital record: here again, the "indirect"[36] takes the controls. This makes a great number indeed of what Malraux described as "fictitious arts," but the adjective perhaps has (for once, coming from him) an excessively negative connotation. "Technical reproducibility" in fact creates *new* forms of art, and only a nostalgia riveted to the past can find nothing but cause for lamentation in the fact.[37]

36. [*Direct* means both "direct" and "live."]

37. There is a bit too much lamentation of this sort, though it is made up for by a goodly number of judicious observations, in the chapter entitled "Splendeurs et misères du microsillon" in René Leibowitz, *Le compositeur et son double* (Paris: Gallimard, 1971). The subsequent arrival of digital recording has not fundamentally altered the situation.

# CHAPTER 13

# The Plural Work

*I*N THIS LAST MODE OF TRANSCENDENCE, THE WORK AGAIN EXCEEDS ITS immanence; however, in this case it does so, not because its immanence has been temporarily or permanently reduced to a lacunary or indirect manifestation and is therefore deficient, but rather by virtue of an operal plurality of an attentional kind. Here it is the work as an object of reception and of an aesthetic relation which takes on different appearances and meanings depending on the circumstances and context. This sort of operal diffraction can take two forms, of which one, physical in nature, characterizes the autographic regime, while the other, which is functional, affects the two regimes equally.

## Physical Transformations

Autographic works, as we have seen, immanate in physical objects or events. Since events have no duration of persistence, they cannot undergo modification (except perhaps for the modification defined, during a conventional "iteration," by the difference between two singular occurrences): hence works of performance are excluded from this category.

The identity of physical objects, which do have a duration of persistence, is defined, we recall, by two parameters: numerical identity (the picture I find on my livingroom wall this morning is—probably—the one that was hanging there the night before), and specific, or qualitative, identity: this picture exhibits certain features, peculiar to itself, or shared with other objects,[1] which an exhaustive description would have to enumerate. Numerical identity is held to be inalterable, barring total destruction (but destruction is never total; the heap of ashes this picture can become will still be *this* picture—and not another—reduced to ashes), but the specific identity of an object of immanence, like that of any physical object, never ceases changing over time, sometimes gradually (patina, wear and tear, various kinds of deterioration), sometimes more rapidly, or all at once (mutilation, collapse). Now, as Prieto has clearly shown,[2] a work exists through the constitutive features of its numerical identity, themselves the end result of a process of transformation. Michelangelo carves a block of marble, Picasso transfers a few ounces of paint from his tubes to his canvas, but their works obviously consist in the effects of this transformational activity: after it has been carved, the block of marble is, numerically, the particular block extracted from Carrara for Michelangelo, the paint that has been applied and the canvas it has been applied to are the particular paint and canvas Picasso was supplied with, but the work of the one consists in the form he has given the marble, that of the other in the way he has distributed the paint. Once transformed by the artist, these physical objects will, without undergoing any change in numerical identity, continue to be transformed by the gradual or sudden effects of passing time. The *Pietà* at Saint-Peter's in Rome, attacked with a hammer in 1972 and then restored as best it could be, remains the same object numerically, but its specific identity has twice changed, passing from intact to damaged, and then from damaged to restored. *The Company of Captain Frans Banning Cocq,* gradually darkened by dirt and then carefully cleaned, has, at least once in a period of some three centuries, been dealt a similar fate. The "unique" physical objects these works consist in are only

1. In fact, it undoubtedly shares *all* these features with other objects. It is only the set of all of them which characterizes it.
2. Luis Prieto, "On the Identity of the Work of Art," trans. Brenda Bollag, *Versus* 46 (1987): 34–35.

unique, then, as far as their numerical identity is concerned. In qualitative terms, they are unique only for the purely hypothetical immutabil-
ity of an instant; for the duration of their persistence, they are temporally
plural, in consequence of incessant, more or less perceptible alterations.
We call this aging.

Sudden variations come about as the result of accident (broken statues, torn canvases, buildings demolished by earthquakes, fires, storms) or
deliberate attack: vandalism; the consequences of revolts or acts of war,
like the bombardment of the Acropolis, Dresden, or Coventry and the
burning of the Tuileries under the Paris Commune; the pillage of artworks to some practical end (buildings used as quarries—Cluny, Jumièges
ransacked by the speculators of the *Bande noire*—or statues melted down
to make cannons); the rectification of details, like the grape-leaves the
Church ordered placed on "shocking" nudes, the enlargement or reduction of paintings to adapt them to new surroundings, and so on.[3] But, as
is well known, such suddenly inflicted damage is not the only kind, and
is not always the hardest to repair. Leonardo used to say, with strange
naïveté, "Poor music—hardly has it been played than it vanishes into thin
air. Varnished, and thus rendered immune to change, painting endures."
It would be hard to pack more mistakes into so few words: it is easier
to render a piece of music immune to change (through notation) than a
painting, as is attested by the state in which a painting like, precisely,
the "poor" *Last Supper* of da Vinci himself "endures"; the painter's ill-
advised technical innovations often took a very heavy toll, and in very
short order. For a fresco, painting, sculpture, or building, to "endure" is
to age, under the impact of untold factors: unforeseen chemical reactions,
heat, freezing cold, damp, dryness, wind, light, dust, worms, insects, bac-
teria, and various kinds of pollution and mold, the results being erosion,
grime, oxidation, craquelure, rivelling, fissuring, crumbling; frescoes fall
off walls, canvases sag, polychrome sculpture fades, wood and paper turn
to dust, and so on.

I do not mean to suggest that these effects necessarily constitute so
many pure calamities. Some are occasionally welcome: "patina," Gide

3. An instance of destruction that may be chalked up to pure stupidity: at Mirabeau's funeral,
in 1791, someone conceived the idea of heightening the emotional impact of the ceremony
by firing off a salvo in the middle of the church of St. Eustache; a number of stained-glass
windows fell out and were smashed to pieces as a result.

liked to say, "is the masterpiece's reward." I am not sure I am sorry that the polychrome statues of Antiquity have lost their color; again, it is well known that the color of corten steel can be darkened through subjection to controlled oxidation and then maintained at the level of coloration desired by the artist (but for how long?). Nor do I say that these processes are all equally irreversible: the remedy is called, of course, restoration. Like all remedies, it is often more dangerous than the disease, either because the effect it produces is the opposite of the one desired (to render them more resistant, certain outdoor sculptures are injected with resins, but this can make them swell up and shatter), or because it is excessive: the nineteenth century of Viollet-le-Duc, Baltard, and Abadie was the golden age of vulgar restoration (consider Carcassonne, Pierrefonds, the seventeen turrets added to the Church of the Saint-Front in Périgueux), whence occasional derestorations, like that undertaken in our own day in the Church of Saint-Sernin in Toulouse. But the twentieth century is not entirely beyond reproach: one's evaluation of the results of a restoration is a matter of aesthetic judgement, and one can (I do not say must) still prefer the mysterious *Night Watch* of yore to the luminous *Company* that it has at least temporarily become, just as one can mourn the grime now gone from the Sistine or Brancacci Chapels.

If I cite these well-known cases, about which opinions diverge, it is merely to illustrate a universal phenomenon: (specific) identity never stops changing, either spontaneously or as a result of external action, so that the life of a work of art is never one of undisturbed tranquillity. Moreover, we need to add to our list the practices of reutilization that so often accompany (when they do not simply take the place of) efforts at restoration: churches, train stations, palaces, or warehouses are made over into museums, hotels into ministries, factories into universities or shopping malls, markets into theaters—so many examples of "salvaging" or usurpation that alter not only the details[4] of the material features of the buildings thus re-converted, but also their overall functioning, and, consequently, their meaning.

4. Some of these "details" can be substantial: see (but you can only see one of them, as the other has now been covered over by the extension carried out under Louis-Philippe) the two successive, identical façades of the Luxemburg Palace, or the cathedral placed, to the great displeasure of Charles V, inside the mosque in Cordoba (the result is not, however, devoid of a certain charm).

But the features that define the identity of an object are not restricted to the "internal properties" of physical makeup, form, and function: they are also properties, external if one likes, of emplacement and relation to a site and an environment. A unique object is by definition located in only one place, and this place always affects its basic character, if to varying degrees. The impact it has can be symbolic: for lack of imagination, perhaps, we have a hard time imagining the Eiffel Tower anywhere but in Paris, the Parthenon anywhere but on the Acropolis, the Sydney Opera House anywhere but in its port, Piero della Francesca's frescoes anywhere but in Arezzo, even the series of St. Georges by Carpaccio anywhere but in San Giorgio dei Schiavoni, and the *Regents* and *Women Regents* anywhere but in Haarlem. The impact of emplacement can also be aesthetic in the true sense of the word (if the distinction is meaningful): think of the Salute at the mouth of the Grand Canal, the Sanctuary at Delphi framed by its mountains, or Gozzoli's frescoes set like jewels in the Medici Chapel. Mankind did not have to wait until the contemporary period to discover the importance of site specificity*, even if certain artists today carry it to the extreme of conceiving works that make no sense at all when removed from the place where they have been installed—like the pictures painted by Martin Barré a few years ago, each of which represented the precise point where it stood in a certain Left Bank gallery.

Yet it so happens that no work is physically untransportable, so that, for centuries, people have, for well or ill, been tearing paintings, sculptures, and monuments from their original sites in order to exhibit them elsewhere, especially in museums, whose very existence and functioning depend on that possibility. Even buildings are subject to this Elginism, whether what is involved is pillage or a desire to save them from destruction: consider the Crystal Palace transported, after the 1851 exposition, from Hyde Park to Sydenham, where it burned down in 1936; the cloisters of Languedoc packed off to Fort Tryon Park (Manhattan), Abu Simbel saved from the waters, one of the Pavillons of Baltard removed to Nogent, London Bridge carried off to Arizona, Dendur placed under glass at the Metropolitan—and there are doubtless many other examples. Every one of these transfers annuls one meaning and imposes another. The life of certain works is punctuated by the symbolic ruptures accompanying the shock waves of History. Thus *Guernica* was painted in Paris for the Spanish Pavilion of 1937, found refuge during the war first in Norway, then in London, and subsequently in New York (for forty-two years), whence it was "repatriated" to Spain in 1981, only to become the object of a new war, between the Prado and the Centro de Arte Reina Sofia (the second of which ultimately triumphed), scandalizing the Basques, who maintained, not unreasonably, that the painting's place was in the martyred city. With each transfer came a new context and thus a new meaning. I will not reconsider the fate of the dispersed sets of works mentioned earlier—except perhaps to add that even a unified work can be dispersed after being divided up: Monet's *Luncheon on the Grass* (1865), attacked by mold one winter, was cut up into three pieces in 1884; the left third is now on exhibit (Orsay) alongside the middle section, the height of which has been reduced, so that the left third cannot be reattached to it. As for the right third (which took up and reworked a figure from Manet's painting of the same name), it has been lost.

I have already mentioned the uncertainties about the extent to which works of art constitute integral wholes; they are exacerbated by such separations. These uncertainties, in turn, relativize the cardinal distinction between the two types of identity. For determining the numerical identity of an object presupposes, it seems to me, the possibility of establishing the object's limits. This does not create much of a problem in ordinary situations: when, like Prieto, I have two "identical" pieces of chalk before me, I have no trouble distinguishing them as the one on the left and the right, and I can just as easily distinguish both of them from the table they lie on. Arthur Danto jocularly wonders about the status of a sculpture that adorns the head of a stairway in Columbia University's Arden House; it represents a cat, or perhaps a cat chained to a banister, or perhaps a cat, a banister, and a stairway, and so on and so forth, until the whole campus, city, and, finally, universe have been sucked into the metaphysical "hole in the sand" this work represents.[5] When a statue begins to show signs of erosion, we are at least fairly certain that it is *that* particular statue which is deteriorating and undergoing a change in specific identity. But when a temple takes to the road, should we say, "This temple is changing its site," or rather, "This complex work (temple +

5. Arthur C. Danto, *The Transfiguration of the Commonplace: A Philosophy of Art* (Cambridge: Harvard University Press, 1981), p. 102.

original site) is disappearing as a result of dispersion"? Frankly, I have no idea, but one thing is certain: when, today, we look at *The Last Supper* in its site in Milan, we no longer see much of anything, and yet we know that what we are looking at is what *The Last Supper* has become. What *The Battle of San Romano* has become is something no one can look at, unless he has one eye in Florence, the second in Paris, and the famous third in London.

I note further that it is not necessary to move works to change their sites, since the site itself inevitably changes, and not always for the better. Saint Paul's Cathedral by Wren still stands where it has always stood in the City*, but can we therefore say that it has remained in situ? And the Parthenon? And Notre Dame in Paris? At the rate things are going, UNESCO will soon have to move the Pyramids to put them back in the desert. There is no certainly no lack of space, or of manpower to do the job.

Because they are bound up with the materiality and extension of time and space, these unceasing changes in (specific) identity are inevitable, and oblige us to take note of a fact that can be formulated as follows: *these unique works are plural*. We can no more look at the same painting or walk into the same cathedral twice than we can bathe in the same river twice: an autographic work, which is at all times defined, for its public, by the present state of its object of immanence (the only *The Last Supper* I can see today is the painting *The Last Supper* has become), never ceases to undergo changes in its specific identity as this object of immanence changes, whereas the numerical identity of the object remains, by definition, stable and constant. *The Last Supper* is still *this* particular work painted by Leonardo between 1495 and 1497 on *this* particular wall of the refectory of the Monastery of Santa Maria delle Grazie in Milan, but its specific features are no longer the ones its creator sought and obtained. It might be said that several works have successively come to immanate in one and the same object, if we understand by "work" that which, in an object, performs an artistic function: I look at the same wall as Leonardo's contemporaries, but I no longer see the same "fresco" on it. This situation, be it recalled, is characteristic of material objects. Unlike physical individuals, ideal individuals are inalterable; exhaustively defined by its specific identity, a text is immune to (or incapable of) all modification, and thus immune to all plurality, since it cannot change by an iota without becoming another text. I can, then, very well read the same text or the same score twice, or rather—if I am dealing with the same copy, or two textually identical copies—I cannot do otherwise. It is, however, possible for me (but this holds, as it happens, for autographic works as well) not to "read" it—or, more literally, not to *understand* it—the same way. In this case, of course, it is not the text or score that has changed, but its reader. This change is, again, inevitable, for the reader is not, for his part, an ideal individual—and the public even less, for it has nothing of an individual about it.

## Plural Receptions

We will conclude, then, with a consideration of the functional (attentional, receptional) plurality of works—or, to put it more simply, the fact that a work (independently of the physical modifications that only autographic works inevitably undergo in the course of time) never produces exactly the same effect twice; in other words—but this amounts to the same thing—is never invested with exactly the same meaning. I use the word *meaning* in its broadest sense, which covers not only the denotational values characteristic of the "representational" works of literature, painting, or sculpture, but also the exemplificational and expressive values (Goodman) characteristic of the merely "presentative" (Souriau) works of music, architecture, or abstract painting, which, if they do not (as a rule) denote anything, nonetheless do have meaning.

I will take as my starting point an elementary, well-known example, Jastrow's duck-rabbit,[6] already referred to. In question here, we remember, is an ambiguous figure,

6. The drawing may be found in Joseph Jastrow, *Fact and Fable in Psychology* (1901) (rpt. North Stratford, N.H.: Ayer, 1979), and in Ludwig Wittgenstein, *Philosophical Investigations,* 3d ed., trans. G. E. M. Anscombe (Oxford: Basil Blackwell, 1968), p. 194. See also Ernst Gombrich, *Art and Illusion: A Study in the Psychology of Pictorial Representations,* 5th ed. (Princeton: Princeton University Press, 1977), p. 4. The drawing is doubtless part of a broad graphic folklore that also includes Necker's cube and Roger Price's droodles*—for example, the two concentric circles that are supposed to represent, by way of his sombrero, a Mexican viewed from above.

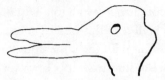

which can be read either as the head of a rabbit facing right, or the head of a duck facing left. We have only one (physical) line, but two (functional) drawings;[7] if a purely "syntactical" description is unambiguous, a semantic description is necessarily equivocal, or, more precisely, two such descriptions are possible, unless we choose between the two readings on the basis of the author's declared intention ("I meant to represent a rabbit, and nothing else"). Such a choice is not, however, always possible or even relevant—if, for example, what is at issue is a randomly drawn line, or if the question posed is, "What does this drawing represent *for you?*", or, a fortiori, if the line is purposely ambiguous, as in the present case. Homonyms provide another elementary example; for instance, the French words *pêche* [peach] and *pêche* (the favorite masculine sport, according to Howard Hawks). Syntactically, from the phonic as well as graphic point of view, we have the same signifier; semantically, the two signifieds are distinct, and therefore, by the Saussurian definition of the sign as signifier + signified, we have two distinct words—with, incidentally, different etymologies. In our two examples, graphic and verbal, one and the same syntactical object can fulfil two semantically distinct functions.[8] This functional ambiguity is the image *in nuce* of our third mode of transcendence: several (functional) works for a single (syntactic) object of immanence. For example: a single painting, in which you can see, depending on the context, a portrait of Mona Lisa or *L.H.O.O.Q. Shaved;* or a single text (to refer to a famous fable) in which you can read, depending, again, on the context, an old work by Cervantes or a more recent work by Pierre Ménard, the French symbolist poet. Or again (if these examples are too fictional or conceptual to convince you), a single text which you read as a promising work

7. See Virgil Aldrich, *Philosophy of Art* (Englewood Cliffs, N.J.: Prentice-Hall, 1963). Aldrich, like Wittgenstein, use the term "seeing as"* to describe competing interpretations of the same line. See George Dickie, *Aesthetics: An Introduction* (Indianapolis: Bobbs-Merrill, 1971), p. 56.
8. Certain puns, which I will let readers discover for themselves, are the verbal equivalents of Jastrow's ambiguous drawing.

by the novice Émile Ajar, only to discover not long after that it was a stylistic exercise by the old hand Romain Gary. This functional definition of the work has been strikingly illustrated by Nelson Goodman (I will come back to this). Yet Goodman has twice rejected such a definition, in terms that, as always, merit attention.

In his already cited response to objections raised by Richard Wollheim, Goodman wrote in 1978:

> Wollheim is tempted at one point to go so far as to claim that two identically spelled inscriptions ought to be considered instances of different works, but wisely stops short of this. To deny that I have read *Don Quixote* if my copy, though correctly spelled in all details, happens to have been accidentally produced by a mad printer in 1500, or by a mad computer in 1976, seems to me utterly untenable.

Returning to this passage in 1984, Goodman adds the following paragraph:

> But further questions do arise here. What constitutes correct spelling needs careful specification; for only in regard to a language is a physical mark a letter, and the same marks may spell different words in different languages [an example that Goodman gives elsewhere, and to which we shall return: *chat* in English and in French]. And Borges questions whether even sameness of spelling in the same language is enough to identify a work: did Cervantes and Ménard, writing the same words in Spanish, write the same work or even the same text? I am currently (1983) exploring some of these matters for a paper on interpretation and identity.[9]

The article announced here is entitled "Interpretation or Identity."[10] It argues that, while we never have access to the world, but only ever to (variable) *versions of* the world, we nevertheless have access, not to variable interpretations of a text, but to the text itself, which is defined in exhaustive and stable fashion by its syntactic identity. Further, since a literary work is itself exhaustively and exclusively defined by its

9. Nelson Goodman, *Of Mind and Other Matters* (Cambridge: Harvard University Press, 1984), pp. 140–141.
10. Or, "Can the Work Survive the World?" Nelson Goodman and Catherine Elgin, *Reconceptions in Philosophy and Other Arts and Sciences* (1988) (Indianapolis: Hackett, 1990), p. ix.

text,[11] we have, really and absolutely, access to the work, so that the relativistic dissolution of the world does not extend to works; in this sense, the work* survives the world*. But this identification of the work with its text (which goes back, as we have seen, to *Languages of Art,* and assumes precisely what must be proven) has perhaps not been demonstrated, concedes Goodman, with a burst of openness that does not last long: "Is there only one work for each text? To answer that we must first be clear about what constitutes *identity of text*. That identity is a matter pertaining solely to the syntax of a language—to the permissible configuration of letters, spaces, and punctuation marks—quite apart from what the text says or otherwise refers to."[12] It will be seen that the question of the relation (identity or not) between work and text is here simply resolved, more summarily than ever, by defining the identity of a text without providing any definition of a work, as if supplying the first definition rendered the second superfluous—which again boils down to assuming the thesis to be demonstrated. We are caught in a circular argument: one might as well argue that a horse is a house on the sole basis of the definition of a horse, without bothering to define a house, "since it's the same thing!"

Wishing to offer a little illustration of a doctrine so blithely established, Goodman proceeds to give an example—a rudimentary one, since "texts, of course, can be of any length" (I think so too). His example is the English word "cape," perfectly analogous to the French *pêche,* since it sometimes designates what a Frenchman calls a *cap* [the geographical term], and sometimes what he calls a *cape* [the garment]. In terms of the linguistic theory I invoked a moment ago, we again have two distinct, homonymic words, that is, two words sharing a single signifier. Once again, however, Goodman, assuming what he should demonstrate (here, the identity of sign and signifier, though what is at stake is still the same

---

11. It is, specifically, this proposition that I wish to contest, for I wholeheartedly subscribe to the previous one: under the above-mentioned conditions of correct establishment, a text has only *one,* unalterable (syntactic) identity. What I reject is the identification of a work with its text, and therefore the conclusion, drawn from two premises only one of which is correct, that the semantic (functional) identity of the work is as unique as the syntactic identity of its text. As I see it, the work is an interpretation, and thus, in the Goodmanian sense, a "version" of the text; our relation to it is at least as multifaceted and shifting as our relation to the world*.

12. Goodman and Elgin, *Reconceptions,* p. 58.

nominalist postulate), cuts off debate: "Although ambiguous, 'cape' is a single word. Inscriptions that refer to land masses are spelled the same as inscriptions that refer to outerwear." Note the asyndeton between the two sentences, which elide a "because" that would, perhaps, stick out a bit too sharply. "Cape" is, then, just one word, which is ambiguous and "susceptible of two correct literal interpretations";[13] it is not two homonymic words. The example implicitly suggests, by extension, that "cape" cannot be regarded as emblematic of the situation in which two works share the same text.

Conversely, in the case of interlinguistic homonyms, like French *chat* (cat) and English *chat,* Goodman rightly concedes that we are dealing with two distinct words, because, on the one hand, this common inscription corresponds to two different vocal emissions (homographs, but not homonyms in the strict sense), and, on the other, because "a text is an inscription in a language. So its identity depends on the language to which it belongs . . . . [This] is not a case of two works having the same text but of two works with different texts."[14] This time, the conclusion seems to me to be absolutely correct: French *chat* and English *chat* are two distinct words—but so are *fils* and *fils* ["son(s)" and "wires"; the two words are not homophones], or, conversely (to take two words that sound alike but are spelled differently) *saut* [leap] and *seau* [pail]. Here we clearly have two different forms for two different meanings— two "texts" for two "works"—because in the one case there is no phonic identity, and no graphic identity in the other. Yet it seems to me that the argument lacks force for that very reason. One can just as well show that the text of *The Red and the Black* differs from that of *The Charterhouse of Parma,* so that each of these two works has its own text. This would not be wrong, but to be right is not necessarily to be relevant: what needs to be proven is not that two distinct works *can* have two distinct texts (so obvious a proposition requires no proof), but rather that two distinct works *cannot* share the same text—just as, in my view and that of others, two distinct words can share the same signifier. It therefore seems to me that, of Goodman's two arguments, the first proceeds from a mistaken analysis, while the second is beside the point. But I am well aware that one can defend correct opinions with false arguments,

13. Ibid.
14. Ibid., p. 59, p. 60.

through ineptitude or carelessness. Hence the weakness of Goodman's first two arguments is not enough to prove him wrong.

The next argument is based on an imaginary, but not impossible, situation: without prior arrangement, twins on holiday in two different countries send their parents two literally identical reports (for instance, "This is a magnificent country!"). One might suppose, says Goodman, that this example is another illustration of the hypothesis "two works for the same text," but not so: the fact that a single text can have "two different applications or interpretations"[15] is not enough to show that the same text can constitute two different works. Granted; but this does not prove the contrary either. However, it does seem to me to prove, at a minimum, that the same text can convey two different pieces of information, and thus constitute two different messages: for example, "Greece is a magnificent country" and "Norway is a magnificent country." I am not sure that a message is always a work, but I am even less sure of the opposite.

Finally, Goodman comes to the case, already mentioned, of Borges's short story, "Pierre Ménard, Author of the Quixote,"[16] which is so famous and so frequently commented on that I will assume everyone knows it. Let me simply recall that, for Borges, Ménard's text, although literally identical with Cervantes's, constitutes another work simply by virtue of the fact that it was produced three centuries later, so that the same sentence, commonplace in the seventeenth century, is archaic in the twentieth, while the same opinion, which had such and such a status in the seventeenth century, acquires another in the twentieth. Here, Goodman limits himself to rejecting this view:

> We contend, however, that the supposed two works are actually one....What Ménard wrote is simply another inscription of the text. Any of us can do the same, as can printing presses and photocopiers. Indeed, we are told, if infinitely many monkeys were to type for an infinitely long time, one would eventually produce a replica of the text. That replica, we maintain, would be as much an instance of the work *Don Quixote* as Cervantes' manuscript, Ménard's manuscript, and each copy of the book that ever has

15. Ibid., p. 61.
16. In Jorge Luis Borges, *Labyrinths: Selected Stories and Other Writings,* ed. Donald A. Yates and James E. Irby, trans. James E. Irby et al. (N.p.: New Directions, 1964), pp. 36–44.

been or will be printed. That the monkey may be supposed to have produced his copy randomly makes no difference. It is the same text, and is open to all the same interpretations, as the instances consciously inscribed by Cervantes, Menard, and the various anonymous copyists, printers, and typesetters who produced instances of the work. Questions of the intention or intelligence of the producer of a particular inscription are irrelevant to the identity of the work.[17]

We see once again that Goodman, after affirming, correctly but pointlessly (no one, certainly not Borges, has maintained the contrary), that only one text is involved here, assumes that that is enough to show that there is only one work. But this is to beg the question* yet again, and to take for proof precisely what needs to be proved.

From this discussion, as long-winded as it was necessary, I draw only the following conclusion for the moment: Goodman's argument does not, on my view, attain its objective, which is to show that there is no distinction between a work and its text, or, more generally, between a work and its object of immanence. That the argument fails to hold up is not, of course, adequate proof that the distinction is valid. Moreover, I am not certain that it is the sort of thing that can be proven—it seems rather to fall into the category of those methodological decisions that turn out, when tested against the facts, to offer more advantages than disadvantages. To say that an object of immanence whose function changes—for example, a text whose meaning changes—becomes another work is neither "true" nor "false," but rather the result of a choice that bears, in sum, on the definition of the concept "work," approached from this angle. Since this *is* a question of opinion, I can do no better than to pass along the remarkably farsighted opinion of R. G. Collingwood, a philosopher who is, today, rather unjustly neglected:

> Works of art [can]not be produced by accident . . . Some . . . point out that if a monkey played with a typewriter for long enough, rattling the keys at random, there is a calculable probability that within a certain time he would produce, purely by accident, the complete text of Shakespeare. Any reader who has nothing to do

17. Goodman and Elgin, *Reconceptions,* p. 62.

can amuse himself by calculating how long it would take for the probability to be worth betting on. But the interest of the suggestion lies in the revelation of the mental state of a person who can identify the "works" of Shakespeare with the series of letters printed on the pages of a book bearing that phrase as its title; and who thinks, if he can be said to think at all, that an archaeologist of 10,000 years hence, recovering a complete text of Shakespeare from the sands of Egypt but unable to read a single word of English, would possess Shakespeare's dramatic and poetic works.[18]

Though I do not subscribe to the whole of Collingwood's "idealist" theory, I do believe that he here very accurately draws the dividing line between the text, defined in terms that are already "Goodmanian" ("a series of letters"), and the work, which commences at the point where the text begins to *function,* that is, to serve as the object of a reading and to carry a meaning. The (written or oral) text as purely "syntactical" object is only potentially a work, and can become one only under various attentional conditions, "knowing the language" among them. The point of the old story of the monkey at his typewriter[19]—which has nothing farfetched about it if we content ourselves with a more modest performance, such as typing the word *monkey*—is that, given enough time or luck, a monkey (or any random mechanical device) can write a word, page, or book; it does not prove that he can *read* the word, page, or book, since reading (this is too often forgotten) calls for greater competence than writing. Indeed, Goodman himself says[20] that a poem is not made to be merely looked at, but to be read (he says the same, incidentally, about a painting, and is clearly right there too, though in a different way). Now, if a text, and, in general, an object of immanence, must be looked at (perceived), a work is that which, in an object of immanence, must be *understood.*

18. R. G. Collingwood, *The Principles of Art* (1938) (Oxford: Oxford University Press, 1958), p. 126.
19. Which Arthur C. Danto, *The Philosophical Disenfranchisement of Art* (New York: Columbia University Press, 1986), pp. 39–40 revamps by imagining—a nice example of Blast Art*, this—that a powerful explosion in the quarries of Carrara one day accidentally produces a replica of Bramante's *Tempietto,* on which lands, no less accidentally (why make things simple), a replica of Michelangelo's *Pietà with Saint Nicodemus.*
20. Nelson Goodman, *Languages of Art: An Approach to a Theory of Symbols* (Indianapolis: Bobbs-Merrill, 1968), p. 241.

Goodman is right again, I believe, when he says that to read the simian or Ménardian copy of *Don Quixote* is still to read *Don Quixote*—but only if we take the verb "to read" in one of its senses (the most basic); it has at least three. To read is, first of all, to identify, letter by letter, the "syntactical" string of a text; this is something a machine can do quite well, and that I can do even in a language I am ignorant of, as long as I am familiar with its writing system (assuming it is phonetic). Reading is, second, to perceive, word for word and sentence by sentence, the literal meaning of this string; here, the simian copy of *Macbeth* is enough for me, or at least for Collingwood, though it will not be enough for Collingwood's future archaeologist, who will not know a word of English. But to read is, again, to perceive, beyond the literal meaning of the string, many other things, having to do with what we call interpretation. Often enough, what is meant by the word in this third sense comes into play even in the reception of the simplest messages (a telegram that runs "I'm fine" does not tell me much of anything if it arrives without the sender's name). Reading in this sense is absolutely indispensable to the reception of works (literary or otherwise), which are not merely objects of immanence, but objects of immanence produced by human beings: identifying them[21] depends, for example, on identifying their producer, with all that entails. To identify a text (for instance) is one thing, to identify the work that immanates in it is quite another, for the work is the way the text *operates*. Hence "to read the simian copy of *Don Quixote*" can have at least two meanings. On the first, I go to the Très Grande Bibliothèque[22] and request Cervantes's *Don Quixote,* without asking for a particular edition. The librarian, who has only the simian copy, hands it over to me for a few hours, without, in his turn, indicating the nature of this copy. I now simply proceed to read (or reread), as Goodman quite rightly says, Cervantes's *Don Quixote.* On the second meaning, a friend one day says to me, "Take a look at what Jimbo plunked out last night." In this case, I react in one of two ways: if I recognize this text as that of *Don Quixote,* I am astounded by the phenomenal coincidence (or suspect that my friend is having me on); if I do not know *Don Quixote,* or have forgotten it, I am astounded by

21. More or less precisely, to be sure; I do not know *who* "wrote" *The Song of Roland,* but I at least know that it was not Joseph Bédier, and that is relevant to my reading.
22. [Name for the new French national library in Paris.]

Jimbo's phenomenal literary talents; in neither of these two hypothetical (sub)cases, however, can it be said that I have "simply proceeded" to read *Don Quixote*. I do not even think it can be said (in the second case) that I have read it unawares, because I do not think one can "read a work" unawares; the expression is, to my mind, meaningless. The most one can do is read a text without being aware that it is the text of this work. Similarly, one can look at a painting without being aware that it is the *View of Delft,* or listen to a piece of music without being aware that it is *The Saint Matthew Passion;* that is all well and good, but it is not the same thing as (I do not say it is worse than) looking at the *View of Delft* or listening to *The Saint Matthew Passion*. For although, following (or not) Collingwood, Borges, or Goodman, I am basing my reasoning here on examples drawn from literature, it seems to me obvious that the distinction in question (between the work and its object of immanence) applies to all the arts, if we simply adjust a few frontiers. Only the literary work requires, from the outset, that its reader have linguistic competence (and, in the written mode, competent knowledge of a writing system), whereas music requires scriptal (notational) competence only when it takes the form of a score, an architectural plan calls for more technical reading skills than a sketch, and so forth.

But let me return to the inexhaustible story of Pierre Ménard, whose threshold of pertinence we would do well to specify. When we say (this "we" does not include Goodman) that *pêche* and *pêche* are two distinct words, we are placing ourselves at the level of literal meaning: the first word designates a kind of fruit, the second a sport. If we had only to distinguish between a literal meaning ("Fido is a dog") and a figurative one ("Mr. X is a dog"), we would no longer be dealing with "two distinct *words,*" but with two acceptations (literal and figurative) of the same word.[23] If the *Don Quixote* by Cervantes and the one by Ménard did not have, on the whole, the same literal meaning—or if, by a miraculous coincidence (at this stage of the game, we do not need to be niggardly with miraculous coincidences), one was in Spanish and the other in an extraterrestrial language in which the very same series of letters did not at all have the same meaning—I think we would have to say, not that we

23. I am not forgetting the gradualistic, fluctuating nature of this distinction (are *trombone,* the musical instrument, and *trombone,* of the kind used in the office [a paper clip], one or two words?). It does not, however, invalidate my distinction.

had the same text twice, but merely that we had the same "syntactical" string of letters (sameness of spelling*) twice, as in the bilingual example *chat*/chat. Cervantes's *Don Quixote* and Ménard's have the same text, in the full sense of the word, because they have not only the same graphic or phonic identity in common, but also the same literal meaning. Their identity accordingly runs deeper than that between *pêche* and *pêche,* which have only their "syntactical" elements in common; like the identity between "dog" and "dog," it also encompasses a certain (but only a *certain*) identity of meaning. Indeed, when Cervantes and Ménard write, "Truth, whose mother is history, rival of time, depository of deeds, witness of the past, exemplar and advisor to the present, and the future's counselor," they both mean (this, at least, is what is implied by Borges's commentary) the same thing on the literal level. Coming from Cervantes, however, "this enumeration is a mere rhetorical praise of history"; Ménard, for his part, "a contemporary of William James [and precursor of, among others, Nelson Goodman], does not define history as an inquiry into reality but as its origin. Historical truth, for him, is not what has happened; it is what we judge to have happened."[24]

The difference between the two sentences (with the same text) does not, then, reside in the disparity between two literal meanings, as in the case of *pêche/pêche,* but rather in that between two interpretations of the literal meaning, determined by two different historical and philosophical contexts. By the same token, the difference between "monkey" as typed by Jimbo and "monkey" as typed by his master does not derive from a difference in denotation, but, rather, from the fact that the second word is typed in very ordinary fashion by a human being, while the other is typed by an animal; if I once jump as high as Sergei Bubka does on a good day, no sensible person will conclude that the same performance is involved in both cases. To put it in (misappropriated[25]) Goodmanian terms, the two words (or two sentences) are, as texts, identical by virtue of their syntactical and semantic/literal identity, but differ, as works, by virtue of the disparity between their "histories of production"; this genetic difference gives rise to a difference in meaning beyond the

---

24. [Borges, *Labyrinths,* p. 43.]

25. Misappropriated, because I am applying them in a non-Goodmanian way. For Goodman, the "history of production" is irrelevant to the identification of allographic works; for me, it is irrelevant to their textual identity, but eminently relevant to their identification as works.

identity of literal meanings. In a word, the two sentences by Cervantes and Ménard denote the same thing (and hence are, to that extent, "the same sentence"), but they do not have the same connotations, for the two reasons put forward by Borges: one, which I evoked a moment ago, being that the same opinion does not have the same resonance in two different periods; the other that the style of this sentence, standard in the eighteenth century, is archaic in the twentieth.

I have just used the word "connotation" to refer to what distinguishes the two sentences, but it cannot be applied with equal propriety to the two differences underscored by Borges, given the definition of the term, which I take for granted here. The stylistic difference between the (supposedly) standard character of Cervantes's sentence and the (again, supposedly) archaic character of Ménard's is clearly a matter of connotation in the strict sense, since it is the *way* the idea is denoted which gives rise to a secondary (stylistic) meaning different in each case. But the difference I have termed "philosophical" is not of quite the same kind; I would be rather inclined to call it *transnotation,* for it depends, not on *the way* the idea is denoted, but on *what* the idea denoted (according to Borges) denotes in its turn, as a symptom denotes its cause—in Cervantes's case, a rhetorical tradition, the influence of Pragmatism in Ménard's.[26] Now a sizeable number of the secondary significations resulting from these contextual changes consist in transnotational values. If, today, a new Pierre Ménard were to rewrite *The Cid,* Ximena's sentence, "I hate you not!",[27] would retain its original denotational value (that she does not hate, or even, by litotes, that she loves the murderer of her father—for the meaning, literal or figurative, of these words has not changed since Corneille's day), but the sentiment they express would, perhaps, no longer have the same ideological value for the public; it would now evince, not a shocking lack of filial piety, but the triumph of love over the moral code of the vendetta (for example), and/or a gulf between two generations. It will perhaps be objected that we do not

26. This notion of "transnotation" is quite close to what I called "evocation" in *Fiction et diction* (Paris: Seuil, 1991), p. 120 [tr. *Fiction and Diction,* trans. Catherine Porter (Ithaca: Cornell University Press, 1993), p. 110], and, doubtless, to what Goodman calls "multiple reference"; see Nelson Goodman, "When Is Art?," in Goodman, *Ways of Worldmaking* (Indianapolis: Hackett, 1978), pp. 57-70, and "On Symptoms of the Aesthetic," in Goodman, *Of Mind and Other Matters.*

27. [Pierre Corneille, *The Cid,* in *The Cid, Cinna,* and *The Theatrical Illusion,* trans. John Cairncross (Harmondsworth, England: Penguin, 1975), p. 75 (line 963).]

have to imagine a literal remake* à la Ménard in order to find such differences of interpretation, and that this interpretation of the text of *The Cid* simply contrasts the attentional reactions of the public of Corneille's day (attested by the famous Quarrel) with those of the modern public[28]—in other words, that it counterposes two "readings" of the same text. That is perfectly correct; indeed, it is precisely what I am driving at.

The case of Pierre Ménard's *Don Quixote* is not only fictitious, but highly implausible, inasmuch as it assumes that a twentieth-century writer could produce [*producir*], and not reproduce, a literal replica of a seventeenth-century text without copying or previously memorizing it, thanks to a palingenetic miracle as improbable as Jimbo's fortuitous exploit. But we need to understand that this replica could also result from much less supernatural processes, such as plagiarism (Ménard, in this case, would recopy *Don Quixote* and coolly publish it under his own signature, in the hope of hoodwinking his readers) or provocative misappropriation à la Duchamp: the same process, but with the intention, this time, of scoring the success that comes with a "conceptual" gag. In both cases, of course, a text that is syntactically and literally identical with Cervantes's takes on a very different transnotational meaning, inasmuch as it results from a very different "history of production"—in short, a very different artistic *act*. And the fact that, in both cases, Ménard manages to produce, laboriously or mechanically, a "new copy" in which Nelson Goodman could perfectly well "read the *Don Quixote* of Cervantes," in no way affects the difference in meaning, entirely deliberate in this instance, that radically distinguishes these three works, as strictly homotextual as can be.[29] I am

28. It is, moreover, probable, and even attested, that "the" public of 1637 was in fact divided, and that the opinion of the censors of the Academy was not shared by the majority of the play's spectators, as its success goes to show. The debate over *The Princess of Clèves* bears witness to a similar difference of opinion. On the literal level, everyone understands that Madame de Clèves confesses her passion for Monsieur de Nemours to her husband. However, this confession is a sign of conjugal sincerity for some, while for others, it constitutes a very tactless way of going about things; a decent woman is not supposed to upset her husband.
29. In his essay "L'infini littéraire: l'Aleph," in Maurice Blanchot, *Le livre à venir* (Paris: Gallimard, 1959), p. 118 [tr. "Literary Infinity: The Aleph," in *Selected Essays,* ed. Gabriel Josipovici, trans. Sacha Rabinovitch (New York: Harvester, 1982), p. 224], Blanchot observes that the "memorable absurdity" of the story of Ménard "is no more than what takes place in the case of a translation. (I am inclined to say that it is rather the opposite, but Blanchot's taste for the *coincidentia oppositorum* is well known.) A translation gives the same work in two languages. In Borges' story we have two works in the same language"—I would prefer to say, "in the same text."

happy to admit that the last two cases are still hypothetical, if it is granted in return that they are perfectly possible—and even, these days, depressingly ho-hum. The reference to Duchamp is perhaps enough to indicate that this type of practice is conceivable in all the arts; the reader will recall the terms in which Borges evokes, at the end of his tale, the sort of benefit literature can reap from judicious recourse to the "technique of the deliberate anachronism and the erroneous attribution. This technique, whose applications are infinite, prompts us to go through the *Odyssey* as if it were posterior to the *Aeneid* and the book *Le Jardin du Centaure* of Madame Henri Bachelier as if it were by Madame Henri Bachelier. This technique fills the most placid works with adventure. To attribute the *Imitatio Christi* to Louis-Ferdinand Céline or to James Joyce, is this not a sufficient renovation of its tenuous spiritual indications?"[30] Let us note in passing that one of these suggestions—the minimalist misappropriation which consists in "attributing" a work to its actual author—is a technique that has been applied for several centuries now; it is by no means the least effective.

We will perhaps again be met with the objection (this "we" takes in Borges and a few others, including, without a doubt, Arthur Danto[31]) that these "mental constructs" are merely figments of the imagination. I am not certain that their imaginary nature is sufficient grounds for disregarding what they have to teach us, but I will point out nonetheless that cases of "disattribution" (and of "reattribution") are common in all the arts; I wonder if we receive the *Letters of a Portuguese Nun* quite the same way as before, now that we know it is by Guilleragues, or, again, *Momo,* now that it has been restored to Romain Gary, or the "disattributed" Rembrandts or Van Meegeren's fake Vermeers. Indeed, Nelson Goodman himself has shown how the revelation that the Van Meegeren paintings were not by Vermeer has changed our perception of the master of Delft by modifiying his corpus.[32] Again, do we look at the same slightly dirty sheet of paper the same way after learning that it is noth-

---

30. [Borges, *Labyrinths,* p. 44.]

31. Who, contrary to Goodman, accepts (and integrates into his thesis; see *The Transfiguration,* chap. 2) the Borgesian interpretation of the Ménard case.

32. Goodman, *Languages of Art,* p. 111; *Of Mind and Other Matters,* p. 196; cf. Danto, *Transfiguration,* p. 43.

ing less than a drawing by De Kooning himself, erased by none other than Rauschenberg? Or the same painting by Brueghel, before and after reading its title, *The Fall of Icarus?* Or the countless apparently "abstract" works by a Klee, Brancusi, Motherwell, or Nicolas de Staël, which need only be given a referential title to take on symbolic value?

These cases, artificial or marginal, if one likes, illustrate a more general fact—namely, the dependence, and thus the contextual variability (depending on period, culture, individual, occurrence) of the reception and functioning of works. Denotational values (verbal or pictorial) are doubtless the most stable, although words, at least, can change their meanings, as today's young readers of Montaigne or even Racine often learn to their dismay. But connotational and transnotational values, or, more generally, those Goodman calls exemplificational and expressive, are, to a great extent, culturally and linguistically determined. Doubtless the fact that the *Mona Lisa* is in the category "oil on wood" or that *Phaedra* is a "play in verse in five acts" does not depend on any cultural context, but it is not certain that these technical characteristics still retain their original (weak) meaning, now that most paintings are on canvas and most plays in prose: what once barely merited attention has become a noteworthy feature. Generic determinations largely depend on categories particular to a given period: for us, the elegiac, lyric, or tragic no longer designate the same features they did for an ancient Greek or Roman. The fact that we call the *chansons de geste* "medieval epics" (and the *Roman de Renart* a "beast epic") would surely have surprised a seventeenth-century poetician. As to the "novelistic" overtones we find in the *Odyssey,* they owe much to the late appearance of a genre of which classical Antiquity had not the faintest notion, and which apparently took shape, in the first centuries of our era, in the absence of any awareness of its revolutionary effect on existing categories—but, as everyone knows, to speak of this "genre" in languages which possess the distinction between novel* and romance* does not have quite the same meaning as to speak of it in others that do not. Similarly, the way in which, for us, Lulli, Gongora, or Bernini exemplify Baroque art doubtless owes more to our vision of art than to the vision of these artists themselves and their contemporaries. This is the moment to invoke Malraux again: "Works of art are restored to life in our world of art, not in their own."[33] As to expressive values or values of metaphoric exemplification, they depend, by definition, on relations of equivalence-by-analogy, many of which are rooted in culturally determined categories. The relation light=happy, dark=sad probably does not have the same force in cultures for which white is the color of mourning; the relation major=happy, minor=sad clearly depends on the (tonal) system of the modern European tradition; it does not apply in cultures whose modal scales are structured differently. Hence it is not very likely that a painting by Monet or Rembrandt, or a composition in C major or A flat minor, has, in the full sense of the word, universal expressive value.

Moreover, we do not have to travel great distances, culturally or historically, in order to find such attentional variation in the attribution of symbolic values. Here are the commentaries two great twentieth-century writers, both French, and writing within fourteen years of one another, make about the same painting:

> But an art critic having written somewhere that in Vermeer's *View of Delft* . . . a picture which he adored and imagined that he knew by heart, a little patch of yellow wall (which he could not remember) was so well painted that it was, if one looked at it by itself, like some priceless specimen of Chinese art, of a beauty that was sufficient in itself . . . . At last he came to the Vermeer which he remembered as more striking, more different from anything else he knew, but in which, thanks to the critic's article, he noticed for the first time some small figures in blue, that the sand was pink, and, finally, the precious substance of the tiny patch of yellow wall.

and:

> The *View of Delft* . . . in which the trapezoids and triangles—the masterfully individualized roofs and retreating gables—fall into line, led by a body of immaterial water and divided down the middle, under a little arching bridge, by the fanning out of the third dimension, like a parade of theorems on horseback.[34]

33. André Malraux, *Le musée imaginaire* (1947) (Paris: Idées-Art, Gallimard, 1947), p. 234 [tr. *Museum without Walls*, trans. Stuart Gilbert and Francis Price (Garden City, N.Y.: Doubleday, 1967), p. 234].
34. Marcel Proust, *La Prisonnière* (1921), in *À la recherche du temps perdu*, vol. 3, (Paris: Pléiade, Gallimard, 1988), p. 692 [tr. *The Captive*, in *Remembrance of Things Past*, vol. 3, trans. C. K. Scott Moncrieff, Terence Kilmartin, and Andreas Mayor (New York: Random House, 1981),

I am not taking much of a risk when I describe the first vision as detailed and painterly*, and the second as formalist (a geometric tendency, to the point of calling the water "immaterial"), or when I draw the inference that the painting sustains these two modes of perception (and, doubtless, would sustain still others) equally well, if only because two spectators [*récepteurs*] can direct their attention to different features of the same work. "I do not claim," says Jean-Marie Schaeffer, "that the properties of a work change with its audience; the work is what it is, but those who respond to it do not all 'mobilize' the same properties."[35] This selectivity is, in some sort, the passive condition for attentional variations; their main active cause is doubtless the ongoing evolution of artistic language itself, which has a constant retroactive impact on the perception of earlier works: "Every great art modifies those that preceded it," says, again, Malraux;[36] or, if one prefers an author who is more in*: "The fact is that each writer *creates* his precursors. His work modifies our conception of the past, as it will modify the future."[37] Everyone knows how much Cubism has changed our perceptions of Cézanne (and perhaps of Vermeer, at least in Claudel's case), or Abstract Expressionism our perceptions of Monet, Gauguin, or Matisse; we no longer listen to Wagner in the same way after Schönberg, or Debussy after Boulez; nor do we have the same appreciation of Baudelaire after Mallarmé, Austen after James, or James after Proust—while Proust himself found that Madame de Sévigné had a "Dostoyevskian side" to her, one the contemporaries of the Marquise doubtless missed. Michael

---

pp. 184–185]; Paul Claudel, *Introduction à la peinture hollandaise* (1935), in *Œuvres en prose* (Paris: Pléiade, Gallimard, 1965), p. 182. It is not hard to find similar differences in interpretation; for example, between Fromentin's and Claudel's interpretations of *Night Watch,* or Chateaubriand's and Michelet's interpretatons of Gothic cathedrals.

35. Jean-Marie Schaeffer, *L'art de l'âge moderne* (Paris: Gallimard, 1992), p. 385. I am inclined to construe this to mean that the object of immanence is what it is, and that every "mobilization" of properties constitutes a different work.

36. Malraux, *Le musée imaginaire*, p. 222 [tr. p. 222–223].

37. Jorge Luis Borges, "The Precursors of Kafka," in *Other Inquisitions, 1937–1952,* trans. Ruth L. C. Simms (Austin: University of Texas Press, 1964), p. 108. But Borges (in the wake of others, like Curtius or Eliot) has often elaborated on this theme—for instance, in these terms: "One literature differs from another, prior or posterior, less because of the text than because of the way in which it is read: if I were granted the possibility of reading any present-day page—this one, for example—as it will be read in the year two thousand, I would know what the literature of the year two thousand will be like." "A Note on (toward) Bernard Shaw," in Borges, *Labyrinths,* p. 214.

Baxandall clearly demonstrates the illusory, or excessively one-sided, nature of the notion of "influence," which, in the case of two successive artists X and Y, mechanically attributes to X an impact on Y, although, when we examine their relationship more closely, we notice that "the second is always the more lively reality": each artist chooses his predecessor, whom he draws in his own direction, so that "each time an artist is influenced he rewrites his art's history a little."[38] He rewrites it, first of all, for himself, but also, and inevitably, for everyone else, with the result that the history of art is always "experienced" in reverse, starting from the present.

The simplest (albeit paradoxical) formulation of this state of affairs seems to me to be the following: "A book changes by virtue of the fact that it does not change, while the world does."[39] As we know, texts, by virtue of their ideal character, are the only objects of immanence which "do not change," in the strict sense, though, in many respects, all works "change" unceasingly, each in its own way. But the change we are concerned with here is of a different kind, and does not spare the most inalterable works—spares *them,* perhaps, even less than the others. In establishing our relation to the works of the past or to works come from elsewhere, our sole choice is between, on the one hand, the spontaneous anachronism (or "anatopianism") which induces us to receive ancient works, or works of remote cultures, in the light and from the standpoint of our time and place, and, on the other, an effort at adjustment and restitution that consists in recovering and respecting their original value— in seeking out, as Malraux would say, "what they *once* said" behind "what they say to *us.*" But, as everyone knows, this effort can in its turn be dated and situated: seventeenth-century historians (and painters) made no effort to correct their anachronisms; as Caillois more or less says, not all cultures have their ethnographers. Be that as it may, neither a naively anachronistic attitude nor an attempt at adjustment place us, vis-à-vis these works, in the situation of their producers and contemporaneous public. There is an effect of cultural parallax that one cannot adjust for without first being aware of it; but this awareness produces another

38. Michael Baxandall, *Patterns of Intention: On the Historical Explanation of Pictures* (New Haven: Yale University Press, 1985), pp. 59–60.
39. Pierre Bourdieu, citing the Sinologist J. R. Levenson, in Roger Chartier, ed., *Pratiques de la lecture* (Paris: Rivages, 1985), p. 236.

such effect. In any event, the work is "brought back to life" or lives on in a "world of art" different from its own. Wölfflin's famous remark to the effect that not every art would have been possible in every period[40] holds not only for the creation, but also for the reception of works. In question here is not impossibility in the physical sense (Poussin or Hokusai *could* have painted *Guernica*), but cultural signification: the function of an act changes when it is taken out of context, and the truth of the matter is that, in art, not everything has the same *meaning* in every period and culture. "There are beautiful things still waiting to be composed in C major," Schönberg liked to say; but, to the best of my knowledge, he did not compose them, and, in any case, the key word in this sentence (as in many others) is plainly the word "still."

For several pages now, I have had the disagreeable impression that I am merely rehashing what have been truisms, not merely since Malraux and Borges, but since Benjamin, or, in a more ponderous, backward-looking mode, the Heidegger of "The Origin of the Work of Art" ("the Aegina sculptures in the Munich collection, Sophocles' Antigone in the best critical edition, are, as the works they are, torn out of their own native sphere . . . World-withdrawal and world-decay can never be undone. The works are no longer the same as they once were," etc.); or even since Hegel's *Aesthetics,* in which the "death of art" means, among other things, that "art, considered in its highest vocation, is and remains for us a thing of the past. Thereby it has lost for us genuine truth and life, and has rather been transferred into our ideas, instead of maintaining its earlier necessity in reality and occupying its higher place," etc.[41] It is perhaps to leap from truism to hyperbole to speak of *operal plurality* in connection with these matters of functional variation—which are in themselves obvious, though we are not obliged to interpret them in unrelievedly apocalyptic fashion. It nevertheless seems to me impossible to define a

---

40. Heinrich Wölfflin, *Principles of Art History: The Problem of the Development of Style in Later Art* (1915), trans. M. D. Hottinger (New York: Dover, 1950), p. 11.

41. Martin Heidegger, "The Origin of the Work of Art," trans. Albert Hofstadter, in David Farrell Krell, *Basic Writings from* Being and Time *(1927) to* The Task of Thinking *(1964)* (New York, 1977), p. 167; G. W. F. Hegel; *Aesthetics: Lectures on Fine Art* (1832), trans. T. H. Knox (Oxford: Clarendon Press, 1975), vol. 1, p. 11. Schaeffer, *L'art de l'âge moderne,* p. 427, is right to remind us that awareness (here critical) of the effects of the Museum and what would soon be called Elginism goes back at least to Quatremère de Quincy, *Lettres sur le projet d'enlever les monuments de l'Italie* (1796) and *Considérations morales sur la destination des ouvrages de l'art* (1815).

work without including functional traits in the definition. A work is an object of immanence *plus* a certain, potentially infinite, number of functions. Every time the actual set of these functions is modified—even if the object itself "does not change," or changes in some other way— the resulting work is modified. Whether one conceives it (first mode of transcendence) as something operating through several different objects, or (second mode) as something operating through a lacunary, indirect manifestation, or (third mode) as something operating through the same object in diverse ways, depending on the context, the relation of "transcendence" between the work and its object of immanence can in every case be defined in functional terms: the work, as its name partially indicates,[42] is the *action* performed by an object of immanence.

With this, we have crossed the threshold of what will make up the subject-matter of a future volume, which perhaps authorizes me to break off here. Before closing, I should simply like to point out that this functional definition of the work of art, which here seems, by virtue of certain of its consequences, to counterpose Borges, or Collingwood, or Danto, and many others, to Goodman, nevertheless finds its counterpart *in* Goodman, so that the present chapter is also a sort of *Goodman vs. Goodman*. For, let us not forget, Borges and Danto are not alone in constructing arguments around pairs of physically indiscernible but functionally distinct objects, like the two *Don Quixotes* or the two series of Brillo boxes. It is, after all, *Languages of Art* which counterposes, functionally, the two indiscernable objects constituted by a scientific diagram, on the one hand, and a drawing by Hokusai on the other. Here the context determines not only the *type* of artistic function, but also the presence or absence of an artistic function. And it is again Goodman who shows us that one and the same object can function as an object of art or not, depending on the symbolic function it fulfils.[43] It is difficult to reconcile propositions of this sort, and a number of others,[44] with the refusal, in evidence elsewhere, to distinguish between, for example, a text as a mere "syntactic" object and the work it constitutes, or does not con-

42. And as the adjective I have attributed to it, "operal," plainly shows: something that is *operal* is something that operates.
43. Goodman, "When Is Art?", p. 178.
44. See especially the recent introduction of the notion of implementation*, in Goodman, *Of Mind and Other Matters*, p. 142 ff., and in "L'art en action," *Cahiers du Musée national de l'art moderne*, no. 41 (Fall 1992), pp. 7–14, where this notion, defined in 1984 as "all that

stitute, or constitutes in some other manner, according to whether its significance changes. That contradiction perhaps rests on (or boils down to) another, between an ontology which considers it a point of honor to be as purely nominalist as possible, and an aesthetics that is basically (and commendably) pragmatist, in which "function may underlie status."[45] You will have understood which choice I believe is dictated by the facts; but I will reserve my treatment of this point until later, along with my supporting argument, if I can make one.

It is, then, less than ever a question of concluding now; at most, it is time to turn the page, or, rather, to notice that the page has begun to turn on its own. In a provisional or preliminary way, when all is said and done, this volume was devoted to the modes of existence of works, with a view to a future examination of their modes of operation. Only this aim justifies the effort spent on the present preliminary study, sometimes arid because of its conceptual abstraction, sometimes ponderously empirical, owing to a welter of examples: if works of art were not what they are—objects of an aesthetic relation—we would not, perhaps, have much cause to study their modes of existence, at least as I see it. I am, then, well aware that I have inflicted too long an approach upon such readers as have, improbably, borne with me, given that the goal is still no more than a promise, and the raison d'être no more than a hypothesis. But it seems to me—and I hope I have shown—that of the two modes of existence considered in the preceding pages, the second already had a great deal to do with the modes of action that will soon concern us, time allowing. If immanence, in its two regimes, does indeed belong to the order of being ("what kinds of objects are involved?"), transcendence, in its diverse modes, is more of the order of "doing" or "acting," since it hinges on the variable relation between the object of immanence and the effect it has (or fails to have) on its audience—an effect which, of course, we have yet to describe. If immanence defines, in some sort, the work at rest (or, rather, in suspension), transcendence already shows us, if only on the horizon, the work in action, and art at work.

---

goes into making a work work," is also christened (this is the more memorable term) *activation;* the notion embraces not only the conservation and recovery of works, but also the means of acting "indirectly" which are provided it by reproductions and even "verbal commentaries." This is, of course, our second mode of transcendence.

45. Goodman, *Of Mind and Other Matters,* p. 145.

# Bibliography

Adorno, Theodor W. *Quasi una fantasia* (1963), trans. Rodney Livingstone. London: Verso, 1992.

Aldrich, Virgil. *Philosophy of Art*. Englewood Cliffs, N.J.: Prentice-Hall, 1963.

Alpers, Svetlana. *Rembrandt's Enterprise: The Studio and the Market*. Chicago: University of Chicago Press, 1988.

Arasse, Daniel. *Le détail*. Paris: Flammarion, 1992.

Aristotle. *De Poetica (Poetics)*, trans. Ingram Bywater. In Richard McKeon, ed., *The Basic Works of Aristotle*. New York: Random House, 1941, pp. 1453–1487.

Barthes, Roland. "De l'œuvre au texte" (1971). In *Le bruissement de la langue*. Paris: Seuil, 1984, pp. 69–78. [Tr. "From Work to Text." In *The Rustle of Language*, trans. Richard Howard. New York: Hill and Wang, 1986, pp. 56–64.]

——. "La mort de l'auteur" (1968). In *Le bruissement de la langue*. Paris: Seuil, 1984, pp. 61–68. [Tr. "The Death of the Author." In *The Rustle of Language*, trans. Richard Howard. New York: Hill and Wang, 1986, pp. 49–55.]

——. "Le théâtre de Baudelaire." In *Essais critiques*. Paris: Seuil, 1964, pp. 41–47. [Tr. "Baudelaire's Theater." In *Critical Essays*, trans. Richard Howard. Evanston, Ill.: Northwestern University Press, 1972, pp. 25–31.]

Baudelaire, Charles. *Les fleurs du mal*. In *Œuvres*. Paris: Pléiade, Gallimard, 1975, vol. I, pp. 1–145. [Tr. *The Flowers of Evil*, trans. and ed. James McGowan. Oxford University Press, 1993.]

Baxandall, Michael. *Patterns of Intention: On the Historical Explanation of Pictures*. New Haven: Yale University Press, 1985.

Beardsley, Monroe C. "The Aesthetic Point of View" (1970). In John W. Bender and H. Gene Blocker, eds., *Contemporary Philosophy of Art: Readings in Analytic Aesthetics*. Englewood Cliffs, N.J.: Prentice-Hall, 1993, pp. 384–396.

——. *Aesthetics* (1958). 2d ed. Indianapolis: Hackett, 1981.

——. "Languages of Art and Art Criticism." *Erkenntnis* 12 (1978): 95–118.

Beardsley, Monroe C., and William K. Wimsatt. "The Intentional Fallacy." *Sewanee Review* 54 (1946): 468–487. Also in *The Verbal Icon*. Lexington: University of Kentucky Press, 1954, chapter 1.

Benjamin, Walter. "The Work of Art in the Age of Mechanical Reproduction" (1935). In *Illuminations,* trans. Harry Zohn. New York: Schocken, 1969, pp. 217–251.

Berlioz, Hector. *À travers chants* (1862). Paris: Gründ, 1971. [Tr. *The Art of Music and Other Essays,* trans. and ed. Elizabeth Csicsery-Rónay. Bloomington: Indiana University Press, 1994.]

Binkley, Timothy. "'Piece': Contra Aesthetics." *Journal of Aesthetics and Art Criticism* 35 (1977): 265–277.

Blanchot, Maurice. *Le livre à venir.* Paris: Gallimard, 1959. [Partial translation in Gabriel Josipovici, ed., *Selected Essays,* trans. Sacha Rabinovitch. New York: Harvester, 1982.]

———. "Le musée, l'art et le temps" (1950). In *L'amitié.* Paris: Gallimard, 1971, pp. 21–51.

Borges, Jorge Luis. *Labyrinths: Selected Stories and Other Writings.* Ed. Donald A. Yates and James E. Irby, trans. James E. Irby et al. N.p.: New Directions, 1964.

———. *Other Inquisitions, 1937–1952* (1952), trans. Ruth L. C. Simms. Austin: University of Texas Press, 1964.

Boulez, Pierre. *Par volonté et par hasard.* Paris: Seuil, 1975.

———. *Le pays fertile.* Paris: Gallimard, 1989.

Cabanne, Pierre. *Le siècle de Picasso* (1975). Paris: Folio-Essais, Gallimard, 1992. [Tr. *Pablo Picasso: His Life and Times,* trans. Harold J. Salemson. New York: Morrow, 1977.]

Caillois, Roger. *Les jeux et les hommes.* Paris: Gallimard, 1958.

Cerquiglini, Bernard. *Éloge de la variante: Histoire critique de la philologie.* Paris: Seuil, 1989.

Chartier, Roger, ed. *Pratiques de la lecture.* Paris: Rivages, 1985.

Chastel, André. "Le tableau dans le tableau" (1964). In *Fables, formes, figures.* Paris: Flammarion, 1978, vol. 2, pp. 73–98.

Claudel, Paul. *Introduction à la peinture hollandaise* (1935). In *Œuvres en prose.* Paris: Pléiade, Gallimard, 1965, pp. 169–204.

Clérin, Philippe. *La sculpture: Toutes ses techniques.* Paris: Dessain et Tolra, 1988.

Cohen, Ted. "The Possibility of Art." In Joseph Margolis, ed., *Philosophy Looks at the Arts.* 3d ed. Philadelphia: Temple University Press, 1987.

Collingwood, R. G. *The Principles of Art* (1938). Oxford: Oxford University Press, 1958.

Danto, Arthur C. "The Artworld." *Journal of Philosophy* 61 (1964): 571–584.

———. *The Philosophical Disenfranchisement of Art.* New York: Columbia University Press, 1986.

———. *The Transfiguration of the Commonplace: A Philosophy of Art.* Cambridge: Harvard University Press, 1981.

Dickie, George. *Aesthetics: An Introduction.* Indianapolis: Bobbs-Merrill, 1971.

———. *Art and the Aesthetic: An Institutional Analysis.* Ithaca: Cornell University Press,

1974.

———. "Defining Art." *American Philosophical Quarterly* 6 (1969): 253–256.

———. "Defining Art II." In Matthew Lippman, ed., *Contemporary Aesthetics.* Boston: Allyn and Bacon, 1973. pp. 118–131.

Dickie, George, and Richard Sclafani, eds. *Aesthetics: A Critical Anthology.* New York: St. Martin's Press, 1977.

Duthuit, Georges. *Le Musée inimaginable.* Paris: Corti, 1956.

Duve, Thierry de. *Résonances du ready-made.* Nîmes: Jacqueline Chambon, 1989.

Eco, Umberto. *The Open Work* (1962). Trans. Anna Cancogni. N.p.: Hutchinson Radius, 1989.

Edie, James M. "Husserl's Conception of the Ideality of Language." *Humanitas* 11 (1975): 201–217.

Escal, Françoise. *Le compositeur et ses modèles.* Paris: PUF, 1984.

Fabius, François, and Albert Banamou. "Rodin, Claudel, Barye et autres bronzes. Attention danger." Interviewed by Isabelle de Wavrin. *Beaux-Arts* 71 (1989).

Gaudon, Jean. "De la poésie au poème: Remarques sur les manuscrits poétiques de Victor Hugo." *Genesis* 2 (1992): 81–100.

Genette, Gérard, ed. *Esthétique et poétique.* Paris: Seuil, 1992.

———. *Fiction et diction.* Paris: Seuil, 1991. [Tr. *Fiction and Diction,* trans. Catherine Porter. Ithaca: Cornell University Press, 1993.]

———. *Introduction à l'architexte.* Paris: Seuil, 1979. [Tr. *The Architext,* trans. Jane E. Lewin. Berkeley: Quantum Books, University of California Press, 1992.]

———. *Palimpsestes.* Paris: Seuil, 1982.

———. "Le regard d'Olympia." In *Mimesis et semiosis: Littérature et représentation. Miscellanées offertes à Henri Mitterand.* Paris: Nathan, 1993, pp. 475–484.

Georgel, Pierre, and Anne-Marie Lecoq. *La peinture dans la peinture.* Paris: Adam Biro, 1987.

Glickman, Jack. "Creativity in the Arts." In Joseph Margolis, ed., *Philosophy Looks at the Arts,* 3d ed. Philadelphia: Temple University Press, 1987, pp. 168–185.

Gombrich, Ernst. *Art and Illusion: A Study in the Psychology of Pictorial Representations.* 5th ed. Princeton: Princeton University Press, 1977.

Goodman, Nelson. "L'art en action." *Cahiers du Musée national de l'art moderne,* no. 41 (Fall 1992): 7–14.

———. *Languages of Art: An Approach to a Theory of Symbols.* Indianapolis: Bobbs-Merrill, 1968.

———. *Of Mind and Other Matters.* Cambridge: Harvard University Press, 1984.

———. *Problems and Projects.* Indianapolis: Bobbs-Merrill, 1972.

———. *Ways of Worldmaking.* Indianapolis: Hackett, 1978.

———. "When Is Art?" In David Perkins and Barbara Leondar, eds., *The Arts and Cognition.* Baltimore: Johns Hopkins University Press, 1977, pp. 11–19. Also in Goodman, *Ways of Worldmaking.* Indianapolis: Hackett, 1978.

Goodman, Nelson, and Catherine Elgin. *Reconceptions in Philosophy and Other Arts and Sciences.* Indianapolis: Hackett, 1990.

Grasselli, Margaret Morgan and Pierre Rosenberg. *Watteau, 1684–1721.* Washington, D.C.: National Gallery of Art, 1984.

Grésillon, Almuth. *Les manuscrits modernes: Éléments de critique génétique.* Paris: PUF, 1994.

Hanslick, Edouard. *On the Musically Beautiful* (1854), trans. Geoffrey Payzant. Indianapolis: Hackett, 1986.

Hegel, Georg Wilhelm Friedrich. *Aesthetics: Lectures on Fine Art* (1832), trans. T. M. Knox. 2 vols. Oxford: Clarendon, 1975.

Heidegger, Martin. "The Origin of the Work of Art" (1835), trans. Albert Hofstatder. In David Farrell Krell, ed., *Basic Writings from* Being and Time *(1927)* to The Task of Thinking *(1964).* New York, 1977, pp. 143–187.

Ingarden, Roman. *The Literary Work of Art: An Investigation on the Borderlines of Ontology, Logic, and Theory of Literature* (1965), trans. George G. Grabowicz. Evanston, Ill.: Northwestern University Press, 1973.

Jakobson, Roman. *Questions de poétique.* Paris: Seuil, 1973. [Partial tr. as "Modern Russian Poetry: Velimir Khlebnikov," trans. J. Rosengart. In Edward J. Brown, ed., *Major Soviet Writers: Essays in Criticism.* New York: Oxford University Press, 1973, pp. 58–82.]

Jastrow, Joseph. *Fact and Fable in Psychology* (1901). Rpt. North Stratford, N.H.: Ayer, 1979.

Kant, Immanuel. *The Critique of Judgement* (1790), trans. James C. Meredith. Oxford: Oxford University Press, 1911.

Kennick, William. "Does Traditional Aesthetics Rest on a Mistake?" *Mind* 17 (1958): 317–334.

Kosuth, Joseph. "Art after Philosophy I and II." (1969). In G. Battock, ed., *Idea Art: A Critical Anthology.* New York: Dutton, 1973, pp. 70–101.

Lalande, André. *Vocabulaire technique et critique de la philosophie.* 10th ed. Paris: PUF, 1988.

Leibowitz, René. *Le compositeur et son double.* Paris: Gallimard, 1971.

Le Witt, Sol. "Paragraphs on Conceptual Art." *Artforum* (June 1967).

Lipman, Jean, and Richard Marshall. *Art about Art.* New York: Dutton, 1978.

Lord, Albert. *The Singer of Tales.* Cambridge: Harvard University Press, 1960.

Lories, Danielle, ed. *Philosophie analytique et esthétique.* Paris: Méridiens-Klincksieck, 1988.

Malraux, André. *Le musée imaginaire* (1947). Paris: Idées-Art, Gallimard, 1965. [Tr. *Museum without Walls,* trans. Stuart Gilbert and Francis Price. Garden City, N.J.: Doubleday, 1967.]

Mandelbaum, Maurice. "Family Resemblances and Generalization concerning the Arts." *American Philosophical Quarterly* 2 (1965): 219–228.

Margolis, Joseph. *Art and Philosophy.* New York: Harvester, 1978.

———. "The Ontological Peculiarity of Works of Art." In *Art and Philosophy.*

Atlantic Highlands, N.J.: Humanities Press, 1980, pp. 17–24.

——. "Works of Art as Physically Embodied and Culturally Emergent Entities." *British Journal of Aesthetics* 14 (1974): 187–196.

Margolis, Joseph, ed. *Philosophy Looks at the Arts.* 3d ed. Philadelphia: Temple University Press, 1987.

Menéndez Pidal, Ramon. *La chanson de Roland et la tradition épique des Francs* (1959), trans. I. M. Cluzel. Paris: Picard, 1960.

Meyer, Ursula. *Conceptual Art.* N.Y.: Dutton, 1972.

Parry, Milman. *The Making of Homeric Verse,* ed. Adam Parry. Oxford: Clarendon, 1971.

Prieto, Luis. "On the Identity of the Work of Art," trans. Brenda Bollag, *Versus* 46 (1987): 31–41.

Proust, Marcel. *Contre Sainte-Beuve.* Paris: Pléiade, Gallimard, 1971. [ Tr. *On Art and Literature, 1896–1919,* trans. Sylvia Townsend Warner. New York: Meridian, 1958.]

——. *À l'ombre des jeunes filles en fleurs* (1918). In *À la recherche du temps perdu.* Paris: Pléiade, Gallimard, 1987, vol. 1, pp. 421–630. [Tr. *Within a Budding Grove.* In *Remembrance of Things Past,* trans. C. K. Scott Moncrieff and Terence Kilmartin. New York: Random House, 1981, vol. 1, pp. 465–1018.]

——. *La Prisonnière* (1921). In *À la recherche du temps perdu.* Paris: Pléiade, Gallimard, 1988, vol. 3, pp. 517–915. [Tr. *The Captive.* In *Remembrance of Things Past,* trans. C. K. Scott Moncrieff, Terence Kilmartin, and Andreas Mayor. New York: Random House, 1981, vol. 3, pp. 1–422.]

Queffélec, Lise. *Le roman-feuilleton français au XIXe siècle.* Paris: PUF, 1989.

Reynolds, L. D. and N. G. Wilson, *Scribes and Scholars: A Guide to the Transmission of Greek and Latin Literature.* 3d. ed. Oxford: Clarendon, 1991.

Rheims, Maurice. *Apollon à Wall Street.* Paris: Seuil, 1992.

Rudel, Jean. *Technique de la sculpture.* Paris: PUF, 1980.

Sandler, Irving. *American Art of the 1960s.* New York: Harper and Row, 1988.

——. *The New York School: The Painters and Sculptors of the Fifties.* New York: Harper and Row, 1978.

Schaeffer, Jean-Marie. *L'art de l'âge moderne.* Paris: Gallimard, 1992.

——. *L'image précaire.* Paris: Seuil, 1987.

——. "Nelson Goodman en poéticien: Trois esquisses." *Cahiers du Musée national de l'art moderne,* no. 41 (Fall 1992): 85–97.

——. *Qu'est-ce qu'un genre littéraire?* Paris: Seuil, 1989.

Schloezer, Boris de. *Introduction à Jean-Sébastien Bach.* Paris: Gallimard, 1947.

Sclafani, Richard. "'Art,' Wittgenstein, and Open-Textured Concepts." *Journal of Aesthetics and Art Criticism* 29 (1971): 333–341.

Shusterman, Richard. *The Object of Literary Criticism.* Amsterdam: Rodopi, 1984.

Souriau, Étienne. *La correspondance des arts: Éléments d'esthétique comparée.* Paris:

Flammarion, 1947.

Stevenson, Charles L. "On 'What Is a Poem." *Philosophical Review* 66 (1957): 329–362.

Strawson, P. F. "Aesthetic Appraisal and Works of Art." In *Freedom and Resentment and Other Essays.* London: Methuen, 1974, pp. 178–189.

———. *Individuals: An Essay in Descriptive Metaphysics.* London: Methuen, 1959.

Urmson, J. O. "Literature." In George Dickie and Richard Sclafani, eds. *Aesthetics: A Critical Anthology.* New York: St. Martin's Press, 1977, pp. 334–341.

———. "What Makes a Situation Aesthetic?" *Proceedings of the Aristotelian Society,* supplementary vol. 31 (1957). Also in Joseph Margolis, ed., *Philosophy Looks at the Arts.* New York: Scribners, 1962, pp. 13–27.

Valéry, Paul. "La conquête de l'ubiquité" (1928). In *Œuvres.* Paris: Pléiade, Gallimard, 1960, vol. 2, pp. 1284–1287. [Tr. "The Conquest of Ubiquity." In *Collected Works,* trans. Ralph Manheim. New York: Pantheon, 1964, vol. 13. pp. 225–228.]

———. "Poésie et pensée abstraite" (1939). In *Œuvres.* Paris: Pléiade, Gallimard, 1957, vol. 1, pp. 1314–1339. [Tr. "Poetry and Abstract Thought." In *Collected Works,* trans. Denise Folliot. New York: Pantheon, 1958, vol. 7. pp. 52–81.]

Vallier, Dora. *L'art abstrait* (1967). Paris: Livre de Poche, 1980. [Tr. *Abstract Art,* trans. Jonathan Griffin. New York: Orion, 1970.]

Walton, Kendall. "Categories of Art." *Philosophical Review* 79 (1970): 334–367.

Weitz, Morris. "The Role of Theory in Aesthetics." *Journal of Aesthetics and Art Criticism* 15 (1956): 27–35.

Wittgenstein, Ludwig. *Philosophical Investigations.* 3d ed. Trans. G. E. M. Anscombe. Oxford: Basil Blackwell, 1968.

Wölfflin, Heinrich. *Principles of Art History: The Problem of the Development of Style in Later Art* (1915), trans. M. D. Hottinger. New York: Dover, 1952.

Wollheim, Richard. *Art and Its Objects.* Cambridge: Cambridge University Press, 1968. 2d ed. Cambridge: Cambridge University Press, 1980.

Wolterstorff, Nicholas. *Works and Worlds of Art.* Oxford: Clarendon, 1980.

Ziff, Paul. "The Task of Defining a Work of Art." *Philosophical Review* 62 (1953): 58–78.

Zumthor, Paul. *Essai de poétique médiévale.* Paris: Seuil, 1972. [Tr. *Toward a Medieval Poetics,* trans. Philip Bennett. Minneapolis: University of Minnesota Press, 1992.]

———. *Langue, texte, énigme.* Paris: Seuil, 1975.

———. *La lettre et la voix.* Paris: Seuil, 1987.

# Index